Praise for Stephen Reddy's

a ball with no points

" Reddy nailed it, big-time! It's one of the best books of this kind that I've read, and I've read a lot of them…part remembering a historic event, and part a trip down memory lane. It's not a basketball book. It's a memoir of another time and place. I really, really loved it."

> **– Bruce Johnson, WHS class of 1963;**
> **longtime Westfield sports historian**

"I LOVED IT! Reddy tells a great story…compelling and content-rich with a 'feel good' aspect. Honesty and authenticity as an author comes through on each page."

> **– Bill Kane, former WHS player, class of 1977**

"Steve has done a great job in capturing the joy and heartache of high school sports. A great coming of age story of life in the early '70s and how a group of small town guys were emotionally tied together forever. The book is not about winning and losing as much it is about friendship and growing up. As someone who witnessed the Westfield team of 1972 and who played against the players in the book it was a nostalgic trip back to a time when things seemed so much simpler. Great book for all who grew up that era as well as for anyone who played high school sports."

> **- Jim Baglin, star player for Plainfield HS and Susquehanna U;**
> **legendary coach for Mendham HS with 685 career wins**

More praise...

"OUTSTANDING!"

"Anybody who has ever laced up a pair of basketball sneakers should read this book. The story is of the Westfield NJ high school basketball team's record setting 1971-72 season. But it is so much more – it's about dedication, camaraderie, and friendship. The author, a starting guard on that wonderful team, has written a compelling account of the special season. Readers will find themselves rooting for the Westfield Blue Devil players as they develop into a close-knit team while pursuing excellence."

- Jay Jorgensen, 2-time Academic All-American Basketball Player at FDU; accomplished author

"...an exquisite look back at a championship season...It's a love letter to basketball and a celebration of friendships lasting half a century."

- John Belis, longtime sportswriter for The Courier-News

"Steve Reddy sank a clutch shot with his attempt to bring back the fond memories of the greatest season in the history of the Westfield High School boys' basketball program...a wonderful story telling version regarding a team that sacrificed stardom to jell into one group who shocked New Jersey. I often felt while reading this terrific piece that I was back sitting as a youth in the Westfield High gym and in awe of a collection of players who will be forever hailed. Three cheers for what Steve Reddy delivered and I guarantee that this classic can be enjoyed by not only people with roots to Westfield but by anyone who appreciates what the result is when a team works as one determined unit."

- Bruce Moran, WHS Class of 1976; former editor and writer for The Star-Ledger and current Westfield Athletic Hall of Fame Trustee

More praise...

"WOW!"

"This is a wonderful story of human emotion and triumph for any athlete that ever dreamed of winning a title. But as we are often reminded, victory doesn't always come without heartache. Sit back and enjoy the thoroughly entertaining story-filled ride that Steve Reddy so deftly weaves."

- Dave Miller, Former TV Executive for ESPN and NESN

"Fantastic story. Steve Reddy brings you back to a great era of sports in the early seventies, when Union County was king in football and basketball. Really enjoyed reading about all the hard work the kids put in at the Gumbert basketball courts. I remember it like it was yesterday."

- Glen Kehler, WHS Class of 1975; star running back for WHS and Rutgers U, and son of legendary WHS coach Gary Kehler

"In the early 1970s, Westfield, New Jersey was a football town, with the height of sports excitement happening on those 100 yards during the September-November fall season. But the 1971-1972 Westfield boys basketball team changed all that in a single season, a testament to the coaching, discipline, and athleticism that is detailed in the book. The portrayal of our childhood playground was perfect; it transported me back to those days playing ball out on those courts, making memories that I still reminisce on. The book is a must-read, especially for those familiar with the highs and lows of that acclaimed season."

- Jack Steimel, star player for crosstown rival Holy Trinity, class of 1972

a ball with no points

Stephen D. Reddy

a ball with no points

Copyright © 2021 by Stephen D. Reddy

Published by Dunkin Drive Publications LLC

Library of Congress Control Number: 2021919299

ISBN: 978-0-578 94818-8

Cover design by Jacqueline Reddy

www.aballwithnopoints.com

First Printed Edition: November 2021

To my teammates and head coach of the 1971-72 Westfield High Varsity Boys Basketball Team:

Neil Horne Jr.
Greg Allen (in memoriam)
Mike Cooney
Al "Chip" Danker
Tim Goski
Mark Jackson
Bob Jester
Steve Lee
Scott Novacek
Tom Pfeiffer
Dave Phillips
Larry Simmons

Now it's been more than 30 years
Since we filled those gyms and heard those cheers.
I can still hear them now.

Our gym housed a boyhood dream
Where good players blossomed as a team.
We dared to win and Horne Man showed us how.

Lyrics from **'Ol Westfield High**, June 2003

Contents

Prologue

I had just finished a round of golf on a Friday in June, 2019 and was having a beer at the 19th hole when my cell phone rang. My eyes perked up when I saw Bob Jester's name light up on my screen. Bob was an old high school basketball teammate of mine who had been difficult to get a hold of in recent years, favoring snail mail to e-mail, avoiding texting, and always having a full mailbox that made it impossible to leave him a message. But on this day he was calling me, so I quickly excused myself from the table and answered his call, sensing that something must be up for him to be calling me out of the blue.

Sure enough, Bob relayed to me some sad news: the son-in-law of our high school coach had passed away unexpectedly earlier in the week and there would be church and burial services in Westfield, NJ the next morning. While Bob checked to get the details of the services, I called fellow teammate Larry Simmons to relay the news. Larry, Bob and I quickly made plans to meet in Westfield the next morning for breakfast and then attend the services together.

I had not seen my coach's daughter Cheryl in years and hardly knew her, and had never met her husband, John Wilkinson. The Wilkinsons had settled in neighboring Scotch Plains where John was very active in youth sports programs, just like his father-in-law Neil Horne Jr. had been. Neil Horne Jr. was the reason I had to be there. Neil had been there when my father died in 1995 and again when my mother passed away in 2007. We buried my mom during a snowstorm in February of that year and were fortunate that anyone would brave the conditions that morning, but Neil and Rose Horne were amongst the handful there at Fairview Cemetery as the snow gently piled up.

Neil had been there for them because of a single season I had spent playing for the now retired coach back in the early '70s. My parents had witnessed that season up close, all 125 days of it. The season that took place nearly 50 years earlier had brought much joy and happiness to those of us that experienced it, and for some of the people that were there, it's not an overstatement to say that the season changed our lives.

The three of us made our way into the packed church off Rahway Avenue and took seats near the rear. Over the next hour we listened to close friends and relatives eulogize John Wilkinson, and then waited as family members slowly filed out as the service concluded. As a teary-eyed Rose Horne came down the aisle in our direction, she caught a glimpse of three familiar faces looking right back. Her spirits seemed ever so slightly uplifted by our presence as we took our turns embracing her and offering condolences. We then joined the procession on its way to Fairview Cemetery on the other side of town.

Funerals make you think. They make you appreciate what you have, perhaps most especially the limited time we have here on earth. The time we still have left and the time we've already had...and all the memories that go with it. When the burial concluded as burials do, with the gathered people dispersing back to their cars and their disparate lives, Bob Jester and I retreated back to my car. A reception was to follow shortly at Ferraros in downtown Westfield. On our way there we decided to make a brief stop at our old stomping ground – Gumbert Park, where playground hoops used to seamlessly complement the three Little League baseball fields situated in the park. We pulled up next to the newer courts, which had long since replaced the older ones where we used to play some 100 yards down the road. We pulled into the small parking area right next to the nearest of four courts that sat side by side and watched as a handful of players were playing some half-court hoops. It was a far cry from what Bob and I experienced at the old courts just down the street where some real basketball magic took place. It was not a stretch to say that those courts were the very reason we were sitting there that very day. I told Bob to roll down his window and tell them "We got next" ....

I suppose that day was the tipping point. I had already started writing this book in my mind, imagining what its contents should include. That was the easy part. The hard part was convincing myself that it would be worth it...that anyone would care...that those memories should be reduced to writing and thereby preserved forever. I thought about the alternative, about not writing this book, and the prospect of that season fading into nothingness over time...effectively being buried without a headstone. In the end I simply couldn't accept that. Those 125 days were too special. The recent resurfacing of previously dormant memories was strong evidence of that. I suppose in some ways writing the book would be a way of saying thanks to all my teammates and coaches who helped make it all possible. For everyone else, it would be a way of sharing everything I've learned from a lifetime of basketball, as a player and a fan, as a starter and a bench player, as a student athlete and a member of the real world, as a parent and a child, as a coach and a player, as a teacher and a student, as a young person and an old one. Perhaps most importantly, it would be a chance to relate a basketball fairy tale, a story of what basketball can be, and once upon a time actually was.

Two weeks later I walked out the back door onto our deck with laptop in hand, then sat down, opened it up, and started typing. I had taken the first step in making sure our story would never be forgotten.

I. Going Home

It was about 10 o'clock on a Sunday morning in June 2014 when I kissed my wife goodbye. I then grabbed my car keys and basketball and headed out to the car, tossed the ball in the passenger seat, and backed out the driveway. I was making another trip down to the Westfield YMCA, like I had done dozens of times before. But this trip would be different. I was 60 years old now and didn't live in Westfield anymore. Instead, I would be making the drive from my home in Bucks County, PA, a little more than an hour away. This time I wasn't driving there to play pick-up basketball, but rather to teach it.

About two months earlier, Neil Horne III had emailed me to see if I would be interested in helping out with a one-day fundraising basketball clinic that would be held at the Westfield Y. I had "known" Neil since he was a little over two years old, since his father had been my high school coach my senior year, and little Neil would occasionally make an appearance at our practices. We took advantage of those occasions and put Neil's young talents to work. Bob Jester and I would spin basketballs on our fingers in spare moments and had gotten pretty good at it – particularly Bob, who could spin two balls at once, one on each hand. Sometimes we would substitute a pen or pencil for one of our fingers and spin the ball on that instead. Before long, we had little Neil holding a pencil tight with both hands with a basketball spinning on top of it.

Neil went on to have a nice basketball career of his own, starring at Union Catholic High School in neighboring Scotch Plains, while playing for his dad, and then later at Cornell University and Williams College. He then followed his dad's footsteps by settling in neighboring town of Westfield and raising a family there. Like many Westfield residents and former athletes, Neil got involved in youth sports within the town. Unfortunately, one of the town's staunch supporters of youth athletics, John Dobosiewicz (or Coach "Dobo" as he was known around town) died prematurely at age 49, leaving behind a wife and four kids. Neil was friends of that family and decided to organize this one-day clinic that would raise funds for the benefit of his surviving spouse and those kids. I figured it was the least I could do to help out and would give me an excuse to briefly revisit Westfield, the town where I had grown up and lived for 20 years.

Neil and I both worked in midtown Manhattan at the time, so in early May we agreed to meet for dinner and discuss some of the details of the clinic. On this particular evening Neil was dressed in a nice dark suit and looked more like a corporate attorney than a basketball player, or even a former one at that. While we dined at a nice steakhouse, Neil filled me in on the other volunteers he had lined up. They all had connections with Westfield and basketball, having either coached or played or lived there at some point, some of whom Neil probably knew more through his dad than himself directly. Russell "Boo" Bowers was the only other participant that I knew, but not well, as Boo had played on an excellent team at WHS and graduated five years after me in 1977. Boo went on become a 2,000-point scorer at American University and a third round NBA draft pick in 1981. Boo's daughter, Tamecka Dixon, who had a nice career in the WNBA, was also scheduled to help at the fundraiser.

The clinic was to have several short segments, with each of us teaching one segment. Neil asked me which one I would like, and I quickly chose dribbling. That was something I had always liked and had become good at. I suppose it was inevitable for me, having watched two older brothers play for WHS and grown up in the era of "Pistol" Pete Maravich, who almost single handedly ushered in a new era of ball handling heading into the early 1970s. I'll never forget the feature article in *Sports Illustrated* introducing Pistol Pete entitled "I Want to Put on a Show," in which he described himself as a skinny kid growing up in the South on a diet of dribbling and ball handling drills that his father had devised for him. I remember being fascinated reading about this wiry little kid doing all these crazy basketball drills, just as he was on the verge of exploding onto the college basketball scene. Of course, he ultimately became the greatest scorer in college hoops history, but I always remember him for his remarkable ball-handling skills. He was one of those people that some would describe as being ahead of his time.

A few days later it dawned on me that I would need polish up my own skills so I wouldn't embarrass myself come the day of the clinic. It had been three years since I had last played any hoops, finally surrendering to ongoing meniscus issues in my right knee despite two arthroscopic surgeries on it. I had barely touched a ball since. Furthermore, it had been years since I had done any sort of dribbling or ball-handling drills, so I needed to do something. To make matters worse, I couldn't find a decent ball anywhere in the house or garage. I had no choice but to run over to the mall and plunk down $40 for a good leather ball – now I at least had a chance with about three weeks remaining before the clinic.

As soon as I got home with my new ball, I did what I did countless times growing up, which was to go down to the basement, put the TV on, pull up a chair, and then start dribbling while sitting on the edge of the chair. First several dribbles with one hand, and then changing hands by pulling the ball under my thighs which extended out beyond the chair, and then several dribbles with that other hand. Back and forth I went, trying to get back that familiar feel of the leather against my palms. After a minute or so, I started reversing hands every single dribble, so every dribble was going under my legs, back and forth, left hand to right hand, right hand to left. This was still second nature to me, even without touching a ball for years. After another minute or two, I started doing figure 8s, where the ball was still going back and forth with each dribble, but now each dribble was going between my two thighs rather than under them. This was a lot harder, but after hitting my legs two or three times with the ball, I quickly got into a rhythm with those figure 8 dribbles, squeezing through that narrow space with every dribble…the rust was falling off already!

A day or two later, I returned to the basement to work on a drill that I could use in the clinic and show the kids. One drill out of many came to mind. It was a simple drill called the Square V, which incorporated several different dribbles and didn't require much space. In some ways it was like a standing version of the drill I had just done sitting in the chair. I would start out standing with knees locked, and bent over just slightly at the waist, and then start dribbling the ball in front of me back and forth left to right, right to left, with the ball always landing directly in front of my feet. If you were doing it correctly, your arms would hang like an ape and sway out a little bit to each side as the ball came into your hand and then return to a hanging position once you finished the dribble. The ball itself would take the path of V, with the ball moving up and down at an angle with each dribble, but always landing in front of you. That was the easy part. Then the drill would shift to the left hand where the ball would go front to back and back to front with every dribble, again following a V path along your left side, with the left arm swinging back and forth along with the ball. Then repeat the drill on the right side. Now for the hard part, the last side of the square. This would be very similar to the first part of the drill with the ball going back and forth in front of you, except this time it would go back and forth behind you. This part of the drill was much tougher to do for any period of time without the ball clipping your heels and being deflected away. But that was the whole point of the drill - if you did it repeatedly, it would start to become second nature and it could be done quite effortlessly after much repetition.

A couple of other twists would make the drill more interesting. First, with the ball back in front of you, you would start dribbling back and forth, left to right, right to left, but this time using only one hand rather than switching hands with every dribble. This was more difficult and less natural, but the whole purpose was to give the dribbler the feel of pulling the ball in different directions relative to the body position, which is what needs to happen in game situations when players are constantly moving and any defender within reach might be trying to swipe at the ball.

The second variation was to go back to the first drill using both arms with the ball going back and forth in front of you, but now you would start stepping forward with your legs one at a time while continuing to dribble the ball. The effect of this, would be that as soon as you moved one leg forward, the next dribble would go between the legs, and then as you moved the second leg forward the next dribble would go behind both legs. Now the next steps would be back to their original position, taking one step at a time, so that the 3rd dribble would be between the legs again, and the fourth dribble would be in front of you. This cycle could then be repeated with every four dribbles with two steps going forward and the next two steps going back, but with all the dibbles landing on the same spot for the floor every time if it was being done correctly. The beauty of this drill was that, with only minimal movement of the body, the player would actually be working on cross over dribbles, between the leg dribbles, and behind the back dribbles even though he'd be doing essentially the same dribble for each one. Yes, even fancy dribbling could be shown to be quite simple!

With the benefit of many years of dribbling practice a long time ago, I was able to quickly perform this drill without much difficulty. The rust was continuing to fall off. I returned to the basement several times over the next three weeks and repeated these drills for roughly 10 minutes at a time. Pretty soon I got to a point where I wasn't making many mistakes and knew I wasn't going to embarrass myself in front of the kids. Still, there was one more thing I needed to do before the clinic, and that was to get on an actual court where I'd have more room and I could dribble a ball up and down a court, trying to simulate game-like situations, like I had done thousands of times before.

Getting access to a basketball court wouldn't be that easy, however, so I quickly settled for a racquetball court near where I was working in Springfield, Mass., which also happened to be the home of the Basketball Hall of Fame. I took my ball in there and started working my way back and forth along the hardwood floor, using all of its 40x20 dimensions. Despite being less than half the length and width of a regulation court, it served its purpose and allowed me to use pretty much every dribble in the book…at least my book. I pretended I was bringing the ball up the court in a game situation with a defender guarding me and changing direction every couple of dribbles…it might be a crossover dribble, behind the back, between the legs, or maybe a spin dribble…they could all be effective ways to change directions and shake free of the defender. I did two of these sessions on the racquetball court, about 20 minutes each, and by the end of the second session, I was feeling pretty good and had worked up a good sweat. The ball felt good in my hands, like an extension of the hands, and I felt like I could do pretty much whatever I wanted with the ball…I still had it!!

While I may have been physically prepared for the clinic as the day quickly approached, I wasn't going to play, so I still needed to figure out what to *say* to the kids. There were, of course, the fundamentals of dribbling that I would try to convey to them. But there were also some nuances that I felt were important that they understand. For example, there was more than one kind of dribble…not every dribble occurs right in front of the player, straight up and down, with the same height and tempo like some robot. No, there were high and low dribbles, soft and hard dribbles, slow and fast dribbles, dribbles in front of, beside, behind and underneath the body, dribbles that are pushed out in front of the body and those that are pulled behind the body, and of course dribbles done at all sorts of angles to the court. Just understanding that all these possibilities exist, perhaps supported with some visual aids, should give any young kid something more to shoot for...both more fun and more challenging at the same time. After all, any kid would get bored pretty quickly just bouncing a ball straight up and down without any variation. He or she wouldn't end up practicing very long and chances are would never become much of a ball player.

The day of the clinic finally arrived, and I proceeded to make the hour-long drive from Bucks County, PA, back to Westfield, NJ. On the way there I would pass through Bridgewater and the little town of Finderne where my wife Susan had grown up and where several of her siblings, cousins and other relatives still lived. I had married into a large, close knit Polish family - Susanna Koterba had been the youngest of five kids and her mom had been one of eight – so keeping track of all her cousins, aunts and uncles was a nearly impossible task for me. I had spent a lot of time in that little town over the years and gotten to know many of those relatives, often at happy events like weddings, graduation parties, and the annual Memorial Day picnic, but also at sadder gatherings at the funeral home just down the street. I think the town came to a standstill when Susan's grandmother passed away not long after I had met her, a testament to how close all these relatives remained to each other despite their large numbers.

Susan had apparently been quite the athlete when she grew up. While I did get to see her belt a few balls and race around the bases in one of her softball leagues, I was never able to witness any of her earlier basketball exploits. She was always fond of telling me and our kids about the day in the 8th grade when her aunt took her on a long car ride to receive an MVP trophy for her CYO league from none other than Austin Carr, who was just about to begin his stellar collegiate career at Notre Dame at the time. Topping that was the incredible story Susan's older brother Andy loved to tell. Late one night in 1956 when Susan was barely two years old, she had been rustled out of bed to come meet the great big black man who had just entered their tiny home – none other than the great Bill Russell! Susan's Uncle Joe had been a friend and co-worker of Russell's dad in an Oakland, CA factory and had just hitched a ride cross country with Bill Russell and his parents. He also ran interference for them during their various stops along the way, making sure there wouldn't be any problems inside either dining or using the rest rooms. It was a reflection of the racial prejudices that were still pervasive across the country, and truly ironic that a factory worker from the little town of Finderne, NJ could actually provide shelter to the college basketball player of the year. The two-time NCAA champion at USF was enroute to the White House where he would meet President Eisenhower, but the Russells would first drive directly to Finderne to drop off our Uncle Joe. Andy now regrets losing the old picture of Bill Russell in their back yard shooting a couple of baskets on the hoop right above their detached garage. Shortly afterward the basketball superstar went on to D.C. to meet the President before competing in the Melbourne Olympics later that year and then ultimately joining the Boston Celtics.

It was just another 20 minutes beyond Finderne to reach my destination that morning. Westfield had been the only hometown I ever knew until the age of 25, having moved there at age 3 from North Carolina. I spent my entire childhood growing up and going to school there, so without any other frame of reference I suppose I just took it for granted. Now, now looking back years after having raised a family myself, I see how lucky I was and understand why so many did and still do consider Westfield an attractive place to call home and raise a family.

Westfield, a town of about 30,000 residents, offered a nice suburban lifestyle with its attractive homes, well regarded schools, a bustling downtown area and plenty of transportation options to Manhattan just 24 miles away. The houses in Westfield were very distinctive - one could drive around Westfield for an hour and not see two houses that looked alike, a far cry from many of the cookie cutter homes that seem so prevalent in many of today's newer communities. From little ranches and cape cods to split levels and larger colonials to huge mansions, it was as if there were a different architect for every home built there. The house across the street from my childhood home looked like a gingerbread house. These one-of-a-kind houses were often situated on relatively small, irregular shaped lots along tree lined streets. The diversity of houses was nicely complimented by a picturesque downtown area that might be worthy of a post card.

The appeal of Westfield as a suburban community has not waned over the years, although one regrettable trend appears to be that many of its newer residents have opted to tear down older homes and construct new larger homes on those same small lots. The house I grew up in on Kimball Avenue suffered that fate in the early 2000s and was replaced by a much larger house that has made the property and street almost unrecognizable to me. My parents used to have an old copy of *House Beautiful* magazine which documented their charming cape cod under construction back in the early 1930s. Now you might find their house listed in *House No More*. Bob Jester also saw his parent's longtime home get knocked down shortly after being sold a couple of years ago.

During the drive I struggled to recall the last time I had been to the Y there, but then it came back to me. I had moved away from Westfield at age 28 to Audubon, PA, some two hours away, to start a new job. Seven years later in March 1990, I was on to my next job, in mid-town Manhattan. Our plan was to move back to New Jersey within reasonable commuting distance of Manhattan, but until that happened, I was facing a 2½- hour commute *each way* from my home in Audubon to Manhattan. To make that more tolerable, I quickly started a routine of staying at my parent's house in Westfield two nights a week, the same house on Kimball Avenue I had grown up in.

By the second week of doing that, I decided it was time to get reacquainted with the Westfield Y on a Monday night after a long day of work, not to mention some serious commuting. So back I went, and while there were mostly unfamiliar faces there, there was one familiar face, and two more that would become very familiar over time.

The familiar face belonged to Jeff Bauer. Jeff was a year older than my brother Tom and seven years older than me. Jeff was quite the athlete and baseball player, but I knew him primarily because I had played on Jeff's team in a basketball rec league in Rahway my first year out of college. Jeff was a natural basketball player, and I was a bit envious. Here was a guy who seemingly just showed up at the basketball court one day and actually played really well – a bit unorthodox, perhaps, but very effective. He played fearlessly, like he belonged, and we won the Rahway league that year, I recall. His mom, Kate Bauer, and my mom also happened to be best friends.

Unfortunately, Jeff and his mom were eventually connected to the two most famous murders in Westfield history. Back in the summer of 1972, the spooky house that John List had lived in before murdering his entire family burned to the ground. Kate Bauer bought the house that was later built on that lot, a house that I had once been in. In 1996, a few years after our reacquaintance at the Y, Jeff was tragically murdered by his estranged wife one day when she walked into his office at the Westfield Leader where Jeff helped her mom run the town's weekly newspaper. She promptly shot him at close range before killing herself.

I also got reacquainted with non-other than Neil Horne III, who I believe had just completed his sophomore year at Cornell. Neil introduced himself to me, because the previous time I had seen him he was likely still a toddler, and I couldn't even have picked him out of a lineup. I'm glad that he recognized me, though, and that we got a brief chance to play together, because it's not every day that you get to play basketball with the son of your high school coach!

I was approaching 36 at that time and still playing pretty good basketball, having never stopped playing for any length of time. The Y was pretty crowded my first night back there, and that meant you better win, or you'd be sitting for a while waiting to get back on the court. I couldn't help but notice one short scrappy guy who was all over the court, very disruptive, very talkative, and pretty cocky. On top of that, his team was winning games. Who was this guy? It turned out he knew of me and all about our high school team, and he gave me the impression that he even went to high school with us. But this puzzled me – I would have remembered him. I would leave there never catching his name or finding out who this person was. I would, however, eventually find out who he was long after I had forgotten our brief encounter at the Westfield Y, and fittingly it happened at the most appropriate time and place, and not coincidentally either.

I had daydreamed my way all the way to the Westfield exit, and before I knew it, I arrived at the Y itself. Though I couldn't remember all the street names surrounding the Y, I had no trouble finding the little side street adjacent to the Y's gymnasium, and the two gym doors that were often opened from the inside in response to banging from the outside...allowing another Y crasher to sneak in for the day. I never snuck in that way but had often snuck in through the boy's locker room by the downstairs desk, which always seem to have a lot of activity around it with people coming and going. Invariably, the desk would buzz people in after they checked in at the desk, and if you timed it right, a non-member could nonchalantly duck into the boys' locker room when that door got buzzed open for someone else.

But no need to be buzzed in this day – I was totally legit for once. I checked in at the upstairs desk and before you knew it, I had meandered down a couple of hallways and entered the Y's main gym for the first time in nearly 25 years...I felt like I had finally returned home! It pretty much looked like I remembered it – one regulation full court, two smaller full courts (which is where all the pickup games would be played) running perpendicular to the main court, with six backboards in total. The sound of bouncing balls and squeaking sneakers permeated with kids shooting around everywhere in the gym. I couldn't resist and started shooting around myself as if I were one of the day campers. The juices were flowing, the body felt good, and I was itching to play a little full court 5-on-5 if only I could.

Neil Horne III quickly spotted me and then introduced me to John Dobosiewicz's widow, for whom this clinic was really being conducted. I hadn't forgotten that, just like I hadn't forgotten the first basketball clinics I had attended on Saturday mornings at the Washington School. I thanked her for her husband's dedicated service to the youth of Westfield and wished her and her kids well in their difficult journey onward without him.

The four-hour clinic would go by quickly and very much according to script, thanks to the organizational skills of Neil III and his determination to make sure it was a successful event. To be sure, the kids got all sorts of great instruction on every aspect of the game by people who had tons of experience either playing or coaching the game, or in many cases both. There were some 60 or 70 kids there, boys and girls, ranging from the third through eighth grade, probably the ages when they can benefit the most from good instruction, not to mention being the most open to it as well. I got to do my little session and demonstrate the "square V" dribble, and explain how they could use it to transform an otherwise more difficult or fancier dribble into a very simple one.

The best part, however, and the part I remember the most, was the last few minutes of the clinic that Neil III reserved for me to talk to the kids about stuff that went beyond the fundamentals. The kids and other coaches all gathered at half court, and I proceeded to tell them about the things that I thought would help them the most to become a better basketball player. I told them that it starts with a belief that you can become a great player. But then you have to do something about it, and that meant practicing a lot, not just once in a while when you felt like it. I brought up the example of how Pistol Pete Maravich had done countless repetitive drills to become an unbelievable dribbler, and how they could do many of those same drills in their own basement. It might even drive their parents crazy with the constant sound of a bouncing ball. I told them that the single most important thing that helped me get better may have been Tim Goski always calling me up and saying: "Come on, Redeye, let's play some one-on-one." I explained that Tim went on to become perhaps the greatest high school player in WHS basketball history, but at the time he still hadn't played in a single varsity game yet. Those simple games of one-on-one made us both better because you pretty much had to do everything – dribble, make offensive moves with the ball, shoot, box out, rebound, and most importantly, play defense. I told them that to become better they were going to have to resist many of the temptations out there that would get in the way of doing the things we had just talked about – constant smart phone use being the most obvious example. Becoming a great basketball player was not something they would be able to push a button for, order online, or achieve quickly in any way. No one becomes great overnight. It takes time, hard work and persistence.

Lastly, I showed them something, hoping it would solidify any impression I might have made on them up to that point, so that maybe, just maybe, it wouldn't all be forgotten a couple of days later. I opened a manila folder and removed a large newspaper clipping, still in nearly mint condition 42 years after its printing, unfolded it, and with two hands help it up for all the kids to see. From where they were sitting, they could only make out the headline, which was all they needed to see. It read in big, bold letters: **"Westfield – the dream comes true!"**

II.   A Dream is Born (Dec 1, 1964 – Feb 28, 1971)

My first recollection of basketball was back in the fifth grade. Tom Pfeiffer and I both went to Wilson School and knew each other since the first grade, and Tom happened to be the best athlete of our class. The two of us, along with a few other Wilson classmates, would often play two-on-two games in one of our driveways. When we weren't playing two-on-two, we might just be shooting around and pretending we were taking the last shot as the clock wound down in the state championship game down in Atlantic City ... 3 ... 2 ... 1 ... Yes, and it counts!!!

That same year my older brother Tom was a junior and starting guard for Westfield High School hoops team. I remember going to many of those games on Friday nights with Pfeiffer and our dads. Tom's dad was a big fan of WHS sports, not to mention one of its most vocal ones. I really looked forward to those Friday night games – after all, who didn't like watching their older brothers play sports for their high school team? They were so much bigger than us at the time -they seemed like gods! It was truly exciting when Westfield pulled off the upset of Scotch Plains in the semis of the Union County Tournament that year, and then followed it up by beating a powerful 21-1 Cranford team in the finals to capture the whole tournament. Winning the Union County Tournament was a big deal, and I remember how excited and proud my dad was later that evening when we got home after the big victory.

Our introduction to the world of hoops continued the following year, with my brother Tom now a senior and my other brother Mark was now a sophomore and one of the starting guards on the JV team, while Pfeiffer and I were now in sixth grade. So now Friday nights were even more special because I would get to watch both my brothers play in consecutive games, with the JV game at 6:30 and the Varsity contest at 8 pm. Those Friday night games were followed by Saturday morning clinics at Washington grammar school. The clinic was for sixth graders, so this was our first chance to learn and compete in an organized way, as the only thing we had played up to that point was driveway hoops at somebody's house. We were in our glory. I remember Tom and I were two of the better players, along with Alan

Deombeleg and a kid named Bob Walchen, who was seemingly two years ahead of everybody else in terms of physical maturity and overall skills.

We would get a rude awakening one Saturday afternoon when one of the parents took an "All Star" team from that clinic to compete in a tournament about a half-hour away. We faced a bigger, faster team from Perth Amboy with several black players, which was all a bit intimidating to me given that I didn't know a single black person – in fact, I don't even remember a single black person being in my grammar school. But it wasn't the color of their skin that was putting us on our heels that day; rather, it was their size, speed and skill that overwhelmed us, as they whipped us by 50 or so and also cracked the 100-point barrier, which naturally brought even more cheers from the raucous little crowd there. Before we limped out of the gym, we watched a few minutes of the next game, which featured neighboring Scotch Plains. I distinctly recall this little point guard who may have been under five-feet tall but seemed fearless and very skillful despite his lack of stature. One play stood out when his opponent had driven down the lane completely past him, but somehow the ball and the kid were now heading down the other end of the court for a lay-up – he had picked his pocket clean! I wasn't surprised to learn the following week that Scotch Plains had won that game, but I was shocked to hear that Scotch Plains then turned around and beat the boys from Perth Amboy who had whipped our butts! That tiny guard must have been even better than I imagined he might be. As it would turn out, I'd be seeing a lot more of him in the years ahead but wouldn't learn his name for another two years.

The next year we graduated to the seventh-grade recreation league on Saturdays at the Washington School where we all got our first taste of playing on an organized basketball team with coaches, refs, scorekeepers … everything. By this time at age 12 or 13, most of us had already played at least one year of organized football and three years of Little League baseball, so basketball was a little behind the other major sports in this respect. Better late than never, though, and the league did help identify the players most likely to be playing for their school teams the next year in eighth grade, whether it be Roosevelt or Edison Junior High.

Meanwhile, my older brother Tom had graduated and was off to college, and my brother Mark was now the big man in our house as one of the starting guards both his junior and senior years on the WHS varsity team. There was also a new head coach in town, Bob Fulton, who had taken over the varsity duties from Bob Stanislow. Hard-nosed defense and hustle were two of his focal points, and at the dinner table I would hear stories about floor burns and running into walls being amongst the things that Fulton expected from his players. Without realizing it, maybe hearing all this helped me prepare, even if subconsciously, for what would come the first day of tryouts for the eighth-grade team.

Sixty kids showed up that first day, a day I will never forget. This was the first school basketball team that any of those 60 kids ever had a chance to make, so many parents probably sent their kids there thinking it was the right thing to do. We soon found out that it was not. Our coach that year would be Richard Gralweski, a rather short, stocky guy with a crew cut that didn't particularly look like a basketball player. But he made it clear right from the beginning that his mission was to identify the 15 players who would make the team.

The weeding out process would be quick, but painful. We did a variety of basketball dribbling and passing drills, interspersed with running, lots of running. That was my introduction to suicides, as they were more affectionately called, and something I was not prepared for. Gralewski would blow the whistle and get everyone on the baseline, broke us into two groups (maybe three that first day), and then blew the whistle again to start the running. Quarter-court, half-court, three-quarters court, full-court, up and back, touching each line along the way, sprinting the whole way. It was relentless, almost never stopping, except for that brief period when the others were doing their running.

Who knows how many sets of suicides we did that first day? Six? Eight? 10? It's hard to count when you're doubled over sucking for air during the only moments when you're not doing the actual running. I'm sure a few kids got sick that day, and a few others just didn't show up the next day. I was one of the better athletes trying out, but I wasn't ready for the onslaught that my body underwent that first day and first week. It was a crash course in conditioning. Not just getting our bodies conditioned, but understanding what it meant to be conditioned. Well, there is no substitute for experience, and I had now experienced conditioning.

Two days later, 15 kids had been cut and likely put out of their misery at the same time, and two days after that another 15. We were now down to 30 kids, with one more round of cuts to go. I figured I was pretty safe, and that after four days our coach should know who I was and wouldn't cut me by mistake, given the sheer number of bodies. I got that confirmation another two days later when I survived the final cut, but Gralewski gave me a little scare that next day when he was handing out practice jerseys after he had told everyone that he could still make further cuts if he thought it necessary. Then, as he handed me my jersey, he said "You could be the last to go." Maybe it was just clever coaching psychology he was applying on me, but whatever his intent it absolutely scared me into taking nothing for granted and playing as hard as I could.

I suppose there was something else working in my favor – an expectation that I not let others down. It wasn't that my parents or anyone pushed me at all, but it just seemed normal that I should do everything my older brothers had done and were still doing at an older age. My father had coached all three of us on the Little League Pirates over a 10-year span, so that experience reinforced the notion that whatever your older brothers did, I should do too.

On top of that, there was something bigger going on in Westfield. There was this football machine that was able to mow down opposing teams from neighboring towns year after year. Not that I knew much about it, barely completing two seasons of Pop Warner football before turning in my shoulder pads for good. But I knew enough that there had to be something special about the head coach Gary Kehler that made those teams keep winning year after year. Saturdays in the fall always seemed like a special time in Westfield, whether you were part of the football team or not. You didn't have to play football or understand trap blocks or 5 holes to appreciate what Kehler was accomplishing year after year on the football field. There was something magical about it. I remember walking to some of their home games - once you got within about a half mile of the field you could hear the stadium loudspeaker, the sounds of the marching band, and the inevitable roar of the crowd whenever the Blue Devils broke another play open. Once there, I would often watch from behind the end zone fence, and seeing play after play where several Westfield players would all be pulling in one direction, and then the next thing you know is that the ball and runner is coming back in another direction seemingly against the grain, or finding that one hole in the line that would conveniently open up at just the right time. This was a well-oiled machine, and Kehler was the master mechanic overseeing it all and keeping it finely tuned.

The varsity basketball teams hadn't been too shabby, either. While they didn't have the same track record or reputation that the football program had, they still had experienced a lot of recent success and had an air of respectability about them – they were also someone to look up to. Without realizing it at the time, growing up with those surroundings was subconsciously preparing me for what I would need to do in the years ahead. The day the suicides came out of the blue, there was no thought of quitting … I had to be one of the last boys standing.

When he wasn't busy conditioning us, Coach Gralewski taught us a lot about playing defense - in particular, team defense. Both he and ninth-grade coach Joe Leonzi explained the proper positioning of each player in relation to the ball, the man you were guarding, and the basket. There should always be a triangle formed by ball-you-man with your back always facing the basket. The further your man was away from the ball, the further you should be away from your man, allowing you to provide more help to the man guarding the ball, if necessary, but also enough time to recover back to your own man if a pass was made to him. You should always have an arm extending into the passing lane between the ball and your man (one side of the triangle), and you should never turn your back on the ball – better to lose sight of your man than the ball. We worked on this constantly. First with players and the ball in stationary positions, and then with each moving. The faster the ball moved, the quicker you needed to react and adjust your defensive position on the court. It was the foundation of good team defense. Coach Leonzi was determined that we execute this the right way. Whenever a player would object that he couldn't get to a certain spot that fast, Leonzi's response was always the same: "Hey, can't do, can't play!"

While the suicides weren't as insane as they were during tryouts, there were still a regular part of our practices on a daily basis. After all, one doesn't get fully conditioned in a week. Suicides were a convenient and often desired form of punishment. I remember one day in ninth grade we had an 11 am practice during mid-winter school break in February, so there was no school that week. Lou Case, who had just moved to town that year, and was now part of our ninth-grade hoops team, made the mistake of walking into practice a few minutes before noon. Worse still was his excuse that he had overslept. That was all Leonzi needed to hear. "Everybody on the line!" Everybody, except Louie, of course. We all got to run suicides for about the next 10 minutes, all except Lou, who had to just stand there and painfully watch. Talk about master psychology! This would make you think twice about letting your teammates down. Thanks a lot, Louie.

There were certain other drills that weren't so pleasant either. A simple boxing out drill was one. Coach would place the basketball in the middle of the circle, with four guys inside the circle, and another four just outside the circle. When the whistle blew, the four inside guys had to keep the other four from getting to the ball within five seconds by boxing them out, i.e., by keeping your body between the offensive player and ball without using your hands or otherwise holding them. It was extremely hard to keep your man from reaching the ball for the full five seconds, and bodies were flying everywhere and often converging at the ball. The drill was effective though – it did what it was intended to do – i.e., teach you how to box out. If you could even get close to succeeding in this drill, you could easily box out for the 1 second required in real game conditions. If you watch an NBA or college game today, the boxing out technique is pathetic or non-existent. Those players obviously didn't play for Gralewski or Leonzi.

Coach Leonzi even had these smaller rebounding rims that would snap into place over the standard 18-inch rim, making it much harder for the ball to find its way through the hoop. We'd be out there in a 5-on-5 half court position, and then Leonzi would then shoot the ball up from various spots on the floor, triggering an all-out scramble to the rebound if you were part of the offensive five, or to keep your body between your man and the ball if you were on defense. I've never seen those special rebounding rims ever since then, but they most certainly served their purpose. It's fair to say that we learned *how* to box out. More important still, we learned *to box out!*

Those drills were tough enough for me, at about 5-foot-6 and skinny as a rail in the eighth grade, but the next one was even tougher. One of the other foundations of good team defense was taking a charge – i.e., planting your body directly in front of an oncoming opposing player and taking it right on the chest as he plowed into your space. Gralewski, of course, had the perfect drill for this. We formed two lines on the baseline, one directly under the basket and one in the corner. People in the corner line had a ball, the others did not. When the whistle blew, the job of the first person in line with the ball was to dribble down the sideline as fast as they could, while the job of the first person in the other line was to sprint downcourt at an angle towards the sideline in order to cut off the person dribbling straight down the sideline. It doesn't take a math major to figure out that you had to run pretty darn fast to make up the extra ground in order to get ahead of the person with the ball, turn your body, and then come to an abrupt stop while planting yourself directly in the path of the oncoming dribbler. Your reward for this all-out effort was to get immediately run over! Unfortunately for me, half the guys on the team were also football players, some of whom probably outweighed me by 30 or 40 pounds. Worse still, some were just plain animals out there. Pete Parken, who would later go on to be a standout wrestler and football player at WHS, appeared to enjoy proving that the player in his path could not deter him from reaching the other baseline!

Coach Leonzi was also a huge fan of taking charges, and even had a system of rewarding players for taking charges with a star that would get sown onto your game shorts if you ever took three charges in a single game, as well as for every five you took on a cumulative basis, sort of like Ohio State football players getting "buckeyes" on their helmets. I took three charges my very first game in ninth grade, so all of those drills was paying off. Perhaps more importantly, it helped me earn the confidence of my coaches despite my skinny frame. Leonzi came to my defense, according to one of my friends, when after history class one day one of Leonzi's students was claiming that football players were better athletes than basketball players. Leonzi would not take sides and wanted to remain impartial, given that he coached both sports, but when the student cited skinny little Reddy as evidence to back his claim, Leonzi responded emphatically: "Hey, Reddy's tough!"

from left, 1ˢᵗ row: S Tebbets, J Havas, P Anderson, T Pfeiffer, S Reddy, J Zimmerman, B Taylor. 2ⁿᵈ row: D Jester, D Reiter, A Deombeleg, B Nelson, N Glenn, D Hylander. 3ʳᵈ row: Coach Gralewski, R Sharp, P Parken, B Conklin, P Hugger

Coaches Gralewski and Leonzi got us conditioned to play real games, whether it was running or getting run over, but it turned out I still wasn't ready for my first real game against another school's team. I played most of that game, scored seven points, lost a close one, and then was so exhausted I went to bed at 7:30 that night.

While we were learning how to play team basketball, we were also learning more about who our opposition was in neighboring towns, like Linden, Cranford, Union, and most of all, Scotch Plains. In some cases, we played two separate junior high schools from these towns. Scotch Plains was the prime example of this, with teams from both Park and Terrill Jr High on our schedule each year with both home and away games, so that we would play Scotch Plains four times each year. They quickly became our main rivals, with each team having their standouts. I'll never forget the first time we played Park at home and they walk into the gym right off the bus with this 6-foot-3 guy, Steve Deck, towering about the rest of us, a full nine inches taller than me. He was not a stiff, either, and combined with other solid players like Jeff Warner and Chris Hahn, Park simply had more size and strength than we could handle. We would lose to them all four times during the eighth and ninth grade seasons, including one blowout loss in their tiny gym where they would full court press us all game, and in eighth grade they hit the 100-point mark and caused the crowd to go nuts at our expense. It was now the second time I had been on the receiving end of a triple digit butt whupping.

We fared a little better against Terrill Junior High, splitting the four games with them over two years. Terrill had a couple of standout players. First, was Eddie Miller, who had an incredible jump shot for someone that age, getting way off the floor and cocking the ball way behind his head as part of his shooting motion. The second was a skinny little kid, skinnier than me, who was a bit of a ball handling and passing wizard that made up for his lack of size. It turned out that his small stature was partially explained by the fact that he was only in 7th grade while I was in 8th, but his advanced skills were corroborated by the fact that he played on both of Terrill's 8th and 9th grade teams that year. Something looked familiar about him, though, and then it hit me – this was the same kid that had caught my eye two years earlier in Perth Amboy making a dazzling steal and subsequent layup. Now he really had my attention. The kid's name was Ray Schnitzer.

From the beginning I was fascinated by Schnitzer's dribbling ability and flair. He had this very slender build and tiny hands that were dwarfed by the size of the ball, yet the ball seemed somehow connected to his hands. While he wasn't being fancy at all with behind the back or between-the-legs dribbles, he had uncanny control of the ball as he drove through traffic with bigger and stronger defenders seemingly all around him. He would often use no look passes to fake out defenses at a time when no look passes were pretty unusual for any player, let alone a seventh grader.

It was during these eighth and ninth grade years that I learned something important that seems so simple – what it means to be skilled at something! Ray Schnitzer was one example of someone with a very good skill, but I actually learned more about skills from the most unlikely of places – eighth grade typing class. I remember being amazed that someone could actually type 60 words a minute...how could a person's fingers actually move that fast in a coordinated fashion? After a few typing classes I started to appreciate the value of repetitive drills for the fingers to get them to move in the right manner at the right time. Just like a dribbler in basketball shouldn't need to look down to see where the ball is going, nor should a typist have any need to look down at the keyboard while typing. At some point I made the connection between the two and realized that practice really did make you more skillful and produce this thing called muscle memory. There was something almost magical about it, that little fingers could move in such an intricate manner to speedily create a perfectly typed page of text, or that the tiny hands of a Ray Schnitzer could make a much larger ball do things that other players couldn't do.

This hit home with me with even greater impact after a ninth-grade team practice when someone mentioned the name of Pete Maravich for the first time and how he was lighting it up in college playing for LSU. Naturally I was curious and wanted to get a glimpse of him, but that wasn't so easy in the pre-ESPN days of college basketball. Eventually there was a Saturday night LSU game that aired on our little black and white TV where I got that glimpse. I remember Maravich toying with the opposition as he played keep-away while putting on a dribbling exhibition over the last 90 seconds. His ball handling skills appeared exceptional, but he also had a flair for the game that almost jumped out of the grainy black and white TV picture. It was only then that I began to fully appreciate what could be done with a basketball.

While our eighth and ninth grade seasons got us acquainted with our opposition and how to play organized team basketball, we also learned a lot more about ourselves. Pfeiffer was still our stud, with a good combination of size, strength, athleticism, and basketball skill. John Havas, Don Reiter, and Neil Glenn were our other starters for much of that time, along with me. Deombeleg and Dave Jester were our other key players. Several of them would go on to distinguish themselves in other sports more so than in basketball – Havas in baseball, Reiter in soccer, Deombeleg in football, and Jester in tennis. But Pfeiffer was the one guy who was cut out to excel in multiple sports as we approached our high school years, and it was pretty clear that his dad, who was seemingly ever-present at every sporting event in Tom's life, would push Tom to do just that.

Back in the late '60s and early '70s it was common for the better athletes to play multiple sports all the way throughout their high school years. The age of specialization at a young age, evidenced by travel teams and AAU competition, thankfully hadn't yet arrived. Kids still had a realistic option to keep playing multiple sports, but that didn't necessarily mean they were good enough to star in all those sports, especially at the high school level when the pool of athletes to draw from was much larger.

As for me, I suppose I made my choice earlier than most, as I was only playing hoops even in junior high. As a 12-year-old sixth grader in Little League baseball, I came out of nowhere and became the home run king with eight homers in our 18 games. The majority of them even came at the expense of the most feared pitchers in the league at the time, including two off of Havas, one off Deombeleg, and even one off superstud Joe Monninger, who would later become the star quarterback for the WHS varsity football team. I was able to get away with it as a skinny 12-year-old, but the next year we moved up to the Pony League and the bigger field where my lack of arm strength would make a real difference. I had such a bad tryout as a 13-year-old that my father's close friend Lank Siebert, who had coached the Rangers for many years and had drafted both my brothers Tom and Mark in prior years, passed me over in the draft despite my impressive resume from just one season earlier. Not surprisingly, I started to lose my love of organized baseball around that time. Maybe in part because I had been cast off, in part because of lack of physical strength, and in part because I had just lost the desire.

At Roosevelt, our eighth and ninth grade hoops teams finished with 8-4 and 8-6 records, so we certainly didn't stand out against our competition. One big win, though, was against Terrill the last game of the season in ninth grade at their place. We had gone down 13-1 before Leonzi called a timeout to stop the bleeding against the Schnitzer and Miller led team, and we scrapped our way back and ended up winning by 10. That game gave me confidence that we could beat a good team and that I could compete with a tough player like Ray Schnitzer.

The summer of 1969 would be my last before entering Westfield High as a sophomore. I suppose the prospect of that scared me into practicing basketball for the first time during the summer. I knew it was something I was supposed to do if I wanted to get better, although like most kids those days, when it was out of season, it just wasn't that appealing to me. I preferred hanging out at Echo Lake, where several of my friends were spending their summers swimming or playing golf. But the prospect of entering high school soon made this summer different and had me concerned, not because high school was a scary place, but because I knew I would face more competition. All the boys from Roosevelt and Edison would be playing for one team now, and like a game of musical chairs, a lot of good players were going to get left out.

So practice I did. Mostly just dribbling and shooting in the backyard. I remember watching the Lunar Landing in July 1969 in our basement, where I would go back and forth between dribbling while sitting in a chair in front of our grainy black and white TV and dashing out the door into our driveway to shoot and dribble around. At one point that summer I broke my left index finger dribbling in the driveway. I remember doing it on a cross-over dribble and somehow hit my left hand against one of my knees, which is a weird way to break a finger, but I managed to do it.

By this time, I was about 5-foot-9, steadily getting taller at the rate of about two inches a year. Unfortunately, I wasn't filling out in other directions, so the extra height was only making me look skinnier, which is exactly what I was. Alan Deombeleg had already given me the nickname "Spider", and though he was the only one who called me that, it was quite appropriate. I must have weighed between 115 and 120 pounds at the time – not exactly football material! So that summer I attempted to do something about it, using the dumbbells and barbells that my older brothers had used in our basement. I had no idea what I was doing or what exercises might be helpful, other than perhaps some arm curls and military presses. Within about two days I had overdone it … nothing serious, just some strained muscles for a novice who had no idea what he was doing and no clue as to the proper technique.

Shortly after that, I was at Echo Lake where I worked as a locker room attendant. Gary Kehler happened to be the pool manager at the time (I guess even the town heroes could use the extra paycheck), and one of his assistant coaches, Bob Martin, was also there on occasion, perhaps planning the upcoming double sessions with his boss. Kehler was always nice to me, skinny little runt that I was, but Martin was another story. One day we were all having lunch at the snack bar and Martin asked me when I was going to hit the weights and put some meat on my bones. I sheepishly explained that I had just started doing weights at home but that I had overdone it and had to take a break, which, as feeble as it sounded, was all true. Martin wasn't having any of it and gave me a look that said: "You're full of shit."

The next thing I knew I was in high school and two short months later basketball tryouts for the JV team began. I was already familiar with a few of the main Edison faces from the Washington School league - namely, Steve Lee, Steve Crane, John Willard, Neil Chamberlain, and, of course, Bob Walchen. By this time Lee looked like the best player amongst them all, with a combination of good athleticism and basketball skills. Willard and Chamberlain, meanwhile, were the best big men amongst the bunch, but "big" just meant they had about two inches on most of the rest of us. There was also Craig Larsen, the smallest kid out there, but an absolute demon on defense. He literally appeared to salivate over playing man-to-man defense, almost frothing at the mouth, shuffling his feet in a hyper rapid manner and getting in your jock. You weren't going to be able to coast against this guy.

Meanwhile, there were a few changes on the coaching front. Bob Fulton, the varsity head coach who had coached my brother Mark for two seasons, had moved on to a new coaching job somewhere in Pennsylvania. His younger brother Cy was then promoted to become the the new varsity head coach. That meant the JV team had a vacancy, which was filled by Ed Tirone, who had coached the Edison ninth-grade team the prior year. Coach Tirone was very easy going on the outside but was no patsy once practice got going. We may have run less suicides that year, but we still did those boxing out drills around a circle, except now you had bigger bodies diving for the ball sitting in the middle – it's a wonder no one ever got a concussion! Tirone also loved pushups, fingertip pushups to be more precise. That's all we did, so only the ends of each finger touched the ground. At the time I thought this was just meant to discipline us or punish us for something done the wrong way. Over time, however, I realized that they made your fingers and hands much stronger, which would make you better equipped to dribble the ball or snatch a rebound or pass out of the air. One day Tirone had us in the pushup position for what seemed like 25 straight minutes while he made it perfectly clear who was in charge. I don't remember exactly what provoked it, but I do remember hurting all over and guys peeling themselves off the floor when it was finally all over.

I was by now a full 5-foot-10 tall and a whopping 120 pounds or so. I managed to beat out my competition for starting guard, or at least enough of it, as Lee and I ended up takings those starting spots. Pfeiffer had a solid hold on one of the forward spots, while the other spot shared between a few guys – Willard, Chamberlain, Glenn, and Lou Case. Peter Hugger was our 6-foot-5 center with gigantic hands that could palm the ball even back in the eighth grade, but his skills were never the asset that his size was, so sometimes we went small and played three forwards.

We had a pretty solid year, going 15-7, making a surprise run to the finals of the Union County tournament, upsetting highly favored Roselle in the second round but eventually losing to a perennially tough Linden team in the finals. Roselle Catholic had the biggest gym in the area and always hosted the last rounds of the tournament back in those days. In the semifinals at that gym, we won a scrappy battle against a favored Jefferson team, and I went to the foul line 16 times, more times than I ever would. I swished the first 11 before finally missing, and finally ended up 14-for-16 from the line, along with only one field goal to give me 16 points for the game. Towards the end of the game, after one of my many free throws, someone behind the basket yells: "Way to go, Twiggy," in a mocking reference to the ultra-skinny British supermodel at the time. Everyone heard it, and many laughed, and I certainly would have too had I been sitting in the stands and not the obvious target of the proclamation. Instead, I pretended not to hear anything. I was having too good a game to let it bother me, and we were close to our second straight upset win on our way to the finals. I filed it away in the back of my brain for later processing.

As part of the JV team, one naturally spends a fair amount of time watching the varsity team play, the team that we would hopefully be joining the following year. They were mediocre, at best, with a 6-13 record that year. They also had one guy who caught my attention, although unfortunately, for the wrong reasons. This kid who was a junior and about 6-foot-2, and may have been even skinnier than I was, if that was possible. Or maybe it was just that he was three or four inches taller than me that made him look skinnier than me. Either way, I couldn't help thinking that I might be looking at a future version of myself, and I didn't like what I was seeing. For the time being, all I could do was make a mental note of it. After all, the middle of the season was no time to think about actually *gaining* weight.

There was one other brief conversation I remember from that sophomore year. Deombeleg, who had decided to forgo high school hoops to focus on football, told me to watch out for a ninth grader from Holy Trinity who was rumored to be transferring to WHS the next year. That ninth-grader's name was Tim Goski. I sort of knew who Tim and his father were from Little League baseball a few years earlier, but had no idea he even played basketball, or how he could be that good to draw the attention of Alan, who wasn't particularly focused on hoops at that point. Alan added that Goski been playing a lot at Gumbert, the local playground where a lot of hoops was being played in the summer. This was something I was completely unaware of simply because I hadn't been there the previous summer. I was a little skeptical though, remembering Tim as a bit on the small side, and for whatever reason I couldn't envision him as a basketball player or someone I would have to compete against. "We'll see about that," I confidently replied to Alan.

The conclusion of our JV season coincided with the first championship run of the NY Knicks that spring, with Willis Reed, Dave DeBusschere, Bill Bradley, and Walt "Clyde" Frazier. Frazier had an epic final game to close out the series, finishing with 36 points, 19 assists and seven steals to lead the Knicks to their first NBA title while giving NY metro area fans something to cheer about after years of domination suffered at the hands of the Boston Celtics.

The ultra-smooth Frazier, who in three seasons had become one of the league's new stars and known for his cool on-court demeanor, was now the pro I most wanted to emulate. Clyde was also known for his quick hands and was rumored to be able to catch flies right out of the air. I started doing this one drill to improve my own hand quickness. The drill required taking two coins, such as two quarters, and laying them on the back of your hand as you extended your hand and arm out in front of you at shoulder height so the palm of your hand was facing down. The challenge was to drop your hand out from under the coins, then to circle your hand back around the falling coins and then catch them <u>one-at-a-time</u> and <u>from the top</u>, catching the nearer one first. This meant you needed to do two loops with your hand, catching one coin from the top at the end of each loop. To start the drill, one must keep their hand and the coins perfectly still and not push them upwards at all; instead, the coins must go straight down. The drill is not easy at all…in fact, very few people can do it. Coins usually go flying all over the place, and most people can't even catch one coin from the top. Perhaps my practice paid off because I got very good at it, and to this day can catch both coins on most tries.

While the Knicks were doing their thing, we learned of another coaching change. Cy Fulton was out as the varsity head coach, not surprising, given the 6-13 record, and his replacement would be Joe Coleman, who had been the head coach at nearby Plainfield. That summer I played in a summer league that had players from several Union County towns and which played the games at Gumbert Park and the Forest Avenue courts in Scotch Plains. I played a little more pick up ball at Gumbert that summer, partly out of fear of the consequences of not doing so, but don't remember running into Goski there. But there were four courts at Gumbert, and I still wasn't going near Court 1, where the older, bigger, stronger, more established players would play, including college players like John Shumate and John Somogyi. Perhaps Tim was over there and I was just being a wimp.

The Fall of 1970 soon came along with my junior year in high school. I was now a full 6-feet tall and had continued my pathetic weight gain rate of a few pounds per year, maybe pushing 130 pounds soaking wet. Whatever plans I had to add more muscle and more weight during the current offseason didn't come to fruition. I didn't need any reminders of that nagging fact, but one September day after school I got the most ignominious one you can imagine. I knew several guys on the football team, including Pfeiffer and Bruce Cant, who were now on the vaunted varsity football team, and I decided to watch a preseason scrimmage after school. Afterwards as I was leaving and heading across the field to the parking lot, I crossed paths with my old nemesis, Bob Martin, who sneeringly greeted me with: "What are you doing here, Reddy? This ball has points on it." I did my best to ignore him and just kept right on walking as if his words meant nothing and warranted no reaction. Of course, that was easier said than done. I knew exactly what he meant. "You don't belong here. You might get hurt if the football hits you. Go back and play your sissy sport." This incident was going to be harder to shrug off or ignore, and given that he was also a gym teacher, our paths would undoubtedly cross again.

Before you knew it basketball season was upon us once again. Among the juniors who were moving up from JV were Pfieffer, Lee and myself. We also had Larry Simmons, a new kid from Newark who had just moved to town to live with his aunt and played on the football team in the fall. Larry was somewhat of a physical stud, with well-defined muscles and an imposing afro hairdo that made him look more like 6-foot-5 than his true height of 6-2. Rounding out the juniors were guards Crane and Larsen, part of the Edison crew.

We managed to improve upon the lowly 6-13 record from the prior year by going 13-10 for the 1970-71 season, at least an air of respectability. Pfeiffer again held up his part of the bargain and started the entire season at one of the forward spots. I had a good game coming off the bench in the fourth game of the year, at Springfield, and managed to harass their top gun, Ed Greassle, into a mediocre game. We narrowly missed the upset of heavily favored Springfield, but I won the starting job from senior guard Eric Hohlman. I started the next seven games, six of which we won, before losing it back to Eric. Even though I was physically outmatched by most of my competition that year, I managed to have a respectable season.

Meanwhile, I think we juniors all had one eye on the JV team that year, highlighted by the presence of Goski after his transfer from Holy Trinity, as well as center Scott Novacek. I had never seen Novacek (aka "Nova") before this season, and while his long blonde hair and big broad shoulders were very distinctive, my first impression was that he seemed a bit stiff and awkward in his movement out on the court. Perhaps unorthodox is a better description, because he was certainly very coordinated and quite a physical specimen. He was also proving to be a real rebounding force around the boards.

Of course, I also got a good look at Goski, the basketball player, to replace the old image I had of a Little League baseball player. Sure enough, Deombeleg's cautionary note to watch out for Goski was not misguided. Tim was maybe an inch shorter than me, pretty lean in the upper body, but well-built below the waist, not plagued with the skinny thighs that I had. More importantly, he exhibited an air of confidence out on the court, and an array of ball handling skills and offensive moves with the ball. He also wasn't at all bashful with his shot.

The JV team excelled that year and finished with an 18-4 record, but it wasn't just Goski and Novacek propelling them. Mike Cooney was a solid ball handler with a nice jump shot, Bob Jester a tough defender and forward who wasn't afraid to mix it up on the boards, and Dave "Moose" Phillips had an uncanny jump shot for a big bulky guy. The one blemish on the JV team that year was their inability to conquer Scotch Plains and Schnitzer, who was still working his magic and led his team to three wins over our JV team that year, with the third and final win occurring in the finals of the Union County tournament. So, 18-4 overall, but an even better 18-1 against all other teams not named Scotch Plains.

Shortly after that tough end to the JV season, the varsity team went into the state tournament against a very strong Linden team that had lost only two games all year. We were big underdogs – after all, Linden had whupped us 104-71 just three weeks earlier, but we played like a different team and took Linden right down to the wire, down by only two inside the last minute and ultimately losing by six points. Pfeiffer played a great all-around game, and Coleman gave Simmons a chance to see what he could do against Linden by starting him. Larry didn't disappoint, and his presence on defense and the boards may have been the biggest reason that game stayed close. Though Lee and I sat the bench that day, there was hope for us juniors that next year would be better once we joined forces with all those upstart sophomores that had just propelled the JV team to a very successful season.

I remember riding the bus back to our gym that day thinking how I hated the abrupt ending to seasons. We had just played our best game of the year and almost pulled off the huge upset, but it was all for naught. There would be no more practices in Westfield's gym for a while. Instead, it would be baseball players, tennis players, and golfers who would take center stage for the next two or three months. I remember staring out the bus window on our way home thinking there would be no baseball for me … or tennis or golf, for that matter. No, I had something else I needed to do, something I had been putting off for too long, and the time had finally come to take care of business.

III.   Paradise and a Parking Lot

"If you build it, they will come."

That's what the Westfield Recreation Commission had in mind when they gave approval to the construction of an outdoor ice skating rink in Gumbert Park that could double as a parking lot, as documented by the Westfield Leader on September 3, 1964:

"The Westfield Recreation Commission Monday night gave approval to plans to build a 75x250 foot ice skating rink in Gumbert Field. In the summer, the rink will be used as a parking lot. It can also be used as a basketball court in both the summer and winter, officials said."

If the Commission was hoping people would come, they got their wish. But they didn't come for the reason expected. No, they came for something that was almost an afterthought of the Commission. They came to play basketball.

My first memories of Gumbert Park in Westfield were from when I was about 6 years old. My older brothers Tom and Mark, were 12 and 10 at the time, playing for the Pirates in Little League games there. My dad was their manager. I remember some of the Pirates' battles against the red jerseyed Giants with their stars Eddie Downs and Bobby Flynn. A few years later I would be the one wearing the green uniform of the Pirates with my dad still running the show. My dad had plenty of company during this period. Al Pfieffer managed the Braves, Sig Goski managed the Cubs, and John Havis's dad managed the Angels, amongst many others. As a 12 year old, I knocked one pitch over the right center field fence at Gumbert field #1 off the Cubs' Alan Deombeleg. Needless to say, that year left me with some great memories of Gumbert.

But while the sounds of kids playing baseball permeated the air at Gumbert, the sound of a bouncing basketball might be heard across the street on the new courts at Gumbert. Four of them, in fact, laying side by side, and essentially surrounded on three sides by the three little league baseball fields that were known as Gumbert #1, #2, and #3. The courts meant nothing to me at the time and would have barely even caught my attention. I didn't think much about basketball during springtime, when Little League games were played, or summertime, when stick ball or whiffle ball would pick up where Little League games left off.

But the courts began gathering the attention of many others over the next few years. What's more, that attention extended well beyond Westfield's borders. Within a few short years of their construction, the cement basketball courts of Westfield would become THE place to play hoops in NJ on summer evenings. This could be said for college players looking to hone their game in the summer, including a few who had a shot at making it in the NBA, top high school players, and younger kids looking to cut their teeth against older players and get them ready for varsity competition.

How this all got started still seems to be a bit of a mystery. After all, Westfield had already had two basketball courts in Tamaques Park. My older brother Tom, who graduated from WHS in 1966, doesn't remember ever playing at Gumbert, although he does recall playing at the Tamaques courts in the summer of '67. What made the Gumbert courts so special? What changed things? Perhaps it was their cement surface which made them smooth and conducive to good dribbling. Perhaps it was that they had normal backboards unlike those weird sheet metal backboards at Tamaques. Maybe it was that the Gumbert courts were a touch shorter at 75-feet…or that there were four of them. Perhaps their more central location right off North Avenue made them a bit more accessible and easier to find for out of towners. Oh yeah, one more thing - there were lights! The lights may not have meant much to the guys who got into the first games at 6 p.m. and got to run early and often, but inevitably some games would continue as the sun went down, especially for those younger kids who had to wait those extra hours for their turn on the best court. In fact, Jay Boyle, who was three years my junior, recalls getting the phone number and calling the town technician who would then come down to Gumbert to get the lights working whenever they failed to come on.

No one that I spoke to amongst those who frequented Gumbert over multiple summers seemed to know the answer as to how it became THE place. It's possible that one of the few people who would likely know – Roselle's Roger Kindel - took the answer with him to the grave with his unfortunate passing in early 2020. Roger, who went on to play at Seton Hall after graduating high school in 1968, was a regular fixture at Gumbert for several summers after that. In fact, his presence there was so hard to miss that many of us would refer to Roger as the Commish. Roger would get the first games organized, settle disputes over who's turn it was to play or which team a certain player should be on, and anything else necessary to keep things running smoothly. After all, there were no adults in the room, so someone had to take charge, and Roger appeared to be in charge ever since I started playing there beginning in the summer of 1970. It may well be that he helped spread the word to local college and high school hoopsters that he knew across the state.

Indeed, if there were a Gumbert Hall of Fame, Roger Kindel would be a unanimous first ballot inductee. Gumbert's reputation grew quickly, as did its list of alumni. While that list is long, there are a few players that achieved great success in basketball that people seem to remember or mention the most when it came to Gumbert. John Somogyi, a '68 graduate of St. Peter's High School in New Brunswick and New Jersey's all-time leading scorer for more than three decades on the boys' side with more than 3,300 points, was one of the early big names to frequent the courts of Gumbert. While I never competed against him, I remember being a bit star struck seeing him on the courts there. Somogyi credits another Brunswick guy, Dave Wohl, who starred at the University of Pennsylvania and went on to a nice career in the NBA that continues to this day in front office positions, for getting him to come to Gumbert as much as he did. Somogyi said that he and Wohl would play a lot together, including a league in Cliffside Park, but found the courts at Gumbert to be a good place to play that offered the most important thing of all – good competition. Somogyi pointed out that it was extremely hard to find an open gym in the summertime in those days that was open for all to come play, so you had no choice but to find outdoor courts to play on. Somogyi also spent time in some tough neighborhoods in Newark where there would be no nets on the rims and he'd be the only white guy there. He would keep his mouth shut and let his game do his talking. Perhaps he and others found the confines of Gumbert Park to be a little less intimidating, not to mention to having chain nets to prove that ball actually went through the rim.

Somogyi said he also spent a lot of time playing with 6-foot-9 John Shumate, a '70 graduate of Thomas Jefferson High in Elizabeth, who went on to star at Notre Dame and play several years in the NBA. This, of course, meant Shumate would also start making regular appearances at Gumbert. Shumate's sheer size and strength made him an intimidating presence on the Gumbert courts. I remember one guy trying to box him out, only to have Shumate jump right over him, dunk the ball with two hands, and then hang from the rim with his legs dangling over the helpless defender's shoulders. Other top Gumbert names that Somogyi and others cited included Mo Layton, who played out of Weequahic ('66) and USC and then five years in the NBA; Brian Taylor who played out of Perth Amboy ('69, and was NJ's second all-time leading scorer behind Somogyi at the time with 2,495 points), who later played for Princeton and then 10 years in the ABA and NBA, and Gary Brokaw, another New Brunswick guy ('71) who went on to play for Notre Dame with Shumate and then played four seasons in the NBA.

Jim Kelly, a '69 graduate of Westfield High who went on to play for Sacred Heart, grew up about a half-mile from Gumbert and also recalls the early days there. Like many others, he remembers starting out on the secondary courts, not quite ready to compete with the bigger stronger players on Court 1. He thinks that the competitive games might have started around 1967, a couple of years after the courts were built, but then continued to gather steam by word of mouth to good basketball players around the state. Kelly also thought Wohl, a '67 high school grad and one of the older players, was a likely ringleader who may have helped recruit or bring several other good players along with him to the courts in Westfield. He described Taylor as very smooth and a freak of nature who once dunked there after taking off from the foul line. He also recalls Shumate showing up with his entourage and how he would bully his way into the lane area, but sometimes getting frustrated by having his pocket picked by little Jimmy Burke. Kelly also reminisced about the supreme talent of Brokaw who he described as so quick that Kelly preferred giving up the ball rather than attempting an offensive move against him.

But to just list the top players that could be spotted at Gumbert would not do it justice. It was the breadth of quality players who made their marks in both high school and college that made Gumbert noteworthy and, more importantly, helped make each of those players better along the way. Any list would be incomplete, but here's a partial list of notable Gumbert alumni based upon multiple sources, including their high schools, graduating year, and college if known:

Bloomfield: Tracy Tripucka '68 (Lafayette)
Colonia: Craig Frank '69 (Trenton State), Tim Kish '70 (Fredonia State), Bo Henning '71 (East Stroudsburg), Steve Solop '72 (Farleigh Dickinson), John Franken '73 (Clemson), Chris Solop '74 (Moravian)
Cranford: Richie Mazzella '72 (Middlesex) Norm Hobbie '73 (Rider)

Dayton Regional: Frank Bucci '70 (Rollins), Howie Alexander '71 (Farleigh Dickinson), Ed Graessle '71 (Farleigh Dickinson)

East Brunswick: Dave Wohl '67 (Penn)

Governor Livingston: Jeff Burdette '70 (Duke), David Corrigan '73 (Moravian)

Green Brook: Jim Pastushok '70 (Wagner)

Holy Trinity: Joe Cullinan '72 (Stonehill), Jack Steimel '72 (UCC), Tom Decker '74 (Mount St. Mary's)

JFK (Iselin): Jay Jorgensen '74 (Fairleigh Dickinson)

Johnson Regional: Chet Miele '68, Joe Dunn '69

Metuchen: Tom Flaherty '72 (Seton Hall), Bob Flaherty '72

New Brunswick: Gary Brokaw '71 (Notre Dame)

North Plainfield: Rich Searl '68 (Duke football)

Perth Amboy: Brian Taylor '69 (Princeton)

Plainfield: Jim Baglin '70 (Susquehanna)

Roselle: Roger Kindel '68 (Seton Hall), Roger Banks '71 (Colgate), Ollie Hawkins '71 (Seton Hall), Lee Hollerbach '72 (Bridgeport), Ross Kindel '74 (Syracuse)

Roselle Catholic: Jim Burke '70 (Brown), Leo Nolan '73 (Fairfield), John Roberts '73, Rick Gomez '74 (Duke, Farleigh Dickinson), Jay Boyle '75 (Seton Hall)

Roselle Park: Neil Pastushok '67 (Wake Forest)

St. Mary's: Frank Labonia '68 (Stonehill), John Sadloska, Pete Davis '69, Bill Kenney '70, Ken Tanke '70 (Biscayne), Ben Candelino '70 (UCC), Jackie Moran '71,

St Peter's: John Somogyi '68 (New Mexico St., Rutgers)

Scotch Plains: Frank Zelesnik '70 (Seton Hall), Randy Hughes '70 (Rhode Island), Ray Schnitzer '73 (Georgie Tech)

South Plainfield: Wolfgang Fengler '70 (Delaware)

Summit: Clark Daggett '69 (Johns Hopkins)

Thomas Jefferson: Earl Foreman '68, John Shumate '70 (Notre Dame)

Union Catholic: Jim Phelan '68 (Boston College), Mike Campbell '68, Mike Allocco '69 (Stonehill), Richie Scialabba '70 (Farleigh Dickinson), Andy Blejwas '70 (Kean), Jim Hydock '70

Weequahic: Mo Layton '67 (USC)

Westfield: Jim Kelly '69 (Sacred Heart), Kevin Kane '69 (East Carolina), Steve Lee '72 (William & Mary), Steve Reddy '72 (Bucknell), Tim Goski '73 (Georgia, East Texas State), Mike Cooney '73 (St. Michaels, VT), Scott Novacek '73 (Bucknell), Bob Jester '73 (Trenton State baseball), Jim Masters '74 (Southeast Louisiana)

Of course, not all these guys were at Gumbert at the same time or even the same year, but there was plenty of competition to go around for a number of years ... and plenty to learn from as well. Many of the older guys could have been found on Court 1, the court closest to the Gumbert #1 baseball field across the street. This had quickly been established as the top court where the best players would play and where, of course, winners would stay on. Sometimes Court 1 losers wouldn't have the patience to wait for their next turn, so they'd take their five and try to get the next five to play them on Court 2, creating a rival court for that particular evening. The more crowded it was, the more likely that was to happen, but others would prefer to wait for their shot at the Court 1 winners. It was basically king of the hill playing out every night.

Jack Steimel recalls that there was also a bit protecting home court involved. Occasionally a group of five out of towners would show up with a stacked team intending to hold court for the evening. This might cause Roger Kindell and assistant "Commish" Jim Baglin to quickly scramble to form their own stacked team out of Gumbert regulars. After all, it was one thing to lose to some of the guys you might see night after night, but quite another to lose to a group of guys invading your home turf in such a manner. The interlopers were often dispatched in quick fashion by the band of Gumbert regulars, sometimes forcing them over to Court 2 to avoid having to sit and wait for their next shot on the top court.

For the younger guys there was usually more waiting involved. For me that meant waiting until I was bigger, stronger and a better player before I would venture near Court 1. For other younger players, it might mean waiting at the court and hope you got picked up as a fifth player on a team that had an open spot, or perhaps waiting until the crowd whittled down and the remaining players actually needed you to play. Leo Nolan, who played at Roselle Catholic and later at Fairfield, recalls one of his first forays onto Court 1 when he was just about to enter high school: "I was young, eighth or ninth grade, and I got into a game that featured NBA player Dave Wohl. Also participating in the game: John Shumate [Notre Dame], Neil Pastushok - Wake Forest, Roger Kindel - Seton Hall, Ken House - Seton Hall, a mainstay at Gumbert, Jim Baglin -Susquehanna, then set winning records at Mendham High School. Exciting moment for me." Talk about baptism by fire … now that took some guts!

Tim Goski was another who wasn't going to let his age impede his development. "I started playing at Gumbert around ninth grade when Pete McGale and I were good friends. I think his older bro Barney took us down there. Of course, we started on Court 4 but marveled at the Court 1 guys. Must have been 69-70." Undoubtedly spurred on by a family of older brothers and good athletes, it wouldn't be long before Goski would be over on Court 1 himself. He would later explain his early aggressiveness this way: "I knew that by getting my ass kicked by the older guys it would make me better (at least that's what Kish told me-ha)". While it was usually intimidating for younger players to play on Court 1 in the beginning, at some point it would start paying dividends if they stuck with it. Goski recalls a big moment for himself: "I remember playing against Jimmy Burke from Roselle Catholic who was a legend and I'll never forget the night I stole the ball from him and went down for a layup. It was like reaching the next level." Jack Steimel, Goski's former teammate at Holy Trinity, recalls Goski's transformation during the summer of 1971. Before that summer, Tim was still a bit more tentative, not quite as confident in his quickly developing game, but in '71 Goski was in full attack mode right from the beginning, always looking to score, playing with more confidence and perhaps more importantly, playing fearlessly, according to Steimel.

There most certainly was plenty of ass kicking that took place on Court 1, and it came in many forms. It might have been the great shooting of John Somogyi, Jim Baglin, or Norm Hobbie, the phenomenal ball handling of Jimmy Burke, the clever passing of Ray Schnitzer, the tenacity of Tom Flaherty or Joe Cullinan, the athleticism of Randy Hughes, the sheer physical dominance of John Shumate, or the toughness of Timmy Kish.

Kish apparently made quite an impression on the younger Goski, who recalls Kish as his favorite all-time Gumbert player: "Timmy Kish was a legend. He was 2-3 years older than us but a wild man. There was gonna be a fight one day at the court between like Kimba and somebody else, some of the big boys and Kish stepped right in the middle of them and he said, with the greatest expertise of profanity I've ever heard, that nobody was going to get in a fight there unless he was in the middle of it. He was about an inch or two smaller than me but really tough. Classic. I really looked up to him. I wanted to be as tough as he was."

One thing was for sure – if you stepped onto Court 1 at Gumbert, it was going to make you tougher. You had no choice. It was either get tough or go home. For one, the players were almost all good athletes and physically tough, so you couldn't let yourself be pushed around. Second, many of the games were pretty intense, or "like wars", as Somogyi put it. They were usually short games, with games usually played to just eight baskets with a margin of two, or first to 11, so you couldn't afford to take possessions off or fall behind much at all. Everyone wanted to win and nobody wanted to sit, so the defense could get very physical when it got closer to game point. In fact, you were more likely to get fouled than get a clean shot off when the game was on the line.

The Flaherty brothers (twins Tom and Bob) certainly didn't lack toughness and always seemed to be in the middle of very physical play. Tom was the skinnier but more talented of the two, while Bob was physically stronger player who appeared to relish any physical confrontations on the court and coming to Tom's defense whenever needed. Tom recalls one time when he dribbled through the legs of Union Catholic star Mike Allocco (the kind of thing that Flaherty was quite capable of and inclined to do when the opportunity was there) and Allocco got pissed off. According to Tom, his brother Bob then jumped between them and shoved the much bigger Allocco who, to Tom's surprise, did not retaliate. While I did not ask Allocco about that specific incident, Allocco separately recalled Flaherty at Gumbert in this way: "Was there ever a game where he did not call 35 shooting fouls or get punched in the mouth??". Needless to say, everyone who played at Gumbert came away with their specific perspective on what took place there. While there may have been no love lost between some of the combatants, the tough competition would pay dividends for most of them. Tom Flaherty made First Team All-State as a senior at

Metuchen, and then followed that with an impressive career at Seton Hall, earning MVP honors there as a senior. In the meantime, Allocco would go on to shatter records at Stonehill College where he is still their all-time leading scorer with 2399 points (not to mention hauling in 1150 rebounds) and got drafted by the Baltimore Bullets and the Virginia Squires.

While the intensity of the games and the competition led to some heated moments on a nightly basis, it was probably a saving grace that the honor system prevailed – i.e., the rule that you called your own fouls and you had to respect that player's call. It didn't mean you had to be happy with the call, and sure enough there was lots of bitching at foul calls not unlike was you see in the NBA to this very day. But you had to accept the call, which helped preserve order on the court when there was no one else to turn to. Some players developed reputations for making cheap calls on a regular basis. Some of those reputations might have been deserved while others weren't necessarily warranted, but I suppose that's just something that comes with the territory.

I certainly wasn't as strong or confident or aggressive as a Tom Flaherty or a Tim Goski when I first started playing regularly on Court 1 in 1971, but once you were there, you had to play like you belonged or everyone would know it and take advantage of you. I wasn't one of the better offensive players back then, so I would have to move more without the ball just for a chance to touch it, and then work extra hard to get a good shot off once I had it. On one occasion I got a shot off over a hard-nosed Ed Graessle around the foul line and called a foul for getting hit on the wrist. He didn't like it and made that clear with some choice language. I hardly ever called a foul there but couldn't back down now, and I didn't. How you carried yourself on the court meant a lot. It was part of becoming a better player. It was part of earning the respect of your opponents.

It's amazing how much we all learned without any coaches around to tell us how to play. When it's either win or sit for a while, you instinctively learn to play tough defense. When there are better players all around you, you learn how to move without the ball to get open. When you know the game might come down to one basket, you learn how to box out and fight for that rebound. Playing at Gumbert, you would learn what your real weaknesses were. If you weren't scoring much or getting the ball much or able to handle the defensive pressure, you would know what you had to work on, whether it was to become a better ball handler, work on your offensive moves, or work on your jump shot. You might think your left hand is good until you see someone with a much better one. You might think your shot is pretty good but you can't get that many shots off, and then you see someone who can work the ball and get their shot off in virtually any situation – then it dawns on you that there are multiple skills that go into making a great scorer or great player.

In fact, there were several players that I played with that turned into great scorers in their respective careers, and you could see evidence of that at Gumbert. Guys like Burke, Cullinan, Flaherty, Hobbie, and Goski. It usually looked like some combination of being confident, aggressive, headstrong, skilled ball handling, good fakes, and sound shooting technique. Some people might watch them and call them "gunners." You might watch some games and see guys like these taking a majority of the shots for their teams. While some observers might look at that as a flaw, a more astute observer might recognize that they shot the ball more because they could or because their team needed them to shoot. It didn't always make everyone happy, but that was playground basketball. The goal was to win, not to make sure everyone took the same number of shots.

Big guys who played at Gumbert often got the short end of the stick because of the relatively short courts and the packed lane conditions, combined with the fact that you might have several of the smaller guys going at each other each time down the court. Often it would seem like the only way the big guys would touch the ball was by rebounding missed shots inside and getting "garbage" points. Naturally, the bigs might sometimes get frustrated or take matters into their own hands. Mike Cooney recalls one time when the 6-foot-6 Ken Tanke decided it was his turn to play guard: "One time he got a rebound and decided to run a fast break. He dribbled over half court, went behind the back, went to the top of the key, made a move around a guy, drove the lane and finished with his patented shake and bake double clutch move. Then he would run down the court yelling 'Shake & Bake!!, Shake & Bake!!' Of course, we would have to pause the game to stop laughing before we could continue." That sounds like the Tanke I remember too.

The players there came in all shapes and sizes, from seemingly every place around. Many of them came together too. After all, we were just kids and only some of us had wheels to get around. Richie Scialabba recalls Chet Miele's blue and white VW van that would regularly bring him, Tanke, Andy Blejwas, Bill Kenney and Joe Dunn over to Gumbert together for the evening's run. A cooler of beer was usually stashed inside as well, which became the reward for a good night's sweat. Sometimes Chet's van would be playing Sweet Georgia Brown, making the beers taste even sweeter.

The sounds of Gumbert were unmistakable. In the background would be sound of baseball chatter all around from any of the three fields close to the courts, with the occasional bleacher cheers, cracks of the bat or call of an umpire piecing the air. You could count on the laughter of young children frolicking on nearby swing sets or racing to get their place in line for the Mr. Softee truck who seemingly owned a parking spot alongside the fence lining one side of Court 1. Indeed, the soothing sound of Mr. Softee's repetitive tune seemed synonymous with summer evenings at Gumbert. Of course, there were always the distinctive sounds of bouncing balls on both the near and far courts, bank shots off fiberglass backboards, and chain nets that rewarded hard earned baskets with metallic "swishes".

There would always be people milling around and watching some of the hoops action. During prime time, roughly 6-8 pm, there would always be players who had "next" hanging out behind the near baseline or sitting on the small bleachers along one side of the court. You could also count on having a few of the Westfield Boosters like Bob Brewster, Ward Gentino, Al Pfeiffer, and head football coach Gary Kehler taking in some of the action a few feet beyond the baseline, no doubt forming opinions about the town's near-term prospects on the hardwood floor. You'd also have a few casual fans or passersby who stopped by to watch, in some cases meandering over from the nearby baseball fields. You might also have the occasional local high school or college coaches observing from a distance, sometimes leaning up against and peering through the chain linked fence that surrounded two sides of Court 1. If you made a good play on court 1, you could be sure there were others who saw it.

Of course, the most discerning eyes for talent would be those high school and college coaches. Gumbert attracted competition and competition in turn would attract coaches and scouts. In the 1960s and '70s, AAU was in its relative infancy and not the forum for recruiting college prospects that it is today. Instead, coaches and scouts would have to search out the Gumberts of the world to find basketball talent that might be able to help their program. As a testament to Gumbert's reputation in the late '60s, Mike Allocco, who would often go head-to-head with Shumate on the courts at Gumbert and ultimately set many records at Stonehill College, was offered a scholarship on the spot one night at Gumbert by Davidson's Lefty Driesell.

I would spend a few summers playing evenings at Gumbert, primarily between 1971 and 1974 during both my high school and college years. I even played there on occasion after my college graduation in 1976, but by that point the incentive to play there was waning considerably. After all, there was no more school team to play for and thus no real reason to want to get better. Besides, by this point most of the familiar faces were gone and it just didn't seem the same anymore. I suppose it was a similar experience for many players who may have frequented Gumbert and spent maybe two, three or four summers there before their life circumstances changed significantly and they moved on with their lives. Naturally, there was a certain amount of turnover each year at Gumbert that meant old familiar faces would disappear and be replaced by new ones.

About a dozen years would go by before I would return to Gumbert. One summer evening while staying at my parents' house in 1990 I decided to return to see what had become of my old stomping ground. Well, not only were the players gone, but the courts were gone too. It turns out they had retired the old courts and built four new ones about a hundred yards down the road on the other side of the street, behind Gumbert #1 baseball field. There were a few players playing there, but the games lacked any intensity, and it was immediately evident that Gumbert was no longer a basketball destination for out-of-town hoopsters. In fact, I'm not even sure if it was getting much action from town residents either. While I don't know what the length of the new courts were, they were considerably longer than the old ones, possibly as long as an NBA court at 94-feet long. That's just not conducive to good playground play. Courts that long normally don't lead to crisp fast breaks, but rather sloppy play with some cherry picking by players too lazy to run the full length of the court and play hard at both ends. Furthermore, the new courts no longer had the appeal of being in the center of all the Gumbert action. Now they had been relegated to the outskirts of Gumbert.

I'm not sure when the Gumbert transformation took place, but it was clear that the Gumbert I knew was history. Perhaps it was a gradual decline that Gumbert underwent, beginning in the mid-to-late-'70s. But I suspect its decline had nothing to do with the courts themselves. Rather, it likely had everything to do with AAU basketball supplanting playground hoops as the primary basketball development forum. It wasn't until a few years later when I personally experienced AAU basketball that my daughter got involved with, but looking back now it is quite apparent the forces that were in play here. Like many other things, this transformation may have come down to money, marketing, and parents being sold a bill of goods that AAU basketball could help take their kid to the next level and increase their chances of a college scholarship. College coaches and scouts were only too happy to encourage participation in AAU tournaments that would provide a convenient forum for them to evaluate talent. Of course, the AAU platform needs volunteers to help it function, and so parents of kids ultimately get involved as coaches, regardless of their level of basketball experience. Unfortunately, this brings politics and bias into the picture, unintended or not. That's not to say that AAU can't provide some great basketball experience or instruction, but it usually requires a big-time commitment, with traveling to various locations for tournaments and often sacrificing whole weekends to be part of them. The Gumberts of the world would naturally be left behind as part of this movement.

The Gumbert I knew was the product of a simpler time. No cell phones and no social media to consume our attention and swallow our time, and few alternatives if you wanted to become a better in the sport of your choice. Somehow Gumbert was able to become a first choice for hoopsters across much of the Garden State. Now Gumbert seems to be a casualty of the times. How can a kid justify spending time at a playground when they could be seen elsewhere by many college coaches who might have a real interest in their future? Gumbert was able to thrive without the help of any adults. AAU, on the other hand, couldn't last for a second without adults running the show or their money to fund its operations. Every Gumbert alumnus that I spoke to lamented the fate of the Gumbert courts and how the Gumberts of the world have fallen victim to the AAU machine that keeps chugging along. No one seems to think that AAU is producing better basketball or better players these days. There's no doubt that this generation's players are better athletes, thanks to better weight training equipment, better gyms, and much greater awareness of the value of weight training, but AAU can't take credit for that. To the contrary, there is a sense that players are relying too much on athleticism and not enough on the fundamentals of the game. Watch a shot go up and see how many players attempt to box out their man, and how many do it with the proper technique? You might find that fundamentals are also a casualty of the times.

I suppose that's just evolution. Things evolve for a reason, whether we like those reasons or not. But evolution takes time. For those of us who experienced Gumbert in its heyday, it gave us what we needed. Again, to a man, Gumbert alumni credited the great competition as the main attraction. Everyone understood and responded to the win or sit framework that prevailed on Gumbert's Court 1. Jim Baglin, a fixture at Gumbert during the period I was there who went on to become a legendary high school coach at Mendham High School, said that Gumbert had such a profound impact on him that he patterned his summer program there after what he experienced there, providing a venue for his current and former players, along with other good local players, to convene and compete in semi-organized pickup games. Last but not least, the lack of politics and adults getting in the way was also an aspect that Gumbert alumni remember in a very positive way.

For me, the memories are clear. The courts at Gumbert that blossomed just as I approached my senior year in high school were a godsend. Little did I realize at the time the role they were playing in my own development; instead, I simply thought of it as a place I had to go if I wanted to become a better basketball player and to be a starting player on my high school team. Only many years later would I be able to fully appreciate what Gumbert meant, both to me and countless others. How lucky was I? To have *THE* place to play hoops in New Jersey just a mile from my house? Right next to the baseball fields where I used to hit home runs? I was very lucky indeed.

Like Joni Mitchell's song said, *"Don't it always seem to go that you don't know what you got till it's gone?"* It may not have seemed like it at the time, but now, looking back, the courts at Gumbert were a little slice of paradise ... and now they are nothing more than a parking lot.

"They paved paradise, and put up a parking lot ..."

IV. A Team is Born (Mar 1, 1971 – Nov 25, 1971)

"It was June of '71 when he came to town
And made his presence felt at Gumbert Playground
Where his boys-to-be refined their skills
And gave the locals their share of cheap thrills."

from *A Team to Remember*, November 18, 2000

The day after our season ended, I measured and weighed myself. I was now 6-foot-1½ and 132 pounds, confirming the obvious: I needed to do something. I began flipping through the sports magazines in our house, namely – *Sports Illustrated* and *Sport*, to see what ads I could find for body building, weight training, or anything else up that alley. I needed some guidance. I wasn't on the football team, so I had no access to their Universal Gym equipment or other equipment the team might have used, not to mention the football coaches who could provide instruction as needed. Furthermore, the football players had each other, a fraternity of sorts, to push, encourage, and motivate each other to do the necessary weight training to get stronger and prepare them for their sport. Many of them were wrestlers too, another sport where strength was paramount. But I had none of that, and no one to turn to … that's how I felt anyway. I was on my own.

I found something in the back of *Sports Illustrated* that I liked, a body building program offered by Joe Weider, who used the moniker "Trainer of the Stars." I had heard of the guy, one of these musclebound guys you see on magazine covers, so I suppose he was one of the more famous ones around. He offered his program for $100, it promised results, and it came with a money back guarantee! As far as I was concerned, it was just what the doctor ordered. The next day at the dinner table I made the request to my father, since I didn't happen to have a spare $100 just laying around. He wasn't so bullish on the idea: "You'll never get your money back," he scoffed in a tone that was both discouraging and indicated that he knew what he was talking about. While he may not have felt the money back guarantee was worth much at all, he still wanted to be supportive of my initiative, and ultimately agreed to take a chance on it and on me. Within a week, the cardboard box with Joe Weider's program arrived in the mail.

I dove into it. There were several pamphlets outlining his exercise program, and several more bonus pamphlets on a variety of topics that Weider thought would be valued by his new pupil. I put those aside for the time being and focused on the exercises. It turned out the Weider program would consist of 15 different exercises, 14 of which would be performed with the use of dumbbells. 15 different exercises with three sets for each, meaning a total of 45 sets to be done for each workout session. They should take a little more than an hour, according to the program, so minimal resting between sets. It all seemed fairly straightforward, fairly easy ... in fact, almost too easy.

I was shocked to learn that I wouldn't even get to use the dumbbells for six weeks! Instead, I would start doing all the exercises using *encyclopedias*! Could that be right? According to Weider, the body needed to be conditioned first with very light weights so that the body would get the maximum benefit once I graduated to iron in the form of dumbbells. It was hard to believe that the encyclopedias were heavy enough to do any conditioning at all ... after all, how much could even the thickest encyclopedia weigh – two pounds?

I decided I would follow the script. Who was I to second guess Joe Weider? The next six weeks several of those big red books got more use than they had in entire lifetime up to that point. By the time late April arrived, the six weeks were up and the books went back on the shelf for good. At this point, I was chomping at that bit to get at those dumbbells! I don't remember what weight I started with, but it was a very small number – maybe five pounds each. I had the smallest weights on each bar that was possible, plus the iron collars that held them in place. I figured it was better not to add weight too abruptly, but rather to add it steadily, about once every week. I usually added a pound or two every week as the calendar progressed through the summer months.

It didn't take too long before I would see some tangible results. Not only was I adding weight to the dumbbells, but to my skinny body, which was the whole point of course. Given my objective, the scale, which had been my enemy, was now my friend. It would be the barometer that would indicate how much Joe Weider was actually helping me. I'm sure within a couple of months I had gained several pounds, even though I didn't feel much stronger given that the weights used up until that point were so light. But any weight gain was an indication that the program was working, at least so far, so that reinforced my resolve to not miss any workouts along the way. Five days a week, three sets of 15 different exercises each day, with 15 repetitions for each set. That meant 3,375 repetitions each week, which took me a solid hour and a quarter each of the five days I worked out.

I went on a couple of vacations that summer, one up to my uncle's cottage on Lake Canandaigua in upstate New York, and another to Lake Winnipesaukee in New Hampshire, where classmate Bill Nelson's parents had a summer home. The dumbbells went with me. Nothing was going to stop the momentum I suddenly had going for me. Nor would any barbs from friends deter me either. "Massive," Dave Jester joked in New Hampshire, referring to my biceps as he watched me do a few curls as part of my routine. He was thinking in absolute terms, while I was focused on relative terms. I knew I was getting stronger and gaining weight. That's all that mattered to me. The fact that I had started from such a low place didn't matter … I was already climbing out of it. Compared to the biceps I started with, my new biceps may well have been massive!

Meanwhile, another head coaching change was announced during the spring – WHS would have its fourth varsity boys basketball head coach in four years come next school year, and I would be getting my fifth head coach in my fifth year of organized hoops. Apparently, Joe Coleman didn't see good things on the horizon, or perhaps he just saw greener grass over in Scotch Plains, where he would become their new head coach. Taking Coleman's spot would be a guy named Neil Horne Jr., who had been the head coach at Ridge High School. We didn't know much else about him other than he had led Ridge to a couple of Group II sectional title games in recent years. There wasn't much else we could do to find out more, no internet to turn to learn more about him, not that we needed to know more … we would find out soon enough.

It was a June evening down at Gumbert when I unexpectedly met our new coach as he was scouting out some of his boys-to-be and mingling with a few of the boosters who would frequently hang out at Gumbert during summer evenings, including the man himself, Gary Kehler. Horne was a tall guy, about 6-foot-5 or so, with a deep commanding voice. He was also pretty young, only 29, although when you're only 17 yourself, 29 seems like a much older person. In any event he seemed very self-assured in those brief initial exchanges I had with him.

The summer of '71 was my first all-out assault on Gumbert, the first summer where I felt at home there. Part of it was based on need – I was running out of time with my senior year just around the corner and had a new head coach to impress. This summer would be my last chance to improve my skills and my chances to make the starting team on next year's varsity which, at least on paper, figured to be a very competitive team. But part of it was based on just feeling more comfortable and feeling like I belonged there on Court 1 where the oldest, biggest and best players typically played. Getting physically stronger throughout the summer certainly helped in that regard.

Then, of course, there was Tim Goski. By the time June rolled around and school was out for summer, Gumbert would have been in full swing, and Goski was a fixture there. I was smart enough to realize that Tim would be my main competition for the two starting guard spots, along with Steve Lee and Mike Cooney. Add the fact that we had a brand-new head coach which just added to the uncertainty. There were no guarantees. I had to do my best to keep up with Goski, which meant I needed to more or less live at Gumbert for the next three months.

That in turn meant that for the first time I would spend some time with and get to know Tim, who was part of an insanely large Polish family. They had something like 12 or 13 kids, with Tim being somewhere in the middle. I would also get to know other juniors-to-be Mike Cooney and Bob Jester, aka "BJ", the younger brother of Dave Jester, who I had played with at Roosevelt. BJ had just had a recent growth spurt of about six inches in one year, propelling him from a guard to a forward virtually overnight. The other likely varsity team members for next season didn't have much presence at Gumbert that summer for a variety of reasons. The football guys needed to chill a bit before two-a-days would start in August. Steve Lee also remembers spending a decent chunk of time on the Gumbert courts that summer, although I have more vivid memories of he and I on the golf course together at Ash Brook during that offseason. Scott Novacek, our future big man who still wasn't even 6-foot-5, was a bit of a mystery guy, and I don't think I saw him the entire summer and still barely knew him at all. The little contact I had with Scott the prior year suggested that this guy was a little different, marching to the beat of his own drum.

So it was primarily me, Tim, Mike and BJ that would be playing pickup games at Gumbert most weeknights, starting at 6, and going to 8 or 8:30 or whenever there were no more bodies left to compete with. Of course, with well-lit courts, the games would often continue until after well after dark. The natural thing to do after a night of hoops in the dead of summer was to find a swimming pool to cool off in. The fact that none of our families had a swimming pool did not prove to be much of a deterrent; to the contrary – it probably provided some added incentive, especially when you consider that I had keys to a Catalina convertible that would allow us to cruise the town in search of one. It didn't take long before we found our favorite one - Mindowaskin Swim Club.

We probably liked it a little too much there, as we hit it three nights in a row one week in July. The third night we got more than we bargained for. We parked the car behind Geiger's restaurant just down the road about 100 yards and then walked towards the club. It sat up on a little bit of a hill, with a large parking lot between Springfield Ave and the pool area. This particular night there was one lone car in the lot, parked far from the pool, with no sign of life anywhere. We quietly proceeded up through the parking lot area to the fence surrounding the swim club, and after a brief check of our surroundings, quickly hopped the fence as we had done the previous two nights. Then off came the clothes and into the pool we went.

Well, it turned out that our scouting of the swim club area was superficial at best, and that we had been overly naïve to think that our antics the previous two nights hadn't drawn the attention of the pool staff and its owners. We hadn't been in the water two minutes before I heard Cooney shout "Somebody's comin', and I ain't kiddin' ". With everyone around me scrambling, I didn't for a second think Mike was kidding, so I made a mad dash for my clothes that were piled up on a poolside bench, grabbed the pile, and then started running towards the back of swim club, across a grassy knoll that sat behind the pool and overlooking it. It was dark and chaotic, but we were all headed in the same direction, away from someone who was in our pursuit with a big flashlight, confirming that Mike was indeed not kidding. The next thing I know we are at another fence at the back of the property, where in a matter of seconds we flung everything over the fence to other side, including our bodies, not knowing what was on the other side, and without regard to whether all our body parts might make it over intact.

The next 30 seconds are a blur, but by the end of that time, Goski and I ended up hiding in some pricker bushes not far from the landing spot near the fence. Cooney and Jester had taken off somewhere, leaving Tim and I to fend for ourselves. I had no clothes on and was holding one sneaker in my hand, and I wasn't even sure if it was mine! Before you knew it, there was a bustle of activity in the area. The bushes we had jumped into lined a little side street that bordered the rear edge of the swim club property. The side street was the shape of a boomerang, and bushes we were hiding in were right at the elbow of the boomerang. Within a minute or two, there were cars coming up this little side street with headlights shining right into the bushes that were the only thing standing between us and a naked nightmare. We couldn't believe they couldn't see us – I guess we chose our bushes wisely! Obviously, this was a very important skill for us to have to take WHS hoops to the next level.

Things were happening fast … more cars where there shouldn't have been any … neighbors outside trying to find out what the heck was going on, and at least person out with what appeared to be a search dog. We could only assume that the police were part of the search effort, along with the pool owners or whoever it was giving us chase. We could clearly hear the one person approaching with dog in tow, getting to within 10 feet us as they walked along the road's edge. Tim and I weren't moving a muscle, but once they had passed us without breaking stride or a single bark, Tim couldn't resist saying "Stupid mutt!" I wanted to laugh but was still too mortified to utter a peep. Within a few more minutes, the authorities, whoever they were, were also walking around in the immediate vicinity while calling out "Steve Peddy, come on out. We've got your stuff." They repeated it a couple of times. So now I am thinking to myself – "Can't this guy read?" But even more than that, it was now clear that we weren't getting away with this, so we spent the next several minutes trying to contemplate our next move.

For a while it appeared to be a bit of a stalemate – they still hadn't caught us but there was also nowhere we could go. After about 45 minutes in our prickery hiding place, BJ ended the suspense by calling us out, saying that they were across the street and had called our parents, or something to that effect. We negotiated for towels before agreeing to our surrender, which BJ managed to secure. Then the three of us gathered outside at a house across the street in the presence of our captors, where our clothes and my wallet were all waiting for us. Luckily, the pool owners had agreed to call off the cops and just give us a lecture in the presence of our parents, who were already on their way over. All things considered, we probably got off pretty easily, and even our parents were more inclined to laugh at us rather than scold us or want to ground us. At one point BJ's dad said something like: "If that's the worst trouble you're going to get into, we can live with that." Amen!

We still didn't know what happened to Mike. It wasn't until the next day we found out he had made it back to our car behind Geiger's with both his sneakers and a tee shirt tied around his waist with one of his shoelaces. He then donned a pair of white painting pants he found in the car and hoofed it back to his home on the south side of Westfield, about four miles from the swim club. When all was said and done, Tim and I probably beat Mike home despite having to endure our failed escape and subsequent lecture.

The next day BJ, Tim, and I played hoops at Roosevelt, where there was an open gym. That's when I realized I hadn't gotten away completely unscathed the night before as I had scratches all over my body from our close encounter with the giant pricker bushes. Still, we could barely stop laughing about our escapades and I quickly forgot about my scratches, which felt more like a badge of honor than something annoying.

A couple of weeks later Mike, Tim and I spent a week at Coach Horne's basketball camp somewhere up in the Northeast corner of Pennsylvania. The three of us attended as counselors at Horne's camp, as the camp was designed for kids in the 12-15 age range. More importantly, it was a chance for Horne to check us all out a little more closely when we got to play pick-up games with the other counselors at night.

There were several counselors there from Verona, NJ, and Clarkstown, NY, in addition to their head coaches who were helping to run the camp along with Horne. One of these other counselors had a car and the great idea of sneaking away for a quick drive across the border to NY where we be much closer to the legal drinking age. We made the trip in the middle of one afternoon, found a rinky dink bar in town, quickly wolfed down one beer - or was it a soda? - and then high tailed it out of there so we wouldn't be pronounced AWOL back at camp ... that would not have made a great impression on our new coach.

While I spent a modest portion of that summer as a part time caddy or playing an occasional round of golf, the rest of my time was largely devoted to my Joe Weider weight training during the daytime five days a week, and to Gumbert most evenings. While I never witnessed it myself, I knew that August meant the beginning of two-a-day sessions for the football team, which must have been a bit torturous on those sweltering August days. I suppose that was what helped separate Westfield football from everyone else. They would put the work in, learn how to play the right way, and then go out there and win.

Before I knew it, summer was over, Labor Day came, and the first day of my senior year had begun. It had been exactly six months since my Joe Weider weight training program arrived in the mail, and four and a half months since I lifted the first set of dumbbells. I stepped on the bathroom scale the morning of that first day of school. The scale read 162 pounds! I had put on exactly 30 pounds in six months! I also had grown another half inch, now standing 6-foot-2. I was still skinny, but a much more respectable skinny than I had been, and much less likely to draw embarrassing comments from the peanut gallery while shooting free throws.

I wondered what my good buddy Bob Martin would think now. What would he say? It didn't take long to find out. The very first day of school I was walking down the hall between classes and here he comes in the other direction with his eyes fixated on me. They become larger as we got closer, and then he had this odd, bewildered look on his face that was priceless! No smile, of course, as that might begin to imply a compliment. No words either, as Martin probably had difficulty putting his own brand of negative spin on what his brain was no doubt having trouble digesting. No words were tantamount to a victory for me. My six months of diligent workouts had just paid their first dividends! Thank you, Joe Weider!! I did my best to maintain a straight face with no expression at all as we passed each other. After all, that's what Clyde Frazier would have done in that situation.

The start of school meant I would start scaling back my weight training. After all, classes and homework would now take up huge chunks of time that were readily available during summer months. Furthermore, basketball preseason was officially here, so while our football brethren were busy doing their thing on the gridiron, Pfeiffer and Simmons in particular, the rest of us would be looking for pickup games after school wherever we could find them. One day we even went over to Scotch Plains for pickup games and a week later they came over to our gym for the same thing. The coaches weren't allowed to say anything, just observe the action and do a little early scouting of our arch-rival. Our nemesis Ray Schnitzer was there with the Scotch Plains boys doing his thing, so I paid extra close attention to his every move, trying to understand what was making him so clever with the ball. "What makes this kid so good?" I thought to myself. "The kid was as skinny as I used to be ... we should be able to beat him," I kept telling myself.

The preseason was my first real chance to observe Novacek up close and get to know him a bit. My first impression was that he was a bit quirky both on and off the court. He did have a good jump shot with excellent form, especially for a big guy, and got great rotation on the ball, while one of his weaknesses was that he did tend to favor going right and dribbling only with his right hand. His real strength, however, was occupying space in the lane with his broad shoulders and giant wingspan, and then going after missed shots relentlessly with his long arms and giant hands. Novacek displayed an uncanny ability to go after rebounds with both arms extended upward and to keep tipping the ball around until his big hands snared it. If this occurred on the offensive end, Novacek seemed equally adept at immediately putting the ball back up without first bringing it back down where defenders might be able to get a hand on it. Scott wasn't cocky at all, but he didn't lack confidence either. He wasn't afraid to go up against anybody or mix it up on the boards as he usually had a physical advantage over them.

Off the court, Scott seemed a bit quirky as well. He would always speak in short, succinct phrases like: "I've got things to do, places to see" and was ever the philosopher who always appeared to be rationalizing something. He might say "our players are better than theirs, so if we just play our game, we should win." Adding to Scott's uniqueness was the intrigue surrounding his father. Scott lived in a big house on Hyslip Avenue. and, according to Scott, his father had a big job in the shipping industry and did business with the Russians, adding to the mystique of the Novacek name. I remember being in his father's car once and seeing a car phone, which was unheard of back in those days unless you kept company with James Bond. The Novaceks also had a separate pool house at the back of their driveway that was turned into a billiards room where teenagers could hang out and plot their weekend escapades in relative privacy.

With Pfeiffer and Simmons preoccupied with their football season, I had no choice but to mingle more with the juniors, whether it be hooping or hanging out after school or over the weekend. Fortunately, being a senior with a car at my disposal most of the time, put me in higher demand amongst the juniors who not yet turned 17 or secured their driver's licenses. When you consider it was a Catalina Convertible, that even made me start to look a bit cool despite my outwardly reserved nature.

I had always been a bit shy and self-conscious, especially when it came to girls, and this only got worse as I approached my 6-foot-1, 132-pound frame during junior year. Just a few short months later, I now sported a semi-respectable body and a very respectable set of wheels to cruise around town in. Now that I was hanging out more with the somewhat cool, confident, and cocky juniors – namely, Goski, Novacek, Cooney and Jester, I certainly had a better chance of breaking through on the social front, although the thought of actually having a girlfriend was still a remote thing for me. Maybe I should have read more of the Joe Weider bonus pamphlets that were included in the weight training program I had acquired. With titles like: *"How to Make Women Like You,"* and *"Be Popular, Self-Confident and a He-man,"* how could I possibly go wrong?

I decided to follow the juniors' lead on the social front, which meant trying to cop six packs of beer on certain occasions. We often used the direct approach, which was to just go into a grocery store, pick one off the shelves and take it to the checkout line. Somehow it worked. Once the checkout girl, who was about our age, hesitated because she felt like she wasn't permitted to ring it up. No problem - Novacek just reached across the counter with his long arms and pushed the button for her. Sometimes acquiring the beer was more fun than actually drinking it! Our beer of choice at that time was usually Hop'n Gator, a fruity malt liquor that was twice as strong as ordinary beer. Drink one of those and you felt it. On other occasions a bottle of Boone's Farm Apple Wine might be the beverage of the evening.

The drinking was rarely to excess, however; instead, it was just more to fit in. Of course, the Catalina Convertible was the easier way for me to fit in, and it was a hit for weekend football games, especially away games like Montclair and Nutley. With top down and wide bench seats, we loaded it up with five or six guys and cruised up the Garden State Parkway to those

Pfeiffer stops a Montclair runner on an end sweep

games in the grandest of styles, blaring tunes like Rod Stewart's *Maggie May* and Cher's *Gypsys, Tramps and Thieves* along the way.

The football team did their part and won close, hard-fought games, including a 7-6 come from behind win at Montclair, on their way to another unbeaten season that fall. Chants of "Na na na na, na na na na, hey hey hey, goodbye" often punctuated each of those victories. It was all very special to be a part of, even if we were just a few unknown hoopsters waiting for our turn to be the focus of attention. The football team, as usual, was going to be a tough act to follow.

Westfield's Vejnoska blocks Montclair's game winning FG attempt

I don't know if it was the convertible, my new physique or my cooler hoops companions, or perhaps all three, but I did get "lucky" with one girl. Not lucky in the sense that a collegiate nerd might get lucky after his first drink of alcohol, but lucky in that I actually got one to look my way and like what she saw. And what a pretty one she was! Her name was Judy Smith, and while I wasn't hip enough to categorize girls as hot or not, in my eyes she was certainly one of the best-looking girls in our class, if not the prettiest of all. Long, straight blonde hair, tallish with a model like figure, and face and smile to match – what wasn't to like? I should be so lucky that she would take a second look at me! Yet sure enough she did, so that fall we went on several joy rides together, sometimes alone, and sometimes with Mike Cooney and Pat Donnelly. One particular day after school I let Mike take the wheel, despite his lack of a driver's license, so Judy and I could be in the back seat while we were getting lost somewhere up in the Watchung Reservation. Don Juan I wasn't, but the circumstances were too perfect to screw it up, so as we finally headed to home, with the lyrics from a future Disney movie started racing through my head: "Boy, you better do it soon, no time will be better … go on and kiss the girl," I did the unspeakable … I kissed the girl. I'm not quite sure where it started, but it ended in front of Judy's house, with Mike patiently awaiting her exit from the rear seat and to be relieved of his driving duties for the day.

There were a few dates along the way, which included the Summer of '42 movie (with the top down, of course), crashing her baby-sitting site one Saturday evening, and even cruising the town one night while stopping every couple of minutes to flop into the biggest piles of leaves we could find along our route. We laughed our heads off at our impromptu silly entertainment that we stumbled upon. I don't remember whose idea it was, but it worked. I remember having to get all these leaves out of the car the next morning before my father happened to see it so he wouldn't ask what the heck had happened in there! In any event, I was a bit smitten with my recent good fortune, but now I had a new set of problems. Do I dare tell anyone about "us," and now that I had her, how would I keep her? My self-consciousness and lack of confidence regarding the dating scene would work against me. Despite hitting it off with who I thought was the perfect girl, that didn't keep me from worrying about what the other guys would say. Would they approve? What did they think of her? What would they think of us? When my best friend Tom Pfeiffer asked me in English class one morning if Judy and I were going out, I borrowed a Scott Novacek line to downplay it: "We're just playin' games." We got a good laugh out of that, but my insecurity with the whole girl scene was still presenting a big challenge to me. Fortunately, there was school, and more importantly a whole basketball season that was right in front of me, so I couldn't dwell too much on either the pros or cons of having a girl who liked to ride my car.

November 15 was the official start of the season, the first day that organized practices were allowed and the first day of the Neil Horne era at Westfield High School. That meant the first day of tryouts, but the two previous seasons had more or less sorted out most of the available spots on the roster. Coach Horne had done his homework as well. By the time tryouts started, most of the likely dozen roster spots were already spoken for. Horne was tentatively holding spots for five football players that were still finishing up their season. Those five were seniors Tom Pfeiffer and Larry Simmons, and juniors Mark Jackson, Chip Danker, and Greg Allen. The juniors had all been reserves on the 18-4 JV team from the prior year. Assuming Horne kept all five of the footballers, that would most likely leave seven available spots for the non-footballers. Those seven spots appeared destined to be claimed by two seniors, myself and Steve Lee, and then the five juniors Goski, Novacek, Jester, Cooney, and Phillips. In addition to those 12 candidates, there were three others who came out vying for a spot on the roster. Two of them, senior Bill Nelson and junior Barry Kaufman, had not made the varsity team the prior season but wanted to give it another go. The third was Joey Cacchione, a junior who had been the third guard on the prior year's JV squad. Nelson and Kaufman were long shots to survive the cut, but Cacchione was a solid player who had a good shot of making the team.

Novacek would be our only real center at a shade under 6-foot-5. Pfeiffer, Simmons, Jester, Jackson, Phillips, and Allen made up the rest of our frontcourt, all in the 6-2 to 6-4 range. Our guards were all in the 6-foot to 6-2 range, except for Lee at about 5-9.

So with our team largely determined, Nov. 15 really represented the first day of practice more than the first day of tryouts. We would have to wait 11 or 12 more days for our footballing teammates to join us, but Horne wasted no time indoctrinating us into his way of doing things. First of all, practices were long. We consistently practiced for two hours and 45 minutes each day, from 3:15 to 6 p.m., sometimes even a little bit longer, with guys shooting foul shots and running suicides at the end of practice. With practices that long, there was time to work on lots of things, both individual and team oriented. Coach Horne was meticulous in planning the practice sessions, making detailed notes prior to each one. Each practice would consist of several short segments, each lasting 10, 15, or 20 minutes, sometimes even as short as 5 minutes, and each one focused on a very specific topic.

Figure 1 below provides a good example. It contains Horne's notes for our third practice on November 17. There were 16 different segments planned for this day, running the gamut from conditioning to individual offensive moves to shooting to individual defense to various team concepts. As indicated in Figure 1, we would often start out practice with a dribbling drill. Some days it would just be dribbling up and down the court using various dribbles along the way with each hand, such as the crossover, reverse (or spin), change of pace, shuffle, hesitation, etc. Other days we might play dribbling knockout where everyone would start with a basketball inside a small area while trying to knock away everyone's else's ball until only one player remained. Dribbling and playing defense at the same time is not easy, so this drill was good for forcing you to use both hands, switching hands, and protecting the ball with your body while using your free hand to knock your opponent's ball away.

A more practical and fundamental drill we did constantly was a full court ball handling and defensive drill. This particular practice we did a half court version of the drill (see drill # 6 in Figure 1). One player would start with the ball at the baseline with another player guarding him, but with his hands behind his back, forcing him to just shuffle his feet. The offensive player would proceed to weave his way up court as if against a full court press, while the defensive player would do his best to hound him and force him to change directions by beating him to the spot. The offensive player had the advantage since no hands were free to knock the ball away, but the drill was extremely tiring for both players. When they reached the other baseline, the players would switch positions and come back the other way. Guys would usually be matched by position and there might be three lines going at once, up and down the court. After a bit of that, the defender was free to use their hands as well, so now it was like a man-to-man full court press. I am hard pressed to think of another drill that was more helpful than this as it forced you to quickly move your feet defensively, and to be able to handle defensive pressure while dribbling the ball up the court, all while getting conditioned. There's no question that it helped us be better prepared for some of the tougher game conditions we might face. Sometimes simpler is better.

Figure 1

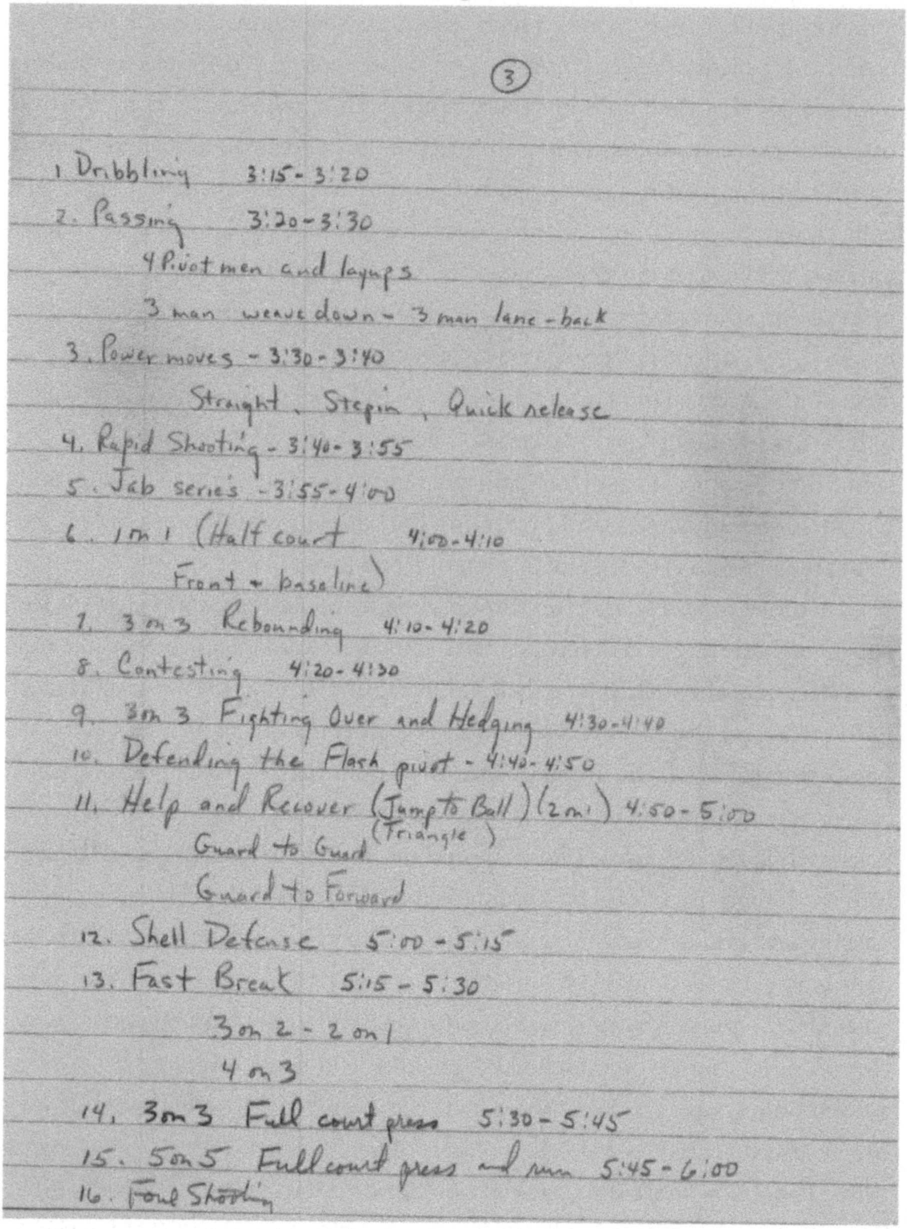

(3)

1. Dribbling   3:15 - 3:20
2. Passing   3:20 - 3:30
   4 Pivot men and layups
   3 man weave down - 3 man lane - back
3. Power moves - 3:30 - 3:40
   Straight, Step in, Quick release
4. Rapid Shooting - 3:40 - 3:55
5. Jab series - 3:55 - 4:00
6. 1 on 1 (Half court   4:00 - 4:10
   Front + baseline)
7. 3 on 3 Rebounding   4:10 - 4:20
8. Contesting   4:20 - 4:30
9. 3 on 3 Fighting Over and Hedging   4:30 - 4:40
10. Defending the Flash pivot - 4:40 - 4:50
11. Help and Recover (Jump to Ball) (2 m) 4:50 - 5:00
    Guard to Guard   (Triangle)
    Guard to Forward
12. Shell Defense   5:00 - 5:15
13. Fast Break   5:15 - 5:30
    3 on 2 - 2 on 1
    4 on 3
14. 3 on 3 Full court press   5:30 - 5:45
15. 5 on 5 Full court press and run   5:45 - 6:00
16. Foul Shooting

Drills 7-11 all focused on different aspects of individual and team defense. Just like the Fulton brothers who had the head coaching reins before him, and like I had experienced with Coaches Gralewski and Leonzi in eighth and ninth grade and Coach Tirone on the JV team, Coach Horne was defensively oriented and paid close attention to details and fundamentals.

For example, in drill #9 on this day we worked on fighting over screens while playing defense, with the defender of the screener hedging against the ball handler. The offensive player always has the advantage in this scenario (just watch any NBA game to see how often pick and rolls are executed and how hard they are to defend), but if the player defending the screener jumps out and reaches out, forcing the dribbler to slow down or take a slightly wider path around the screener, it can buy the on-ball defender enough time and space to recover back into a good defending position. Of course, the hedger, the player jumping out to help his teammate, must then himself recover back quickly to defend his own man who may be rolling to basket at the same time. Horne knew that defending plays like the pick and roll would be important to our overall success. The alternative would be lazy defense, where the defender gets picked and then goes underneath the screen, leaving the ball handler a wide-open shot, or if the hedger doesn't do his job, the dribbler might continue all the way to the basket. Consequently, Horne paid more than lip service to these types of drills throughout the season, but especially during preseason when there was more time for teaching and less focus on any particular opposing team.

For team offensive concepts, Horne kept it simple there too. We ran very few plays or sets. Instead, his emphasis was on sound execution of just basic things rather than trying to get fancy with too many options. For example, he had one motion offense that we would occasionally run, which had 5 players continuously changing spots, screening away, cutting to a spot, popping out, and then the ball being reversed to the other side of the court. All five players would end up in all five spots as the motion offense continued, so positions became moot. The idea was to just wear down the defense, get them to make one mental lapse, and then perhaps a cutter would get open flashing across the lane for an easy layup or short jumper. Still, to keep the defense honest, Horne had one play that we would run out of the motion offense which would start out the same way, but would result with a double screen for one player flashing across the lane, invariably freeing him up for an easy shot.

Most of the time we would not be running a motion offense, but rather a set offense, with a guard up top, two at the corners of the foul line, and two on the lower blocks. While there were a few plays we ran out of this basic set, Horne again wanted us to rely on basic principles rather than set plays. So that meant a lot of passing and screening away. If you didn't get the ball, rather than just stay there you should be screening away for someone else who could then take the spot you just vacated. While this was going on, the ball might get reversed back to the top of the key and then the other side of the court. If the passing lanes were blocked, the ball could be dribbled to the desired spot with the other players moving to rebalance the team's spacing and positioning on the court. The effect of all this was very little memorizing of plays, but instead the implementing of team concepts, such as pass and screen away, keep the floor balanced, don't stand still for too long, and get the ball to the open man whenever you could. Once again, sometimes simpler is better.

Our preseason would only last three and a half weeks, with the first regular-season game scheduled for December 10. In addition to long practices covering seemingly all aspects of the game, and double practice sessions on Saturday at end of that first week, Coach Horne also scheduled five scrimmages against other schools during the preseason. The first of these was scheduled for November 24, the day before Thanksgiving, so would have to play without our five football teammates who would play their final game the following morning. We scrimmaged Vailsburg at home that day, and while it felt good to get out on the court and play real basketball instead of doing three hours or drills, it was a little hard to tell how well we did. We had a lot of players playing together for the first time, running a couple of new offenses for a new coach, and without some of our best players who hadn't been to a single practice yet. If nothing else, it gave Horne a chance to evaluate his new personnel and observe their tendencies in real game situations.

The next day was Thanksgiving Day, which of course meant the final game of the football season in the annual showdown versus Plainfield. This year's showdown would take place in Westfield as the Blue Devils would attempt to wrap up another undefeated season and extend their unbeaten streak to 33 games. They had never lost a game during my three years in high school, with the sole blemish being a 20-20 tie with Rahway two seasons earlier. The game was a close battle played in snowy conditions on a very slippery field and would later become known as the Ice Bowl in Westfield circles. The Blue Devils ultimately prevailed 12-6 with a late fourth-quarter 15-yard bootleg run around left end right after a muffed punt by Plainfield. Earlier in the game each team had scored a defensive touchdown, also on punting plays that were made very challenging by the slippery conditions. Two of my grammar school friends, Bruce Cant and Tom Pfeiffer, were responsible for Westfield's first TD, with Cant breaking through to block a punt and Pfeiffer recovering the loose ball in the end zone for the score. At the end of the frigid morning, the home crowd got what they had been so accustomed to getting – another Westfield victory! Somewhere up in that crowd bundled up in winter jackets, scarves and beanies was a girl I hoped I had won over as well.

That afternoon we would have our traditional Thanksgiving dinner at home with turkey, mashed potatoes, gravy, etc … the whole nine yards. I didn't have to think very hard to appreciate that I had a lot to be thankful for – good health, a nice home to live in, a nice car to drive, a nice girl friend if not a girlfriend, and so far, a starting spot on the varsity basketball team in my senior year, just like my older brothers ahead of me. After dinner it would be a relaxing afternoon of watching more football on TV, but that would also signal the last day of football season, at least for all of us in high school. Now it was time for some hoops. Starting tomorrow it would be our turn to take center stage. The football players would trade in their pads and cleats for shorts and sneakers. No longer would Horne have to think about his team as one that existed only on paper. The day had finally come when we would all take the court together for the very first time.

V. Jimmy V and the Bison

It was late August 1972 when my parents and I loaded up the car and took the three-hour drive to Lewisburg, PA and the campus of Bucknell University, which was to be my home for the next four years. Within hours of dropping me off and getting registered, freshman orientation would begin and last another four days, during which time all the upper-class Bucknellians would begin arriving on campus as well. My first college classes would begin one week later.

That next week, right after classes had begun, I got word that the new basketball coach was calling a meeting of all the basketball "hopefuls." I was a basketball hopeful. The young coach had just been hired in late spring, presumably missing the recruiting window for that year's freshman class, so that year's team would have to be picked from a combination of the prior year's team, which had only won six games, and the basketball hopefuls. There was a catch, however. In 1972, freshmen were still not allowed to play NCAA varsity sports, so any of those hopefuls wouldn't be able to play for the new coach this year. That still didn't deter the freshman hopefuls from turning out in big numbers for the hastily called meeting, during which the brash 26- year-old coach introduced himself to the freshman and upperclassmen alike. His name was Jim Valvano.

I was not familiar with Valvano other than what my father and brother Mark had told me about him earlier that summer. They had both seem him play for Rutgers in the National Invitation Tournament at Madison Square Garden back in 1967. He was one half of a Rutgers backcourt that also included consensus first-team All-American Bobby Lloyd. Rutgers lost in the NIT semis to a Southern Illinois team that featured Walt Frazier, who just three short years later led the NY Knicks to their first championship and established himself as one the NBA's new stars. Valvano had distinguished himself quite well in that tournament, scoring 24 points in defeat in the semifinal game while also guarding Frazier and "holding him" to 26 points.

As one can imagine, the young Jim Valvano had all the same energy and enthusiasm as the older version that the sports world would get to know many years later. He introduced himself by stating that he wasn't like other coaches who liked to play golf or tennis in the off season. No, he just liked basketball. Then he described his college basketball experience at Rutgers where he played alongside "pretty boy" Bobby Lloyd, the good-looking, blonde-haired All-American guard whose job it was to shoot the ball and score points, while Valvano's job was to do the dirty work of playing tough defense against the opposing team's best guard. He accentuated the contrast between the two by imitating Lloyd combing his hair and then shifting to himself into a defensive position trying to get inside the jock strap of his opponent.

Needless to say, his message was getting through, and the energy with which he delivered it was infectious. Valvano went on to describe his father Rocco and the one rule he had established for his son – "Don't ever do anything to embarrass me and I'll never do anything to embarrass you." He then reinforced his message by saying he didn't want to hear about us getting arrested for public drunkenness or taking liberties with a waitress in a downtown bar. He said girlfriends are fine, but that once the season started, we should tell them we'll see them in March. Oh yeah, he also said he expected us all to be going to class and that we should never take for granted the value of a Bucknell education. While he took basketball seriously, he said that basketball should never be the reason that we didn't do well in our classes. If we ever needed help with our schoolwork, he would get us help – help as in tutoring or a teacher's assistance, not help as in helping to circumvent the class requirements. He exuded caring and enthusiasm. By the time the meeting ended, everyone was pumped up and couldn't wait to get out there on the court. Only one problem – it was still the first week of September! We would all have to wait five more weeks before we could play for the new Italian dynamo who was trying to change the face of Bucknell Basketball.

I knew college basketball was going to be a lot different than high school. After all, it would all take place at a new school, with new players playing in front of a new student body that came from towns from around the country rather than my hometown. No, I wasn't in Westfield anymore. But I liked my chances. I had done well in high school and continued to improve and get stronger in the months since my senior year season had concluded. I had added another eight pounds in the last 12 months and now weighed in at 170 pounds, while standing a shade over 6-foot-2. I was used to playing against tough competition, and now had another summer of Gumbert hoops under my belt. Plus, Bucknell wasn't exactly the cream of Division I basketball, so I figured I should be able to graduate to the brand of college basketball that was going to be required at Bucknell.

It didn't take long to see who my competition was going to be, thanks in part to my brother Mark having preceded me at Bucknell and graduating earlier that spring. I met a few guys from my brother's old fraternity, Phi Kappa Psi, four of whom were on the previous year's varsity hoops team, and a couple more were good high school players who now played intramural hoops at Bucknell. So right away I got included in Phi Psi pickup games with a bunch of these upper classman and distinguished myself well right out of the gate. Before long I would start meeting and playing against the other freshman hopefuls that were also part of the Valvano kickoff meeting. I felt confident and ready to go when the season and tryouts formally began on Oct 15.

I was one of four guards who would make the freshman team and the tallest amongst all of them. One guard, Bruce Barr, a super-quick lefty and explosive scorer who played like the Energizer Bunny on offense but not much defense, started the whole year at one guard. I ended up sharing the second spot with another guard from Maryland, who was just a solid all-around player and stood only about 5-foot-8. Despite being only a part-time starter throughout that year, I had earned the nickname "Magic" from some of my teammates, two years before Earvin "Magic" Johnson burst onto the college basketball scene, so clearly my ball handling skills weren't too shabby. Freshman year was effectively a practice year where basketball hopefuls could show what they were capable of in advance of varsity tryouts the following year. Only then would we all find out what Valvano thought of each of us and our abilities on a basketball court. That said, the freshman team still had to endure many of the same long and boring bus rides to places like Lehigh, Lafayette and Delaware. There were even a few smaller schools on the schedule that you had barely heard of, and most of these had gyms whose only distinction from high school gyms was that they lacked the crowds that most of us were accustomed to seeing there. Still, there was a feeling that next year would be better – it would be big time.

By the time my sophomore year rolled around in late August 1973, I had another summer at Gumbert under my belt and I had added a few more pounds to get me to 175, while standing at 6-foot-2½. I was no longer employing Joe Weider's weight training program that had transformed my body two summers earlier, figuring I had perhaps plateaued there, but instead utilized Universal weight machines that were present in both Bucknell's gym and the Westfield Y. I felt like I was physically ready for the challenge of making that year's varsity squad.

Regardless of the state of my own abilities, there would be a new challenge that I would be facing that fall. The first recruiting class of Coach Valvano was about to arrive on campus and, as fate would have it, the NCAA rule preventing freshman from playing on the varsity team had changed in the offseason. So now I would have to beat out upperclassmen, guys I played with the prior year, and Valvano's hand-picked freshman recruits. The last group even included my former teammate from Westfield, none other than Scott Novacek. At least we'd be vying for different positions.

It wasn't long before I got an up-close look at the Valvano recruits during September pickup games down at Davis gym. None of them overly impressed me, except for Tom McClean, a skinny athletic guard from East Orange, NJ, who would get up and down the court with the speed and fluidity of a gazelle, seemingly lighter on his feet than everyone else, and who had equally impressive ball handling and passing skills. There was no doubt he was going to be tough to beat out. In addition to McClean, there were three other guards amongst Valvano's recruits, so regardless of the initial impression they may have made on me, they undoubtedly represented additional bodies that I was going to have to beat out not only to make the starting five, but even to make the team.

Preseason started well enough until I was thrown a curveball – I got sick. It started out with a little bit of insomnia the first week of school. I couldn't seem to shake that, which made playing basketball tougher and got me a bit worried, which only made the situation worse. About three weeks later, things compounded when I came down with a virus which sapped all my energy. Things came to a head when on a Friday night when, just as parties were just getting underway all over the Bucknell campus, I felt like I was going to pass out while walking back to my room and sat down on a bench. A couple of minutes later I asked a couple of students passing by of they could help me to the infirmary, which was nearby. I forced myself to stay awake but felt zero energy or strength. The two students carried me to the infirmary. The physician on duty that evening could not find anything specifically wrong with me but sent me over to the local hospital so I could be observed overnight. The next afternoon my dad picked me up and took me back to Westfield, with no return date scheduled.

Five days later I returned, somewhat refreshed but now two weeks behind in my classwork, with only 10 days until the start of the season and tryouts to make Valvano's varsity squad. I was already a little out of shape from my illness and lack of playing over the two previous weeks. I reluctantly decided to drop one of my four classes to make the process of catching up right before the commencement of the season somewhat less daunting. I would have to take an extra course to make it up sometime over the next couple of years. At least that would give me the chance of putting in the time required to compete on the hardwood floor while also doing what was required in the classroom.

All that assumed I remained healthy, but unfortunately, I continued to battle insomnia which would make me feel like crap at the worst possible time. My parents and I ultimately concluded something that I didn't want to admit, that the cause of my insomnia was most likely tension over making the basketball team. Lack of sleep would make it had for me to do well there, or certainly not as well as I otherwise could, and then I started to worry about getting enough sleep, which then put more pressure on myself each night I tried to sleep. Well, trying to get more sleep or feeling like you have to get more sleep is not a great formula for actually getting more sleep. The cycle would continue to feed on itself.

When Oct. 15 arrived, I fought through it as best I could. I didn't have the best tryout, but not that bad either, and Valvano knew I had been sick recently. When Friday afternoon on Oct 19 came around, I certainly didn't expect any bad news. We all waited out in the hallway outside Valvano's office to be called in to hear something about our status with the team. The wait seemed endless, but finally my turn came. By now, the hallway was empty. I walked into the office occupied by Valvano and assistant coaches

Tommy Thompson and Al Srebnick. I settled into my chair, still unaware of the news that was about to come crashing down on me. "Stephen, Stephen," Valvano started out. "This was a tough one." The rest of the message became somewhat of a blur as a cloud of gloom descended upon me and engulfed me. My eyes welled up and I couldn't hold back the tears while saying something to the effect that I expected to make the team, and perhaps that I deserved to make the team, despite my recent illness. Their collective reply was that I would need to start out on the JV team. They did tell me to prove them wrong, to show that they were making a mistake. They said they would bring me up to the varsity squad if I were to do that. Perhaps they said it as a bit of a consolation message, or because they felt they had to say something positive, or perhaps they truly meant it. Whatever their intent, it was all I had to hold onto as I walked out of that office late on a Friday afternoon. My world as I knew it had just been shattered.

I wiped away the tears during the walk back to my room at Phi Psi. I didn't know what to do next, so I resorted to my security blanket – a basketball. I grabbed it out of my room and headed to an outdoor court at the bottom of the hill and began to shoot around by myself. I suppose it was therapy, a release of stress. But it was also a way to avoid everyone else, to not have to tell them what had just happened. I stayed for what seemed like two hours, until well after dark anyway. I finally returned to my room to face reality. Fortunately, I got a call from Tom Kachar, a friend that I had played with the prior year on the freshman team, suggesting that we drive over to Penn State for a night of pinball at a big arcade there. It seemed like the perfect escape. I went. During the hour-long drive to Penn State I let Tom know about the events of that afternoon. He commiserated with me, and soon thereafter we started pouring nickels into a variety of pinball machines throughout the arcade.

Over the weekend I let my parents in on the news. It was just a couple of days later that I got a letter from my dad with the copy of a poem by Rudyard Kipling called "If". My father said his dad had given him this when he had experienced a setback and thought it might help me too. I was not familiar with the poem but immediately understood why he had sent it. It was essentially a brief guide on how to live one's life and how to deal with difficult situations. I was particularly struck by one passage in the poem:

If you can dream—and not make dreams your master;
If you can think—and not make thoughts your aim;
If you can meet with Triumph and Disaster
And treat those two impostors just the same;

These were indeed welcome words. I would find out years later that the last two lines were also emblazoned above the walkway out onto Centre Court at Wimbledon. This guidance reinforced what I had already decided, which was to accept the outcome, face up to it, and then go out and try to prove that Valvano had made a mistake. The following Monday afternoon, just three days after getting cut and before I had received my dad's letter, I got summoned back to Valvano's office. They wanted to talk to me. What could this be about? Had they changed their mind? I doubted that was going to happen, but what could they possibly want me for? I proceeded back to Valvano's office in Davis gym where the same three coaches awaited me. No, they weren't promoting back up to the varsity squad. Instead, Valvano said he was worried for me and just wanted to make sure I wasn't going to jump off a bridge or something equally dire. I assured them that I wasn't. Furthermore, I told them that I was reconciled to my spot on the JV team and would try to show them that, in their own words, they had "made a mistake." They viewed that as very welcome news and understandably quite relieved at my more upbeat demeanor compared to what they had witnessed just three days earlier. The two teams were now set and the season could now go forward.

It's amazing what can happen when you fail at something that you've been working at for a long time, especially when it all happens in a single climactic moment. It's like the first day after a hurricane has passed through, after the rained has stopped and the wind has died down, things are drying out and the sun finally breaks through the clouds, signaling a new day. Even though your property may have been damaged, you are still alive and healthy, with the whole world is right in front of you, and the worries that had been all consuming are suddenly nowhere to be found. I went back to Kipling's poem:

If you can make one heap of all your winnings
And risk it on one turn of pitch-and-toss,
And lose, and start again at your beginnings
And never breathe a word about your loss;

I started to unwind, to relax. I started sleeping better. After all, I no longer had to worry about getting cut from the team. I also started playing better, a lot better. Unencumbered by any more negative thoughts, I could now play freely and do what my body had been training to do the past few years. I also had some new motivation spurring me on ... to prove Valvano wrong. About three weeks later I would get my first real opportunity to do just that. It was still preseason but getting closer to the opening game. Valvano decided he wanted an inter-squad scrimmage between the JV and Varsity teams, using refs and the scoreboard, to see exactly where his team stood. In the second period (we played 10-minute quarters instead of halves that day), we picked apart their zone defense and I nailed five jumpers in a row, four of which would have been 3-pointers had there been a 3-point line in that era. After the fifth, Valvano said, "Way to shoot, Stephen." Just a minute or two later, as the second period wound down, I hoisted a 35-footer just prior to the buzzer sounding and swished it, capping off a perfect quarter. I was so in the zone that day that I actually shot it from that distance rather than heave it, even though it was well outside my normal range. My teammates all gave me some skin on the way back to the bench. I felt a bit of vindication. It was indeed a good day on the hardcourt.

The season opened a few days later and I continued to play well with my reaffirmed confidence. In the fifth game of the season on Dec. 15, our last game before a two-week break for exams and Christmas, I had a good game against Rider College at their place, scoring 18. But I separated my shoulder slightly in a collision going for a loose ball. Fortunately, all it needed was two to three weeks rest to get it healed. I opted for two, and right after New Year's I was back at Bucknell all ready to go. Bucknell had a 4-1-4 semester configuration, so there were no regular classes during January. Instead, the campus was only sparsely populated with students taking certain optional classes or programs known as "Jan Plan." My Jan Plan consisted of basketball and pinball.

Our next game was Jan. 6 at Drexel, where the field house resembled an armory more than a gym and had one of these weird hard rubber floors rather than a hardwood floor. I managed another good game but missed the potential game winning shot after I dribbled the clock down for the last shot in regulation time. We ended up losing in overtime. Two days later I was playing pinball in downtown Lewisburg when another JV teammate came in and abruptly announced that Valvano wanted to see me. I don't remember what I was thinking, just that I made a beeline back to the gym on campus. There they were again – the three amigos. Valvano didn't hesitate: "Stephen, you've been playing well and we're bringing you back up to varsity. Effective immediately. Great job." I don't remember what I said, but I know what I felt. Vindication!

One thing this meant was being reunited with former Westfield High teammate and friend, Scott Novacek. Scott had already made an immediate impact upon his arrival as a freshman. Still only 6-foot-5, but with broadest of shoulders and his uncanny ability to snatch loose rebounds off the glass, Scott became an unexpected starter right out of the gate and was playing solid basketball. The team was still struggling to get more W's however, with its first set of Valvano recruits and a stronger schedule that Valvano had already incorporated. Scott and I were getting something to eat one night in the Bison, the late-night eatery in the student campus center, and reflecting on our current basketball status. Scott, ever the philosopher, said: "I play basketball because it's good exercise for your body, you make friends, and it's fun." It wasn't like I had asked Scott to justify his reasoning for playing hoops. It was a no brainer for me. He was just stating the obvious. If someone was good enough to play, they played.

The rest of that season I was good enough to play in either the third or fourth guard spot and getting a decent amount of playing time in a few games. The two starting guards were both freshmen and part of Valvano's initial recruiting class at Bucknell. I'm pretty certain I was the only walk-on on the team at that point, with everyone else having been recruited by either Valvano or his predecessor. Yes, I had done reasonably well and achieved something that wasn't easy. But next season, my junior year, would present new challenges. There no doubt would be a new wave of Valvano recruits to enter the picture and replace some of the graduating old guard. I would be up against new competition once again.

Nevertheless, I still felt good about my chances when September rolled around again in 1974. There were indeed six new freshman recruits on the scene, three of which were guards. One stood out in particular, a small, cocky guard from Washington, D.C., named Gerald Purnell. As quick as returning sophomore Tom McClean was, Purnell appeared to be even quicker if that was possible. On top of that, he was a skilled, hard-nosed kid who had a lot of confidence in his ability to score despite his lack of size. He was going to be tough to beat out.

A 3-on-3 tournament was organized in the preseason among all the basketball hopefuls. I'm not sure who organized it because the coaches were not allowed to run any kind of organized practice, but somehow it was set up and I ended up on the same team with Purnell and another one of the freshman recruits, John Callaway. Right away, our team was viewed as stacked and the favorite to win the tournament. The prize for winning was a home cooked dinner at Coach Valvano's house, not a bad incentive to win. Sure enough, form held up and our team cruised through the tournament unbeaten to claim the first prize.

The evening soon came for us to have our coveted dinner. The three of us drove to Valvano's very modest house a mile or so off campus, and were greeted by his wife Pam, who was also the chef for the occasion. They also had a couple of young toddler girls running around the house that I suspect were about two and four years old. I don't remember what we ate, just that it was very good and we all sat at their kitchen table for the meal. Afterward, Valvano, treated us to a little bit of his Frank Sinatra collection. Sinatra, like Valvano, was also a full-blooded Italian with parents that had immigrated and settled in Hoboken, NJ. Valvano played a recording of Sinatra singing *My Way*, maybe from Madison Square Garden, and Valvano went on about him as if he were some kind of God, and that he was in another league than the Beatles or any other groups that we may have liked. Thinking back to that night now, it makes perfect sense that Sinatra would have been his guy and *My Way* his song.

I was not a shoo-in to make the team, although my chances were pretty good after what had happened my sophomore year, despite even more of

Valvano's recruits being in the mix now. A week after tryouts began, I took the walk down to the gym to learn my fate. This year Valvano decided to post a list of names making the varsity squad. There were 13 names on the list. Six of them were sophomores from Valvano's first recruiting class. Five were freshman and his newest recruits. One was a junior recruited by the prior coach. One was a junior walk-on named Reddy. Way to go, Stephen!

The 1974-75 Bucknell Bison in Davis Gym

This team, Valvano's third at Bucknell, appeared to be a lot more talented than his first two, at least on paper. His first two years hadn't exactly set the world on fire, with 8-16 and 10-12 records, but everyone involved was inclined to think that this third year under Valvano would be the charm. Valvano certainly must have since he continued to beef up the schedule. This season Bucknell would be taking on nationally ranked Rutgers for the second straight year, along with Pitt, Penn State, and highly regarded South Carolina in the season opener.

The new season also brought with it some brand spanking new warm up uniforms, featuring Bucknell orange and blue striped bell bottom pants. Picture day in our new getups brought about an unexpected lecture from

Valvano. The whole team clad in our new warmups assembled in the academic quad for our official team photo. When it was all over, I asked if I could hitch a ride with the coaches back down to the gym rather than make the five-minute walk down the hill. I explained that I'd rather not be seen walking across campus in our new eye-catching uniforms; after all, it was the middle of the day on a weekday and people were everywhere going to and from classes. Well, Valvano laid into me big time for being self-conscious about that and for worrying about what others might think. It was a sharper criticism than any basketball-related criticism that he ever bestowed upon me. I knew Valvano was right, of course, and over time learned to appreciate that advice perhaps more than anything else I ever learned from him.

From left - Sitting: A Greenman, J Calloway, S Stettler; Standing: Coach J Valvano, S Reddy, Coach A Srebnick, S Oristaglio, T McClean, S Hebditch, J Griffin, Mgr W Pow, W Gravely, R Clark, J Warner, Coach T Thompson; In the tree: G Purnell

The team hit a little speed bump shortly before the season opener. Our last preseason scrimmage was on a Saturday afternoon just down the Susquehanna River at the university that bears its name. Everything seemed perfectly normal that day, but two days later at the start of practice Valvano announced that Scott Novacek had just let the coach know he had decided to quit the team. It caught us all by surprise and was certainly a blow to the team, as Scott was likely to be a starter again or, at a minimum, get significant playing time. Despite having been Scott's teammate in high school, I just wasn't close enough to him to know exactly what led him to that decision. I could only surmise from our conversation a few months earlier that he wasn't getting the same fun out of it that he had earlier. Years later Scott would clarify that his love of basketball was still intact, but he just wasn't enjoying being part of a losing basketball program, of which Bucknell certainly had a recent history and Valvano was determined to change for the better. If nothing else, this just proved that the college experience was a very distinct one from high school. No, we weren't in Westfield anymore.

The team had no choice but to move on, and a few days later opening day was upon us. We were to play a talented South Carolina team (one pre-season poll even had them ranked No. 1 in the country), coached by legendary coach Frank Maguire, at their place in a new arena with over 13,000 seats. It presumably came about through a combination of Valvano wanting to face some big-time competition and Maguire wanting a piece of cake home game to start their season, so perhaps they were doing each other a favor by scheduling the game. South Carolina was loaded that year. Mike Dunleavy was their star junior guard who went on to a long NBA career. Alex English was their star junior forward who would go on to an ever better, hall-of-fame NBA career, and would in fact score more points in the 1980's than any other NBA player – that's right, more than Michael Jordan, Larry Bird, Magic Johnson, Isiah Thomas, Kareem, and all the rest. They also featured 6-foot-10 Tom Boswell, who would have a brief career with the Celtics, plus 6-4 sophomore Nate Davis who was rumored to have a 39" vertical leap, 6-7 former high school All-American Bob Mathias who we had scrimmaged back in high school, and newcomer Jackie Gilloon, a ball-handling wizard out of Memorial High School in West New York, NJ, who was a Parade Magazine All-American and patterned his game after Pistol Pete Maravich.

The opening game was scheduled for Monday, Dec. 2, four days after Thanksgiving. A snowstorm that Sunday forced us to skip our scheduled practice so we could leave early for Newark Airport in a few vans. We took our flight early Monday morning and settled into our hotel in Columbia, S.C., before our afternoon shootaround in the big coliseum. The adrenaline would be flowing big time when we took the court a little later for the pre-game warmups. I had joked with teammate Allan Greenman that it would be the one night when I wouldn't be afflicted with "white man's disease" and could probably dunk the ball. Unfortunately, even a pre-game dunk would have cost our team a technical foul (it had been banned just a few years earlier in the wake of Lew Alcindor's domination at UCLA) so I wasn't about to find out. It was too bad though, because we were so pumped up by the time we took the court that I could feel my wrist up by the rim as we took our pre-game layups to the tune of Dr. John's "Might have been the right place, but it must have been the wrong time." For one brief moment, we were playing in the big time!

We managed to hold our own that night in front of a crowd of over 12,000 fans. Even though Dunleavy picked us apart with a quiet 28 points and Boswell cleaned up on the boards, we stayed within striking distance the entire way and ended up losing by the very respectable score of 88-74. We didn't play scared at all despite being physically overmatched. At one point their freshman hotshot Gilloon went behind his back three times in rapid succession while advancing the ball just past half court, but Gerald Purnell was in his jock strap the whole way and swiped the ball from him to quickly silence the crowd. I would only play the last two minutes that night, but drained my only shot, a 21-footer from near the top of the key. As we left the court shortly thereafter, Valvano said "Way to knock it down, Stephen," clearly pleased with the showing his team had made that night.

While the loss to South Carolina may have been a moral victory, it wouldn't take long for any good feelings from that effort to be erased from our psyches. Three days later we would lose our home opener to lowly Bloomsburg State, proof that you have to win games on the court, not on paper. A few days later we would take an 0-3 record into our game with Penn State at their gym. This was a hard-fought game that could have gone either way, but we ultimately lost in overtime. Later that night after returning to Bucknell's campus, a few of us headed down to the downtown pizza shop, where Valvano and Tommy Thompson sat at one table. Valvano looked despondent, wallowing in the depths of an 0-4 start and forced to wait two weeks before the next game right after Christmas. No, this wasn't the ACC. At Bucknell, sports programs really would shut down for a full week so student athletes could take their semester ending exams, which was immediately followed by a break for Christmas. Valvano had no choice but to wait for another chance to right his ship.

The mood seemed more upbeat two weeks later as the team reconvened for practice and then the long bus ride to Roanoke, Va., for a two-day Christmas Tournament that included Gettysburg, St. Francis of NY, and the host team Roanoke. It was hard to imagine that the start to our season could have gotten any worse, but a freakish ending to our game with St. Francis turned that into a reality. Another hard-fought game came down to the waning seconds. With two seconds left, we made a foul shot to put us up by one point. St. Francis, without any timeouts remaining, was forced to advance the ball quickly the entire length of the court for a last-second shot. Their desperate inbound pass sailed over the head of its intended target who had broken toward our basket just as the ball was released and landed near half court about 10 feet from the sideline. The ball appeared headed toward Purnell, who could have simply grabbed it to end the game, but inexplicably appeared to step out of the ball's path, almost as if he were afraid of committing a foul. The ball then bounced one or two more times before being picked up by a St. Francis player near the sideline but now in their frontcourt. He turned and in one motion launched a 35-footer and swished it as the buzzer sounded. We were all stunned. We were now 0-5.

After retreating back to the locker room, we all commiserated and felt bad for Gerald while at the same time we didn't quite understand what had just happened. Meanwhile, a shell-shocked Valvano tried to make the best of a bad situation. He acknowledged that Gerald had made a mistake but didn't blame him for it. We would simply have to regroup and get our first W the following night. We did exactly that in the consolation game against Gettysburg, beating them handily to finally stop the bleeding and get in the win column.

After New Year's we would lose again to go 1-6, and then finally kicked into a gear a bit and started winning. In fact, we won nine straight games, including a nice upset win in a Saturday afternoon home game against highly regarded Pitt. We were finally winning the games we were supposed to win, and Valvano's mood was understandably improving as things around from our horrific start. By the time we reached 10-6, little Bucknell would have the second longest win streak in the country, second only to the school that we face in our next game – none other than Valvano's alma mater – the Scarlet Knights of Rutgers!

Along the way, Valvano had promised that if we didn't lose another game before the Rutgers game, he would warm up with the team before the game. Well, we did our part and then he did his. Our home gym was packed that night; in anticipation of an overflow crowd, Bucknell added some end zone bleachers behind each basket to augment the 3,000-seating capacity of Davis Gym. Like South Carolina, Rutgers was loaded with talent, but unlike the Gamecocks, the Scarlet Knights were winning. Rutgers featured Phil Sellers, Mike Dabney, Hollis Copeland and Eddie Jordan, who the following season would propel Rutgers into the NCAA tournament unbeaten at 31-0. Even against us, Rutgers brought a 15-game win streak into the game to trump our nine-game win streak. The student body was rocking in anticipation as we took the floor, led by our fearless leader Jim Valvano in our pregame layups. As with South Carolina, we played up to the occasion, keeping the game very tight for a while and only trailing by 44-41 at halftime. We eventually succumbed to the better talent of Rutgers but didn't disappoint the crowd in the process. The Lewisburg inhabitants were not accustomed to seeing basketball of that quality played in little Davis gym.

The rest of the season was up and down, and we finished with a 14-12 record, losing our last game in the conference playoffs to a LaSalle team that featured 6-foot-10 Joe Bryant who would later have a kid named Kobe. Our losing that year was not for a lack of trying on Valvano's part. I often thought he tried too hard and got too excited for his own good during games. I thought his instruction during practices was excellent, but often during games his passion, emotions, and excitability often appeared to get the better of him. A few of us joked that at times the three coaches on the sideline resembled the Three Stooges, both in their appearance and behavior. Valvano was Mo with his short straight black hair, Srebnick was Larry with his short curly hair, and Thompson was Curly with his short and almost balding look. In certain frantic game moments Valvano would leap out of his chair and grab one of his assistants almost as a reflex action, much like Mo might slap around his two stooges when something went wrong. Years later the image of Valvano running around the court after winning the national championship at North Carolina State would give others a vivid picture of Valvano's excitability. In fairness to Valvano, I believe he became a better coach over time and with more in game experience was better able to keep his cool and coach his team through tight game situations.

It was hard not to like Valvano's passion for the game, and for everything else, for that matter. Our practices were only 90 minutes long, but he made them all count. Even bus rides could be an adventure with Valvano. He once got off our bus after it got hit by a snowball and confronted the thrower, citing a lack of respect on their part for our bus and its occupants. On another occasion a weird debate broke out between a white player who claimed that "90 percent of guys masturbate, and the other 10 percent are liars," and an inner-city black player who insisted he had never even heard of it. Valvano, overhearing the discussion his front row seat on the bus, ventured down the aisle and blurted out that "You guys are unbelievable!" Another coach probably would have ignored the whole discussion, but Valvano was more inclined to get involved with his players. Once in the locker room he noticed a player had an ROTC brochure, and he then proceeded to tell the player what it was like to go into the service or boot camp and getting disciplined for not having perfectly shined shoes or having a tie slightly out of place. "Is that really what you're looking for?" he asked after describing it all in a hilarious manner, in a way that only Valvano could, quite certain that the player didn't know what he might be getting into. In another locker room episode Valvano would relate his now famous Green Bay Packers story, some 18 years before the rest of the sports world would hear it during his dramatic ESPY awards speech. None of us knew at the time what lay ahead for our coach, but with all this powerful charisma, you knew he had the potential to do something special.

I got very little playing time that junior season, stuck in the depth chart behind the prior year starting guards and freshman Purnell, who would lead the team in scoring as a freshman. It was a tough reality to face, being at the height of my basketball abilities while simultaneously spending more and more time on the bench. I had always felt that I would never want to be a senior who rode the bench, having seen a few before me do it. It just didn't seem like that experience would be any fun; after all, I wasn't playing just to earn a varsity letter. Besides, there was a fairly competitive intramural league at Bucknell which my fraternity happened to dominate in recent years. I could help continue that tradition if I chose to forgo varsity hoops during senior year. So as the season neared its completion, I sensed that I might be approaching my last practice, my last game, my last bus ride ... as a member of my school's team. It felt like a piece of me was about to die at the tender age of 20. I felt a bit of gloom on the bus ride home from that last game at Lafayette. My father had been at the game, and I had played very little. I sensed I had reached the end of the road.

I wouldn't have to make that decision right away though. I could take the summer to mull it over. However, a few weeks after our season ended, someone else announced he was done with Bucknell basketball. Valvano was moving on – to Iona College. I didn't know much about Iona, but quickly surmised that they were a bigger school offering him a better deal. Iona would be his next steppingstone on his way to the top of the basketball world. Bucknell had now become his last.

A couple of days after we heard the news, Allan Greenman and I set out to play tennis, but unable to find open courts on campus, we ventured off campus to a nearby Lewisburg playground that had a couple. While we did battle on the tennis court, Valvano appeared at the nearby swing set with his two young daughters. He may not have been a big fan of tennis or golf, but there was certainly more to him than just basketball X's and O's. Family really did mean a lot to him. After our match, Allan and I wished him well in the next leg of his basketball journey. I would never see him again.

Nor would I ever don the orange and blue again in Davis Gym. When the season had ended my junior year, I felt like it was over. That summer I spent three months travelling out West in a van with two other friends from Bucknell. Aside from one or two days in Berkeley, CA at the end of our journey, it would be my first summer in six years without playing any hoops. But when I got back to campus in September, two things had changed that forced me to reconsider everything. First, of course, was that we now had a new coach – Charlie Woollum – which equated to new opportunity. Second, and more importantly, was that Tom McClean, one of our starting point guards the past two seasons, had decided to not play hoops that year so he could focus on training for the Olympics. The fleet footed McClean with a gazelle-like stride was also a stellar track and fielder who became the NCAA 800-meter champion and would ultimately narrowly miss making the Olympic team. McClean's absence moved me up on the depth chart and gave me a realistic shot at being the third guard which would bring meaningful playing time, certainly more than I had seen the prior year.

It came down to the last weekend before I walked into Woollum's office to let him know that he wouldn't see me at tryouts. I couldn't stand the thought of sitting on the bench during senior year, or even the possibility of that. I suppose, being somewhat conservative in nature, that I chose the sure thing.

A few weeks later intramurals started up and I would play my first game for Phi Psi. We were loaded and the odds-on favorite to win it all. I remember that first game when I received a short outlet pass near the right sideline. I had seen my opponent out of the corner of my eye as I looked back to catch the pass. With my momentum already taking me up court, in one quick motion I caught the ball and pounded it hard with the left hand as my right foot went forward. I then exploded off both feet into a jump spin dribble, with the ball still in my left hand and whirling around me and extending over the right sideline as I spun while airborne. In one motion I had spun around and past my defender who no doubt had grasped at air where he thought the ball was going to be. I heard some ooohs and laughs from the sideline in my wake as I proceeded down court on the fast break. They had just witnessed the perfect spin move! Later a teammate told me that Coach Woollum had walked into the gym just moments earlier and seen that play, which of course put the biggest smile on his face.

But Coach Woollum was not my coach. I was playing for Phi Psi and for myself now. I thought back to Nova's comment a year earlier – "I play basketball because it's good exercise for your body, you make friends, and it's fun." No, I wouldn't be wearing the orange and blue anymore when I took the court. But I proved that night that I didn't need a coach or a school to play for, and that basketball could still be fun without either. Oh yes, basketball was most definitely still fun.

Our Phi Psi team went 9-0 that season, winning the championship game after falling behind by 11 points early. I graduated from Bucknell a couple of months later. The real world would be my next stop.

VI.   Taking Flight (Nov 26 – Dec 31, 1971)

"The rumors were flying, the hoopsters were good;
How high they would soar was not yet understood,"

from *A Team to Remember*, November 18, 2000

It was 9:30 am on Friday, Nov. 26 when we reported for practice, still minus our football teammates. Horne decided to give them one day off to ease their transition into their new sport, so the rest of us would have to wait one more day for them to join the team. In the meantime, Horne still had 10 bodies to work with, plus the JV squad that included promising players in sophomores Jimmy Masters and Buddy Robinson. We did double sessions that day, finally ending at 3:30.

We reported back for practice the next morning, along with the football five - Pfeiffer, Simmons, Jackson, Danker, and Allen - fresh off their one-day vacation from football. They would now need to get their basketball muscles going. Naturally, that would take a little time, but Horne was in no rush. We still had two weeks until our season opener. He would use all of it to get the football five fully acclimated and size up all of his personnel.

We went almost three hours that Saturday morning, giving the football five a full dose of Horne's routine and methods. But we weren't done yet that day. It was another double session, and the afternoon session would be a scrimmage game against Clarkstown, NY, a team from Long Island whose coach was friends with Coach Horne. It was their camp that Goski, Cooney and I had worked at during the summer, so the preseason scrimmage between their respective squads was no doubt agreed upon during that summertime collaboration.

It was just what we needed because Clarkstown sported one of the most highly touted big men along the East Coast in 6-foot-6 Bob Mathias, a junior at the time who would eventually play for a talented South Carolina team. Unfortunately, Horne wouldn't let the football guys play that day – it was just too soon, but it would still be a great test for our center Scott Novacek. Horne told Novacek before the scrimmage that he wouldn't see anyone all year as good as Mathias, and that he would need to put a body on him to keep him as far away from the rim as possible. Scott held his own that day and while Mathias showed us some of his skills, he did not dominate inside the paint that day.

Being shorthanded that day also meant more playing time for the rest of us, and Goski was more than happy to pick up the slack and show what he could do against some of his former campmates. Having spent the prior three summers living at Gumbert, Tim wasn't about to be intimidated by anyone from Clarkstown. When he was at the foul line getting ready to shoot free throws, one of their guards, apparently still smarting from some of the nighttime counselor games at summer camp, resorted to calling Tim frail. Without hesitation, Goski responded with a sneer: "Come meet me in the parking lot after the game and see how frail I am." While we were still just in our infancy as a team, I could see that the confidence of Novacek and Goski was going to be a real asset. It was reassuring to know our team was loaded with guys who wouldn't back down from any opponent. Of course, the challenge still remained for Horne to harness that confidence and use it to our advantage. After all, we weren't playing at Gumbert now … no, we were representing our school as the Westfield High School Blue Devils varsity basketball team.

Two days later we would have our second full practice with all the football players included. We still had 15 on the roster, so some cuts were still to come, most likely after a few more practices and Horne had a chance to evaluate everyone. Still, Horne was in no rush to insert the football five into scrimmage situations, so the next day when a tough Roselle team came to our gym for a scrimmage, Horne for the second time had them sitting in the bleachers watching rather than playing. They still weren't ready in Horne's mind. More importantly, though, was that Horne felt they would learn more by sitting down and observing what was happening out on the court, rather than struggle out there against a strong opponent while not yet in basketball shape and not yet sure of what we were trying to do as a team. It was a shrewd move when the temptation would have been to throw them into the fire right away – after all, it was only a practice game. The football five didn't exactly get a day off though, as they had to show up for a 7 a.m.

practice with Horne to finish getting them caught up on various team concepts.

Not only was Roselle a very strong team, but we knew a few of them from Gumbert. Lee Hollerback was a fairly slender but skilled 6-foot-6 center who also had long blonde hair to somewhat rival Novacek's. Mike Johnson was a very polished 6-4 forward who was clearly one the best players in Union County, and whom we had faced two years earlier during the county tournament. At guard they had a rising star in sophomore Ross Kindle, who a few years later helped lead Syracuse to a Final Four spot in the NCAA tournament. Ross was also the kid brother of Roger Kindle who starred for Roselle a few years earlier and was a strong crafty guard who still held fort at Gumbert every summer and was the unofficial czar of pickup games there.

Even though we had to play them shorthanded, we still made a good showing out of it. In these scrimmages the score was typically kept on the scoreboard for each quarter and then reset back to 0-0 for the next quarter. We played four quarters that day (scrimmages often went longer than that if the coaches desired), and Roselle won the first, second and fourth quarters by slim margins in each case, but in the third quarter we blew 'em out by double digits. Goski and Novacek were key in that stretch, with Tim showing a bit of his playground tendencies at times. It was perhaps a sign of things to come. Goski had developed exceptional offensive skills on the cement courts down at Gumbert and, importantly, played with a confidence and fearlessness that matched those skills. Horne's challenge was going to be how much leeway to give Tim to deviate from a team oriented offensive set and revert to an attacking playground style of play that leveraged his own individual skills.

The results against Roselle were encouraging. Next came two more days of practice with our full squad before we would go up to Cliffside Park to play them in a Friday night scrimmage. After the first of those practices Horne decided to make those necessary final cuts, and Bill Nelson, Barry Kaufman and Joe Cacchione all learned that they did not make the final roster. As Horne would explain later, while he felt Caccione was the better basketball player, he felt Chip Danker was the better athlete, so he chose the latter for what was essentially the fifth guard spot. The other four footballers

- Pfeiffer, Simmons, Jackson and Allen completed our 12-man roster. The latter two certainly didn't have the same level of basketball skills as the starters did, but they would still be important parts of the roster in the roles they would play every day in practice. With all the defensive and rebounding drills that we did every day, these guys, along with Jester, Phillips, Cooney and Lee, didn't make it easy on the starters. It seemed like there were constant mini wars breaking out going for loose balls and rebounds, and Jackson set the hardest picks I can ever remember – it was like running into a brick wall!

1971-72 Varsity Boys Basketball Team

Left to right – Back: Coach Neil Horne Jr., Trainer John D'Andrea, Mike Cooney, Steve Reddy, Steve Lee, Tim Goski, Greg Allen, Chip Danker, Coach Bill Dunkle. Middle: Bob Jester, Dave Phillips, Tom Pfeiffer, Larry Simmons, Scott Novacek, Mark Jackson. Front: Managers Paul Leifer, Mike King, Brad Chazotte

Having Pfeiffer and Simmons in the lineup was going to make a real difference. Not only were they exceptional athletes, but their mere presence on defense made us a tougher team to score on or rebound against. While we weren't a tall team by any means, no one was going to push us around. Furthermore, we had guys that went after missed shots and loose balls like they meant something. As good as Novacek was in keeping both his arms up going after rebounds, Larry Simmons was equally adept at jumping quickly and snatching balls off the glass with one hand. On the offensive end Tom and Larry gave us more balance. While neither had the offensive skills of Goski or the pure shooting ability of Novacek, and Simmons was usually a reluctant shooter, opponents couldn't take them for granted either. This was especially true given the offensive sets that Horne was implementing with many interchangeable parts and where any given player might end up in any position on the court. It was indeed a team-oriented offense where individual skills would be muted a bit to improve the chances of getting better shots.

There were more than just the physical attributes that Pfeiffer and Simmons brought to the table, however. There was also invisible tension between the senior and junior classes that I think we all sensed below the surface. It wasn't spoken, but you could sense it. I know I could.

Pfeiffer had heard about how much Goski had improved and seen Novacek show flashes of brilliance as a sophomore on a JV team that had gone 18-4, which was better than what we had done during our JV year. But neither of them had played a single varsity game yet, and hadn't they lost three times that JV season to a Ray Schnitzer-led Scotch Plains team? Tom and I never had that much of a problem with Schnitzer. I could tell that Tom was taking a "show me" attitude toward Goski, Novacek and the rest of the juniors. Those other juniors were no slouches either. Jester, Phillips, and Cooney were also largely responsible for that 18-4 record and promised to be valuable contributors to our current team. Meanwhile, Larry Simmons may not have been saying much, but he wasn't backing down from anyone either. Lee and I were the other half of the seniors that one way or another were going to keep the juniors honest. Thus, there was an ever-present tension that fueled our intra-squad competitiveness., and it made for some heated battles during our practices. Guys were fighting for playing time. Sometimes tensions would rise to the surface and boil over a bit. But Horne was there to oversee it all. It was his job to manage it, harness the talent that was there, and get the most out of it.

On Friday, Dec. 3, one week before our first regular-season game, we rode up to Cliffside Park to face an opposing team for the first time with all 12 players dressed and ready to go. It felt a little bit like a horse being trained for the Kentucky Derby and then about a week before the big race the trainer tells the jockey to run the horse a little harder, to let her open up her stride. I don't remember what the scoreboard may have reflected, but the extra horsepower that our team now had was clearly evident at various times throughout the scrimmage. Yes, we were making a lot of mistakes, but there were enough good things happening to make us feel good about where we were. We were now starting to see how we would handle all sorts of in game situations, like full court presses, zone defenses and out of bounds plays. There was a lot to execute and a lot to improve upon, but there were also signs of our potential, and at long last the football players were fully on board and integrated into the team.

Horne gave us Saturday off, somewhat out of necessity, as most of the seniors would be taking SATs and ACTs that day.

On Monday we would return to our practice routine, with Horne again adding more special offenses, defenses and plays for specific game situations, as exhibited in Figure 2 below. These included a 3-1-1 half court zone press, a 1-1-3 zone defense, and last second shots against either a zone defense or with us talking the ball out near half court. Horne knew that some of these situations would never materialize in real games, but one of them might, and he knew it might make the difference between winning and losing. Horne had it all planned out … seemingly down to the minute … so one thing was certain - Horne had already thought it through and knew what he wanted to spend practice time on.

At the close of practice that Monday, Horne called us all up into his office. With our opener at Berkeley Heights just four days away, it was now time to elect captains. Horne pronounced that only seniors were eligible, which only left four of us. We were to write one name down on a piece of paper for the vote. After the votes were cast and tallied, Horne announced that Tom Pfeiffer would be one of our co-captains and that we now needed to vote again for a second one. Twelve votes were cast again. This time Horne announced that the vote was a 6-6 tie between Larry Simmons and me. We were to vote again. The same result again – another 6-6 tie. Horne then made a decision – we would have one more vote and if tied again, we would have tri-captains. Pieces of paper were handed out one more time. Votes were cast. Votes were tallied. Horne announced the outcome: 7-5. Larry Simmons would join Tom Pfeiffer as our second co-captain.

Figure 2

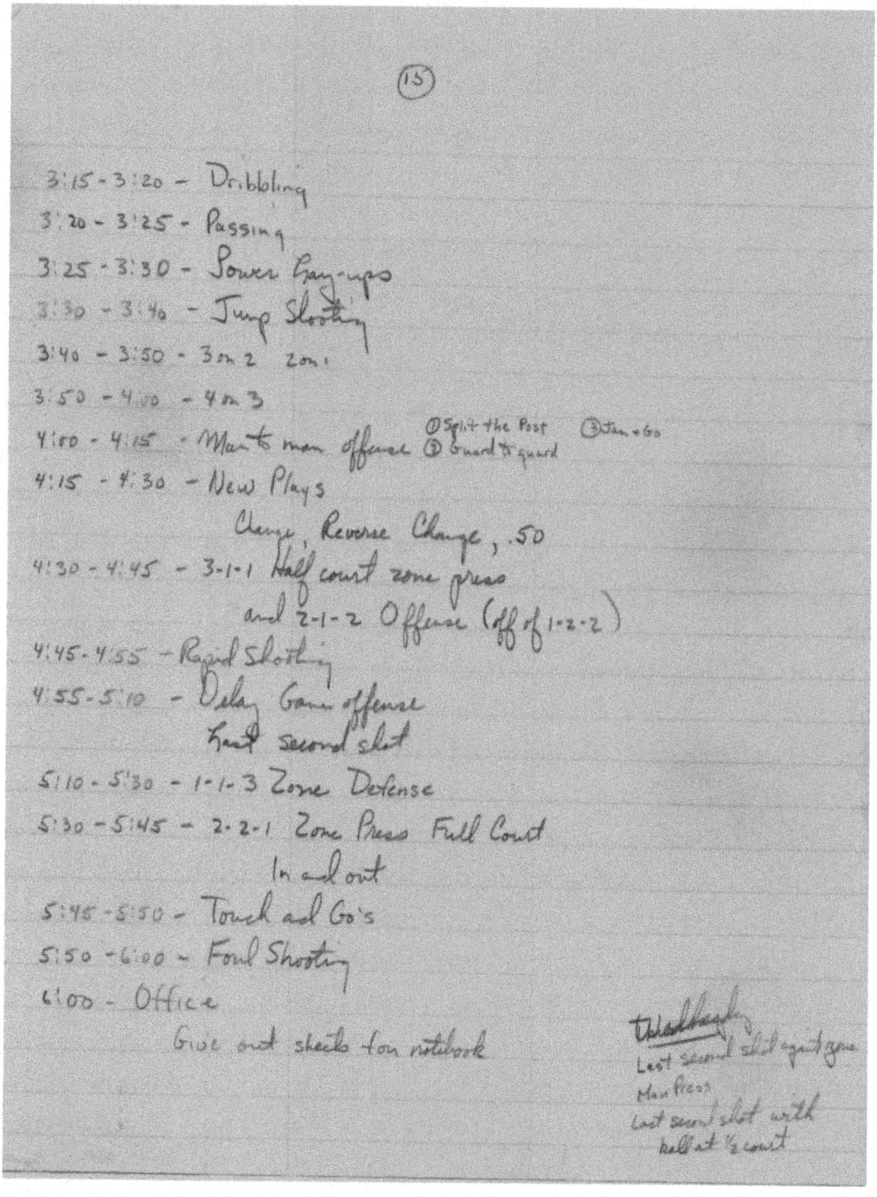
(15)

3:15 - 3:20 - Dribbling
3:20 - 3:25 - Passing
3:25 - 3:30 - Power Lay-ups
3:30 - 3:40 - Jump Shooting
3:40 - 3:50 - 3 on 2 zone
3:50 - 4:00 - 4 on 3
4:00 - 4:15 - Man to man offense ① Split the Post ② Guard to guard ③ Jam + Go
4:15 - 4:30 - New Plays
Change, Reverse Change, .50
4:30 - 4:45 - 3-1-1 Half court zone press
and 2-1-2 Offense (off of 1-2-2)
4:45 - 4:55 - Rapid Shooting
4:55 - 5:10 - Delay Game offense
Last second shot
5:10 - 5:30 - 1-1-3 Zone Defense
5:30 - 5:45 - 2-2-1 Zone Press Full Court
In and out
5:45 - 5:50 - Touch and Go's
5:50 - 6:00 - Foul Shooting
6:00 - Office
Give out sheets for notebook

Wednesday
Last second shot against zone
Man Press
Last second shot with
ball at ½ court

A mix of emotions swirled over me at that moment. While I had spent very little time, if any, thinking about being co-captain prior to that date, I would be lying if I said it didn't mean anything. After all, my two older brothers had both been captains of their respective teams during their senior years, so it would only be natural to want to follow in their footsteps, at least subconsciously. The way it happened was a little bit of a stunner, not to mention a little bit of a mystery. Only one person knew, at least at that moment, who had changed their vote. But all of that was trumped by what I had done myself, which was to vote for Larry Simmons each of those last three votes. I somehow managed to fool myself into thinking there was some form of weird etiquette that said you don't vote for yourself. I'm sure I got that confused with something else, like letting others go ahead of you through a doorway. Whatever it was, I was now second guessing myself for what I had just done.

The next day during school I remember passing Larry in the hallway and feeling a little bit of resentment. Larry had voted for himself, I now knew. He hadn't made the same dumb mistake that I had. But then I did something smart. I decided to accept it and focus on the season that was immediately before us. What happened in that vote happened and there was no point in reliving it anymore. While I couldn't avoid hearing how some people had voted that day, I never asked to find out how everyone voted or who ultimately changed their vote. I didn't want to know. It might have changed my opinion of that person forever, rightly or wrongly. It was better for me and the team that I not know that. Besides, I had brought it all upon myself and finding out who voted for whom wasn't going allow me to shift blame or responsibility to someone else. While ignorance wasn't necessarily bliss here, it was the better way to go. It was better for our team. I had to put it behind me.

That day we would travel to Maplewood to play Columbia in our final preseason game. We played six quarters, with both coaches wanting to give their players a thorough test before their quickly approaching opening games. When all was said and done, the scoreboard read 110-91 in our favor. Even over six quarters, 110 was a lot of points, and everybody felt pretty good about the team's showing. Of course, Horne wasn't about to admit that. We were just getting started and this was no time to pat ourselves on the back.

That evening I was sitting at the dinner table with my mom and dad, and for some reason I felt compelled to make a prediction. "This team will be better than either of Tommy or Mark's teams," I announced, directing it primarily to my dad. That drew a big belly laugh from him, the type of laugh that I had never heard from him before. It was almost as if I had said, "The Vietnam War has been the most important war in American history" to someone who had spent two and a half years at sea on the battleship *USS North Carolina* during World War II, like my dad had. It wasn't that he didn't think we had a good team, but he just didn't think I had that perspective to make that judgment. After all, my older brother Tommy had played on a 16-7 team with players like Bob Felter, Jerry Richards, and Pete Mavraganis and won the difficult Union County Tournament, while Mark's senior year team had gone 15-8 and won the Watchung Conference title, the only time it had been done in the past 10 years. No, we were going to have to prove to my dad what I had predicted. He had been around long enough to know that talk was cheap.

At school the next morning, word began to spread quickly of the gruesome List murders that occurred in a big house up on Hillside Avenue. Five bodies had just been discovered the night before. More details would emerge the next morning in the Westfield Leader, which stated that John List had apparently murdered his wife, three children and mother about a month earlier and then taken off somewhere. He had notified the school superintendent that the kids would have an extended absence from school for a family trip, which gave him a head start for his getaway. Concerned neighbors had noticed lights going out one by one and notified police, who made the gruesome discovery. They would find his car the next day at JFK. News like that would be shocking anywhere, but especially in a town like Westfield, where things like that just didn't happen. The List house, which stood up on a hill further back from the street than most Westfield houses, immediately took on a mystique of its own. It would burn to the ground the following summer, adding to the mystique. List appeared to get away with it, at least for a long while, but was eventually caught in Virginia in 1989 with the help of the TV series *America's Most Wanted*.

For the last two practices before our first game Horne shifted into regular-season mode. We would spend about 15 minutes each day reviewing Berkeley Heights' offense, though I'm not quite sure how Horne knew what it was, especially at the outset of the season. We also spent a little more time on various press situations, out-of-bounds plays, last-second shots, and foul shooting. The final day before our first game, we concluded practice with 20 minutes of foul shooting, the most of any practice, before winding up at 6 p.m. Horne then gave us our instructions for the next day: Be at school at 5 p.m. wearing jackets and ties.

Preseason was now officially over.

December 10, 1971

At about 5:15 we were all on the bus enroute to Berkeley Heights to face Governor Livingston Regional High School. The junior varsity game was at 6:30 and our game would follow at 8pm. It promised to be a relatively easy opening game for us. We would hardly set the world on fire that night at the offensive end and shot a paltry 6-for-18 from the foul line, but we dominated them on the boards (53-23) and smothered them on defense, holding them to only eight field goals on 17 percent shooting on the way to a 46-29 victory. That's the great thing about defense – you can be stinking up the joint on offense with bad shooting and turnovers, but if you play good team defense, you shouldn't have any off nights at that end of the court and your team should always be in the game. The little bit of scoring we did get was fairly balanced, with Simmons and Novacek each getting 10, Pfeiffer had 9, and Jester and I each had 7. Goski had a very inauspicious varsity debut in which he committed five times as many fouls as he scored points, which is to say that he fouled out with only a single foul shot to his credit. Fortunately, we didn't need his scoring that night. No one was too worried about Tim's poor start; we all knew that would change for the better. I think Tim was more embarrassed than anything.

Word got out that someone was hosting a party, so a few of us decided to head over there once the bus had returned back to the high school. After all, we were now supposed to be the cool guys, the center of attention. The party was already in full swing given that we didn't arrive until about 10:30. Moments after I walked through the door, I saw the girl who was the center of my attention. There she was, Judy Smith, standing with another guy. I immediately got this sinking feeling. It looked like she had come there with him, that she was "with" him. I didn't know who he was, hadn't seen him before, and wasn't even sure if he went to our school – I guessed not. A few minutes later, Laura Saunders, who was Judy's best friend, came over to me and reassured me that he "was just a friend." Being the novice dater that I was, I did not feel reassured.

The next morning as I got ready to go to practice, I remember a strong feeling of ambivalence – there were all these good vibes flowing from our team and the new season and its prospects, mixed in with my totally uncertain, very tenuous status as one of the cool players who could claim a girlfriend as his own. I didn't like the latter feeling. Fortunately, practice would soon force me to focus on the more comfortable of the two subjects.

Saturday night Pfeiffer and I decided to head over to Hillside to do a little scouting of Scotch Plains, who had had their way with us the past four years. We had lost to them twice each of the last two years and had also lost to Park Junior High all four times we had played them. Our only success had been managing to split our four games with the Terrill Junior High teams that featured Schnitzer and Eddie Miller. All told, Tom and I had a lousy 2-10 record against all those Scotch Plains teams the past four years. Add to that the fact that our juniors had just gone 0-3 against Schnitzer's JV squad the prior year to spoil an otherwise great 18-4 season. Needless to say, Scotch Plains had our number, and they were the team that we circled on the calendar. We were to play them the following Friday night at home in just the third game of the year. Just six days to go until what we thought of as our biggest game of the season.

We took our seats at the very top of the bleachers in Hillside's gym, which were tall bleachers that were only present on one side of the court. The gym wall was our backrest. The first thing we noticed as Scotch Plains took the court was that Schnitzer, or "Ray Ray" as some called him, had gotten a haircut, courtesy of his new coach and our previous coach Joe Coleman. Up until that point, Ray Ray had looked like a miniature version of Pistol Pete Maravich, with somewhat longish and floppy hair, and clever ballhandling skills to justify the comparison. But Coleman apparently didn't care about that and decided that a little more discipline in the form of short haircuts was what would help make them a better team that year. While it may not have been a crew cut that Ray Ray was sporting, it certainly wasn't going to be flopping around any time soon. As soon as Schnitzer made a turnover, I was thinking that Sampson had lost his power when he got that haircut. Surprisingly, Scotch Plains got beat that night, but we weren't going to let their performance cause us to take them lightly the next time we faced them. There was absolutely no risk in that happening.

December 14, 1971

Our home opener was a Tuesday afternoon contest against South Plainfield, nothing to get overly excited about. If we did our job, we should win, simple as that. Things started out as expected and we jumped out to a 22-8 lead after the first quarter, but then we got sloppy. Their press hurt us in the second quarter, and we squandered almost the entire lead – we barely led 30-28 at halftime. Horne gave us a nice tongue lashing at halftime and it paid dividends in the third quarter as we outscored the Tigers 30-4 to put the game away. We cruised home from there for a 73-50 win. For the second game in a row, we dominated the boards, this time by a 50-24 margin, led by Simmons with 16 caroms. Novacek led us in scoring with 21 points, with the rest of the scoring being pretty balanced again. Goski scored 11 to end his one-game slump.

It was all good enough to beat South Plainfield this day. We would still need to step it against Scotch Plains to beat them on Friday.

December 17, 1971

At 3 p.m., Goski, Novacek, Cooney and I got into the Catalina and headed over to the Blue Star shopping center on Route 22 in Watchung. For our big night home opener against Scotch Plains, we decided we needed to spruce things up a little bit. Our mission was to get a few accessories to complete our game attire. We needed wrist bands, but rather than boring white ones, we thought we'd get them in blue and white, our school colors. Our plan changed once we got to the Two Guys store there, and we saw that we could get red ones too. For some reason our team uniforms, which had been new one season earlier, had a little bit of red trim in them. Not sure where that came from, but it was real. After some quick deliberation, the four of us walked out of the store a few minutes later with red and blue wrist bands and red and blue shoelaces. We would each wear the colored wrist bands and shoelaces, one red and one blue, for the vast majority of the season. Three or four other players would subsequently join us in our color coordination scheme.

On the way back we plotted an opening play to allow Goski to do a number on Schnitzer. It was right out of the playground, but seamlessly woven into the framework of our offensive set. Goski would screen down for Novacek on the right side of the lane. I would pass the ball to Novacek who was now on the right wing, who would immediately dump it down to Goski with Ray Ray pinned on his back. Goski would then "do the Shu," which was a reference to John Shumate, former Thomas Jefferson standout who was now a sophomore starring at Notre Dame and whose shooting motion had the ball cocked behind his head. We had seen him a lot down at Gumbert and sometimes when screwing around Tim would imitate Shumate with an exaggerated cocking of the ball way behind his head. Horne would never know of our little plan because it was a basic play we could call out of our normal offensive set, without the "do the Shu" part, of course. We would get our chance about four hours later.

We took the court about 7:50 p.m. for warmups and could feel the electricity in the gym. It was packed. Adrenaline was flowing. For the past six years, this was what Tom and I had dreamed of … the big game against our archrival in front of a big crowd, only now we were no longer in the crowd…we were why the crowd came.

Tom, Larry and I made a slight detour prior to the opening tap. We left our huddle and walked the 20 feet to shake hands with Joe Coleman, Scotch Plains' head coach and our former coach just a few short months ago. He greeted us with a smile and a handshake.

Horne gave us one other routine for the start of each game. After we broke out of our team huddle, the five starters would go to the near foul line for a final mini huddle just prior to the opening tap … a last moment of pregame encouragement or messaging. Being a players only huddle, we often used our own choice words that were fueled with adrenaline. After that, it was time to play ball.

Which meant, for this game, it was time to call a play for Goski to take on Schnitzer down low. After Scotch Plains turned it over on their first possession, I brought the ball down court and waited for Goski to screen down for Novacek to flash out on the right wing. I hit Novacek about 20 feet from the basket and he immediately dumped the ball down to Goski in the low post. Tim took one quick dribble with his left hand, but then reversed dribble toward the baseline. With two more quick dribbles Goski slithered by Schnitzer along the baseline and laid the ball up from slightly underneath the backboard. We executed the play almost exactly as we had discussed earlier that afternoon in the car, except that Tim got all the way to the basket and didn't need to imitate Shumate with a baseline jump shot.

On our initial offensive play, Goski screens down on Novacek's man

The first quarter had a lot of sloppy play, mostly bad or deflected passes that led to turnovers, but we still got the better of it and led 14-9 at the end of the quarter. This continued through the second period, although the shooting picked up a little bit and we managed to stretch our halftime lead to 31-19. Our front court guys were dominating on the boards at both

Novacek receives the ball on the right wing and looks to feed Goski

Goski now has the ball in low post with Ray Schnitzer defending

Goski beats Schnitzer to the baseline with a reverse dribble

Goski rises up for a layup before the defense can react

ends, and that was the primary reason for our halftime lead. Everyone was contributing on offense with Novacek leading the way with 10 points.

We couldn't stand prosperity, though, and the third quarter would see our lead totally evaporate. Scotch Plains outscored us 28-14 in the period, with their big guy Steve Deck getting nine points. A couple of steals put them into the lead by two points heading into the final period. Scotch Plains maintained their momentum early in the 4th as they stretched their lead to 6 points, forcing a timeout by Horne to stop the bleeding.

Goski stomps his foot in disgust after Scotch Plains takes a 6 point lead

Then we bounced back with six straight to tie it up on a couple of short jumpers by Simmons, followed by two free throws by Cooney. Scotch Plains got the lead back when they hit one of two free throws. We briefly took the lead back with just under four minutes left when Pfeiffer hit a contested shot in the lane, but then the teams traded steals, leading to an Eddie Miller layup and a 56-55 lead. Cooney countered with a nice 15-foot jumper from the foul line – we led by one again with about three minutes to go. Horne had decided to stick with Cooney and leave Goski on the bench at this late

Novacek makes a great block on Eddie Miller's 17-foot jumper

Novacek hauls in the blocked shot with both hands to secure the ball

stage of the game given that we had the momentum while Mike had been on the court the entire fourth quarter.

Novacek then exerted himself with a couple of big plays. First, he snatched a missed shot off the boards and made a quick put back to put us up 59-56. Then just a few seconds later Scott made a tremendous block of an Eddie Miller jump shot by the foul line, and immediately rose up again to snatch the loose ball out of the air with those big mitts of his. But Miller came right back after a missed Cooney jumper to hit a baseline jumper from the right side.

We now clung to a 59-58 lead as we deliberately worked the ball around Scotch Plains zone defense. Finally things broke our way the final two minutes when I hit a driving shot along the baseline with 1:50 left, followed by a Pfeiffer steal of the inbound pass and quick lay in which gave us a five-point lead at 63-58. We were able to run out the clock from there to seal a 66-62 win. We had final conquered Scotch Plains!

Miller had been stellar for the Plainsmen, hitting for 24 points on a variety of jump shots. Ray Ray had 12, but we kept him pretty bottled up and limited his penetration and assists. Pfeiffer led us with 17 and Novacek had 14, while all five starters scored in double figures. Once again, we dominated the boards, this time by a margin of 51-25.

It was a nerve-racking victory that lifted us to a 3-0 record. Scotch Plains would leave with a surprising 0-3 record, not exactly what Joe Coleman had planned on last spring when he bolted town and paved the way for Neil Horne. Having given up a big lead and then to fall behind by six in the last quarter, the opportunity was there for us to collapse and succumb to Scotch Plains again. But it never happened. Something held us together. It wasn't very pretty, but we had finally beaten Scotch Plains for the first time in our last five tries, so we weren't going to complain about how it may have looked. We were finally over the hump, so to speak, so now we could start looking at what lay ahead on the schedule. There were other teams out there ... a lot more ... Horne would soon have us focused on our next hurdle, but first we still had a weekend ahead of us.

Now that the season was underway, our Saturday routine would be a practice (assuming no game that night) coupled with spending an hour or so over at Washington School, where the sixth- and seventh- grade clinic and games were still held on Saturday mornings. The clinics were run by Bob Brewster, one of the most prominent WHS boosters and father of a houseful of successful athletes – Bob Jr., Brad, Daryl, and Roger. The senior Brewster was the founder of the clinic, and he would run it for 21 straight years. Throughout that period the high school varsity team had lent its support to the clinic by having its players show up to help out with coaching and refereeing or whatever might be helpful. After all, many of the varsity players had gotten their real start at this clinic, Tom Pfeiffer and I being among-them, and Horne wasn't about to break with this tradition. It was a great way for the younger kids who may be just starting out to be able to see the varsity players up close, players that they may want to be like someday. It was an easy way for the varsity players to give something back. It was a win-win relationship for the town and its residents.

That evening there were one or more parties slated, so I made plans with two or three other players to meet up and then head over in the roomy Catalina. But first there was one other item that would be added to our agenda for the evening – alcohol. I don't remember who bought it or where we got it from. I just remember what I drank. It was a bottle of Boone's Farm Apple Wine. It would have been bad enough if I had stopped there, but I didn't. A bottle of Strawberry Hill. A whole bottle. More cheap wine. Needless to say - too much wine … way too much.

What happened next is rather painful to recall. Before long, I would be relieved of my driving duties. Fortunately, my teammates were looking out for me, at least enough to not make that mistake. The next thing I remember was stumbling across the lawn of the location of one the parties. I never made it inside. Soon after I began puking my guts out. I somehow managed to not compound the situation by keeping it all outside the car. The next thing I remember is being taking back to Dave Phillips' house. I'm not even sure if he was with us earlier that evening, but that's where we ended up. Moose's older sister then took over the clean-up operation and for the next hour or so helped deal with my drunken condition and prepare me for my ultimate trip back home. I took turns crying, puking some more, and apologizing to Dave's sister for being such a mess. She continued to clean up after me and tend to my needs. I would be forever in her debt. Sometime between midnight and 1 p.m. I would have to make short drive home, a drive that ordinarily take just five minutes.

I would make it home that night without further incident ... well, almost. I successfully navigated our winding driveway around to the back of our house and then into the right-hand spot within our two-car garage. I then proceeded to fall asleep right there. Not sure for exactly how long. Five minutes? Ten minutes maybe. But then something woke me abruptly. It was my mom coming out to see where I was. I somehow reacted quickly and grabbed the antenna that lay in the front seat next to me. It had been broken off earlier in the evening by some rambunctious party goer. I had no idea who had done it, but at least it helped me in this particular moment. "I was looking for this," I stated to my mom, holding it up for her to see. I ambled slowly into the house hoping to bring the night to a close. I appeared to have at least escaped detection at that particular moment.

The next morning I resumed my physical recovery. One night's sleep alone was not enough. I still felt like crap. I had to go to Holy Trinity for an 11:30 mass to get me back in time for a 1 p.m. interview with a Dartmouth alumnus who lived a couple of blocks from us. My brother Tommy had gone to Dartmouth and done well there in basketball, starting for a while under head coach Dave Gavitt, who later had success in the Big East Conference. I must have walked into that interview looking and acting like a zombie and made an underwhelming impression on the Dartmouth alum. Despite having scored 1350 in my SATs, including 800s in my math SATs and ACTs, solid grades, a high class ranking, and a brother who did very well there, I ultimately did not get accepted by Dartmouth. I would spend the rest of the afternoon physically recovering, rehydrating, plodding through homework that I didn't feel like doing, and pondering what I had just done over the previous 24 hours.

I didn't like what I had done, not one bit. It was a pathetic attempt to try to impress others, including one girl in particular. Worse still, I was messing with the success that our team was on the verge of achieving and I risked blowing it all with the stupidity and recklessness that I had shown the previous night. It was very clear to me what I had to do. I decided right then and there: no more alcohol for the rest of the season. I figured it was the best way to put the previous night behind me to the fullest extent possible. Another night's sleep and 24 hours of rehydrating wouldn't hurt either. It would be good to feel normal again.

I walked onto the court Monday afternoon about 3:15 for practice and was greeted by a bunch of unwanted smiles and laughter, both from those who had been with me part of Saturday night and others who had heard about it. I was defenseless and had no choice but to endure whatever ribbing they were going to give me. I surprised some of them just by being there at practice on Monday; that's how bad I had looked two nights earlier. I couldn't wait for Horne's whistle to signal the start of practice. Thank God we were about to play some hoops again. Finally, the whistle came. The nightmare was over. I was back in my safe zone. It was now time to prepare for Springfield, our opponent on Tuesday.

December 21, 1971

For the second Tuesday in a row, it would be one of those lower energy afternoon home games that started at 3:45 p.m. These games generally just didn't have the same crowd energy as night or weekend games when you'd have larger crowds that extended beyond the home team's student body. Instead, the players themselves would have to create the energy in the gym with their play.

Of course, counterbalancing this was that you could always count on Al Pfeiffer, Tom's dad, occupying a seat not far from the court and making his presence felt with his game commentary that would easily pierce through the relatively sparse Tuesday afternoon crowds. The senior Pfeiffer was almost certainly THE most vocal of all Westfield sports fans and was not shy about criticizing any Westfield player or coach if he felt they were underperforming. Al Pfeiffer didn't confine his critiques to just players either. He was once ejected by the referee officiating a Phillipsburg Catholic vs. St. Patrick's state tournament game that was played in Westfield's gym. He was indeed a tough critic, but a fair one as far as I was concerned. Those critiques, combined with any postgame commentary he might direct your way, were enough to ensure that you came to play that day.

Our opponent this day was Springfield, whose high school was known as Dayton Regional. Springfield was not as strong as the previous two years when they touted sharp-shooting Frank Bucci and hard-nosed Ed Graessle.

Those guys were gone now, so we were well positioned to avenge losses of the prior two years. We would do just that, but not before another bad stretch through much of the first half just like we had endured in portions of the first three games. We only led by 23-20 at halftime, before pouring it on in the third quarter and opening up a 23-point lead, which was increased even further in the last period on the way to a 73-43 victory. We seemingly just weren't sharp enough yet to play 32 solid minutes of play without some kind of lapse part way through the game. On the plus side, we continued to dominate the boards as with our three previous opponents, this time by the whopping margin of 55-27, with Novacek leading the way with 21 rebounds. He also led us in scoring with 18, while Goski added 16 and the reserves contributed 20 points. I even managed nine points in my first game since my Saturday night debacle. We went home that night with a 4-0 record. So far, so good.

December 23, 1971

This day would bring a rare Thursday night game, but for good reason. The next day was Christmas Eve. Thursday was the last day of classes before a highly coveted, 10-day Christmas break. So that also meant only one day of preparation for our opponent that night, which was Union High School at their place.

Horne decided to shake things up a little bit this night. He decided to start Mike Cooney in place of Goski, not a move any of us were expecting. But Horne wanted to send a message to Tim. I suspect he felt Tim was playing a little out of control and not staying within the offensive scheme enough. Perhaps he was reverting to his playground instincts a little too much for Horne's liking. Furthermore, Cooney had played well in the first four games, so Horne probably felt it was as good a time as any to get Tim's attention.

Goski got the message. After a few restless minutes on the bench, he came in and lit it up – clearly his best effort of the year with 16 points and 10 assists, including six steals in the third quarter alone when we broke the game open after another slim halftime lead of only 33-28. The 10 assists were especially impressive and exactly what Horne wanted to see. Tim was too good to be just a one-dimensional playground player, and he proved that night that he could be much more. We wore Union down that night, eventually winning by a score of 75-59 with four guys scoring in double figures, and with the whole team again dominating the boards by a margin of 48-17. This marked the fifth straight game we had more than doubled our opponents in the rebounding department. We also had a season high 24 assists as a team, so Goski wasn't the only one moving the ball well that night. Horne couldn't help but be pleased with how we played and the end result, but he also wasn't about to get complacent as our schedule would get tougher over the next couple of weeks.

For the record, Union happened to have a junior that only scored four points against us that night even though he had scored 18 against our JV team the prior year. The kid's name was Ray Liotta. By the end of the game Liotta was undoubtedly looking forward to baseball season, and I'm pretty sure he wasn't asking anyone on our team if this was heaven. For all I know he may have vanished right underneath the bleachers at the end of the night.

Christmas Day came two days later. Our family continued to celebrate in the normal manner, although some of the magic was gone and gradual changes that occurred over the years were plain to see. The days of me and my two brothers waking up insanely early to see what might be under the tree were long gone, and the nature of those gifts had shifted from silly toys and games that might have brought a few days of fun, to more practical things, like clothing, whose value would last well into the new year but certainly did not merit waking up early to discover. The biggest change, however, was the absence of my older brother Tommy, who was now in his second year of law school 3,000 miles away in Berkeley, Calif., after graduating from Dartmouth a year and a half earlier. Christmas mornings of old were now just a memory. Nor would he be around to watch any of my games and see whether his kid brother was any good and following successfully in his own basketball footsteps. But that was life. Life is not symmetric. Even my other brother Mark, who was now in his senior year at Bucknell and much closer to home, would not get to see any of our games this season. The world keeps moving and everybody does what they need to do. Yet I was perfectly content with where I was at that moment, being in high school and getting to play hoops on the high school team ... an unbeaten team, no less ... with guys that had become my best friends...that was all I cared about at that moment. I was in no rush to get to college or the real world. As far as I was concerned, time could have stood still and I would have been perfectly happy.

Two days later began a dream week when classes and homework were out and hanging out with friends and playing hoops were in. I remember Mike Cooney and I talking a year earlier in the aftermath of the Knicks first championship about how cool it would be to have their lives, where they had no classes to attend and playing basketball was their top priority. Well, this week we got to mimic the Knicks and their lifestyle, at least as we perceived it. Our whole days would revolve around our practices or games, with the rest of our time spent on either eating, sleeping, or some leisure activity, just like the Knicks and Walt "Clyde" Frazier would do...and most importantly no homework!

Game-wise it would be a light week for us, with only one game scheduled during the holiday week. No Christmas tournament for us. But that one game promised to be a tough one, indeed our toughest game to date at Roselle Catholic, perennial site of the semis and finals of the Union County Tournament with seating capacity for about 2,200 fans and bleachers that surrounded the court on all four sides. I was quite familiar with their gym by this time from watching my older brothers play in the UCT there. In fact, my brother Tommy's team pulling off a big upset of Cranford in the finals when I was in the fifth grade was one of my first basketball memories. Then my JV team had its best run of the year also making it to the finals, including the "Twiggy" game when I knocked down 14 free throws.

It wasn't just their gym we were familiar with, however. A few of their guys were fixtures down at Gumbert during the summer – Leo Nolan, John Roberts, and Rick Gomez chief among them. Nolan was a smooth 6-foot-4 lefty with a sweet jumper and crafty moves in and around the foul lane area. Roberts, aka 'Guber,' was more of a stiff, robotic player who would just go after the ball and liked to mix it up inside even though he wasn't particularly tall. Gomez was only a sophomore but appeared to be an up-and-coming star, with a little bit of Goski's playground toughness. As a guard, Gomez didn't have Tim's array of offensive moves or fluidity with the ball, but instead would rely on brute strength and sound shooting mechanics to be a real scoring threat from mid-range. That wasn't all though. Their top scorer was Walt Milne, someone we weren't very familiar with, so we knew we would have our hands full this night.

December 28, 1971

Nova and I spent a good part of the afternoon shooting pool in my parent's basement and otherwise killing time before our game that evening at 8. It sure beat the Latin or English class that would ordinarily precede a Tuesday afternoon game or practice. Instead, we would follow a more Knick-like game day routine in the hours leading up to the game. Before we knew it it was time for our early meal and the bus ride to Roselle.

We arrived at Roselle Catholic's gym around 6 p.m. in plenty of time for the JV game at 6:30. Usually our team would sit together in one section of the stands, but tonight was different. The gym was so spacious that there was plenty of seating everywhere at the time we walked in. Besides, it was a Tuesday night and not even a school night, so the vibe was quite different. Scott and I made our way to the top of one of the end zone bleachers where we could lean our backs against the wall.

Given that we had no school that day or the past few days, I should have been in perfect condition for this game, but for whatever reason I just didn't feel that way. After sitting there a few minutes I complained to Scott: "I'm tired, hungry, nervous and stiff – great shape for a game." That even got the philosophical Novacek to laugh rather than try to analyze what might be ailing me. Perhaps I mentioned too many things for Scott to even try. Another great aspect of the Roselle Catholic venue was that it featured a cafeteria that was open during games, so I decided to take advantage of that and fix one of the things that was bothering me with – a hot dog – even though it was only a little more than an hour until our tipoff time. One of the WHS boosters happened to be in the cafeteria and saw me making the purchase and said "What are you doing? You're going to get sick." I shrugged it off, thinking that eating the hot dog was better than not doing so. Scott accompanied me through the food line but settled for something more snack-like and less likely to end up on the floor.

About an hour later the tipoff arrived and any prior concerns about how I felt that night gave way to concerns about our opponent. Roselle Catholic came out of the gate fast and it became clear right away that we would not dominate the boards like we had done with all our previous opponents. We trailed 17-14 after one period. Things got worse in the second as they opened up a 30-18 lead, but we fought back and managed to get it back to a three-point deficit at halftime, 33-30. The third period also started to slip away from us as they built up a 56-48 lead, but even worse than that was our entire front court was hampered with either foul trouble or injury. Both Novacek and Simmons picked up their fourth fouls in that period, while Pfeiffer had three fouls and also sprained his ankle early in the third. We scored the last bucket of the third quarter to trail 56-50.

The up-and-down, back-and-forth battle continued into the fourth. Jester and Cooney were forced into big minutes with all the foul trouble and Pfeiffer's injury. The last period began going our way score-wise as we scored the first eight points, taking the lead back at 58-56, but Novacek fouled out with about seven minutes left. Then things went from bad to worse when they tied the score again and Simmons fouled out with four minutes left. Roselle Catholic was still outrebounding us and now our top two rebounders were sidelined for the rest of the game. Horne felt he had no choice at this point and returned Pfeiffer to the lineup, now saddled with four fouls himself in addition to being hobbled with the ankle sprain.

The next two minutes or so had teams trading baskets three times to bring the score to 64 all, before Cooney made a three-point play the old fashion way. Mike was coming up big this game for us in key stretches of the game when we were shorthanded and now had scored nine points. Milne tapped in a missed shot to cut our lead to 67-66 with just over a minute left. At this point we went into a semi-freeze, but that was a lot of time to try to run out. Sure enough, they forced us into a turnover with 20 seconds to go, then came down court and missed three times at close range before finally converting a fourth try with just 11 seconds left, giving them the lead once again at 68-67. That last offensive rebound gave the home team a rebounding edge of 37-25, no doubt aided by the early departure of Novacek and Simmons.

Horne used our last timeout to set up a final shot. The play was designed for Cooney to hit me flashing out on the right wing and then looking to hit Goski coming off a double screen set on the left side of the lane. The play started out as planned but got bogged down when Nolan was harassing Cooney as he worked the dribble toward the lane area. Mike looked toward the left side where Goski was, but then reversed direction and, with about three seconds left, started driving to his right in my direction, while I was camped out along the right baseline. As he reached the right edge of the foul line, the man guarding me had taken a step up the lane to provide help against Mike's potential foray down the lane. Seeing this, and sensing the clock winding down, I took one step further back from the basket while putting both hands up asking for the ball. Mike saw me and delivered a strike. I caught and let it go with one second left from 15 feet right along the baseline. The ball swished through the net simultaneous with the sound of the buzzer!

I turned into a human pogo stick for the next several seconds as pandemonium broke out and I was mobbed by my teammates (and who knows who else). I kept hopping as we gradually made our way to the visitors' locker room. Needless to say, it was quite the exhilarating moment for all of us but especially for me. In one quick shooting motion I managed to realize every kid's dream of hitting a game-winning shot at the buzzer as well as keep our perfect season going at 6-0. It had been a hard-fought game, just as we had expected, and were most fortunate to walk out of there with a win, especially given that we had been trailing the vast majority of the game. But somehow the basketball gods seemed to be looking over us, and it felt darn good. They say sometimes it's better to be lucky than good. It seemed that maybe we were a little bit of both on this particular night. As for me, in addition to being the unexpected hero who hit the game winning shot, my stat line read: seven field goals and five foul shots for 19 points, the highest point total of my five-year career. If that's what "Tired, hungry, nervous and stiff" translate to, I would take that trade anytime. Finally, it's only fair to give credit where credit is due – the hot dog made all the difference in this game. That's right. The hot dog hit the spot, so I could hit the shot! Take that, Johnny Cochran!

When our bus returned to school, I learned that there was a party in town that night, being a holiday week. I remember being a little embarrassed to even go inside, fearing I'd get some kind of hero treatment. Thankfully, not many people there had been to or knew about the game, so I was spared what could have been an uncomfortable scene. When I returned home a little later even that felt a bit weird, but I couldn't help but smile when my parents described my pogo stick antics immediately after the buzzer sounded.

The next day at practice my teammates insisted that we recreate the final play. 3 … 2 … 1, Cooney hits me with the pass along the baseline. I let it go. I missed the shot. Not enough adrenaline presumably. Or was it hot dog?

The rest of the week was easy. No games, no classes, New Year's Day, lots of college football on TV. We would go into 1972 unbeaten. But while his players may have been relaxing, Horne was not. He was busy getting ready for the most challenging part of our schedule that was just around the corner. We would have three games the next week when classes resumed, with the third being against a tough Colonia squad. The following week would pit us against Cranford and Thomas Jefferson. All three of those teams were better than anyone we had played thus far, with Jefferson being unbeaten and ranked No. 1 in all of New Jersey.

We may have been 6-0 at this point, but it still wasn't clear whether my preseason prediction I had made to my father was looking good or not. After all, we had had difficult patches in all six wins, and two of our wins required overcoming six-point fourth quarter deficits. The basketball gods had indeed been smiling on us thus far, but the jury was still out on our team and our season. Our real test would come early in the new year. 1971 was now history.

VII. School's Out

What does a basketball player do when he no longer plays for his school team but still wants to play?

The next closest thing is the recreation league or intramural league. These can still be very competitive with a high level of basketball being played. They still have zebras with whistles. They still have scoreboards. They still have standings and championships and trophies, and not the participation kind either. But what they won't have is fans or coaches, except perhaps for an occasional girlfriend or two. "Players only, baby," to borrow a phrase from an NBA talk show.

The rec league or intramural league represents somewhat of a compromise between playing for your school team and just playing pure pickup basketball at the local playground or gym. On the one hand, these are still very organized efforts with predetermined schedules of game dates and times, with rosters that are relatively fixed and determined at the beginning of the season. On the other hand, it has in common with pure pickup basketball that the players are playing for themselves and generally for the pure fun of it. The players also generally get to form their own teams, unlike school teams where eligible players will be determined by the school's student body and then hand-picked by one or more coaches.

While pickup basketball offers the greatest flexibility to find good competition when and where it's convenient for you, many players who played on their high school or college teams are used to the organized structure of rec leagues. Of course, they may also still crave the prospects of beating your rival teams on the way to a championship and the bragging rights that come with it. I suppose I was no different coming out of college. Besides, a Tuesday night rec league might guarantee a good run that was going to be hard to find elsewhere at that time of the week. One might have to wait for the weekend to find a good pickup game. Furthermore, an overcrowded gym might mean long waits and having to win to avoid a "one and done" scenario. Perhaps most important of all was that the rec league provided a bridge to help ease the transition into the real world from cushy college environments where one could sleep in late, go to a few classes, play some hoops, and still have free time for socializing and whatever. The real world meant having a regular and rigid work schedule, alarm clocks going off insanely early, commuting, and then finally getting home with a small window of free time. The rec league offered an opportunity to fill some of that precious free time with something of value and the chance to prove that these twenty or thirty something players still had it.

Of course, by the time I graduated college I had already experienced a little of this by playing intramurals during my senior year rather than varsity hoops. My next venture would be playing in a work league at Mutual Benefit Life where I started working in Newark, NJ, right after graduation. It was a very weak league in which I was clearly the best player and averaged close to 30 points a game. It was hardly something to look forward to, however. The league was played in the tiniest of gyms on the sixth floor of a dilapidated building in downtown Newark, required dressing in a dark, cold locker room, and then afterward you'd have to walk in the dark through some pretty seedy areas to make it safely to the train station.

My first league outside of the work was a Rahway league that I got recruited into by Jeff Bauer. It was quite competitive with former high school and college players from the Union County area who were probably all in their 20s. Richie Scialabba, a former Union Catholic standout, was also on the team and we managed to win the league that year. I had about 24 points in the championship game, more than I ever scored in a school game. I was now a bigger fish in a smaller pond. But then, before you know it, there's no more league, or at least for our team. These things are year to year. Leagues and teams have to get organized. Somebody had to take the lead for each team. Rosters and entry fees have to be submitted. Sometimes people don't pay up when they are supposed to. Sometimes people are travelling and communications break down. Things fall through the cracks, and then the next thing you know, you're not on a team anymore.

My Rahway league may have been gone, but within a couple of years I had it more than replaced by three other leagues: a Monday night league in Cranford, a Tuesday night league in Nutley that my boss had played in for years, and a Thursday night league in Clark that Scialabba and a few of his buddies got us into. At the time I was still single and had the luxury of playing in all of them. I got to play with Mike Cooney and Jimmy Masters, who was two years behind me at WHS and had blossomed into a nice player. The Thursday night league had several guys I knew, including Cooney, Scialabba, his Union Catholic sidekick Andy Blejwas, and three pretty big guys – Ken Tanke, Chet Miele, and Howie Alexander.

After just a few months out of college, I started dating Susan Koterba, the girl I would eventually marry. I believe she only came to one rec league game my entire life, but she chose a good one. It was the championship game for the Thursday night league. We were both 24 and engaged at the time. We won the game and then went to one of the local bars to celebrate. At 6-foot-2½, I was one of the shorter guys on our team. We were veritable giants in the bar that night, which made it perfectly fitting when someone ventured over to the juke box and queued up "Short People." We were all blaring it out at the top of our lungs – *"Short people got no reason to live,"* of course directing our vocals to all the short girlfriends who were unlucky enough to be in our presence. To add insult to injury, a couple of beers later, Susan was pronounced the winner of the "Biggest Tits in the Bar" award by Tanke as the testosterone in the bar was starting to run amok. I can't comprehend why Susan wouldn't want to come to any more of my games after that night … with free drinks, prizes, and serenading – what's not to like? Maybe she felt that it just couldn't get any better than that, so she would quit while she was ahead. In any event, she took it all in stride. As for us guys, moments like that were about all we had left to play for.

One thing you always had to worry about with these leagues was having enough guys show up each week. A typical roster might have seven or eight guys who would play regularly, with maybe six or seven showing up most weeks. But occasionally you'd have only five guys for a game, and once in a blue moon a team might show up with only four. That wouldn't necessarily mean a forfeit, however. Three times I had to play on teams with only four players. We won two of them. Remarkably, the opposing teams in those two cases were good teams … we had even lost to one of them previously … but for some reason the box and none defense we were forced to play was able to stop them just enough times. Perhaps the opposing team never knew when to shoot because they always thought they should be able to get off a better shot with the 5-on-4 advantage, so they would never get into a normal offensive rhythm. In one of those 5-on-4 games in the Clark league, we came up with a deflection that forced a turnover with two seconds left, and then on the out of bounds play quickly got the ball back to the in-bounder who banked in a 25-footer to force overtime. We capped off the minor miracle by winning the overtime session. Beers followed immediately thereafter.

The Nutley league was the weakest of the non-work leagues that I played in and was doing it mostly to curry favor with my boss. The last season I played there we improved our team by adding Jimmy Masters to our squad, while another team improved theirs by adding Paul Lape, a slick guard from nearby Bloomfield who had made first team All-State my senior year in high school and then had a nice career at Seton Hall, where he set a Madison Square Garden record for most assists in a game for a collegiate player. I had never seen him play before, but against our team I did get to see one impressive fake behind the back pass on a fast break when he wrapped it halfway around his back, then cupped the ball between his hand and wrist, and then brought it back around in one quick motion to finish the fast break layup. The only better version of that move I have ever seen was the one pulled off by Pete Maravich going full speed right around the foul line. That said, I managed to one-up Lape that particular night as I pulled off what was hands down the best spin move of my life. Our team rebounded the ball and I started heading up the left side of the court as the outlet pass headed my way. My head was turned back to see the ball into my hands, but I had caught a glimpse of Lape heading toward me just before I turned my head back. The moment I caught the ball I pounded it hard with my right hand and then spun like a top clockwise, whipping the ball around my spinning body towards the sideline and then out in front of me. Lape whiffed on what he thought would be a sure steal the moment before I spun. I spun so fast I almost fell over, but managed to keep both my feet and control of the ball as I headed up court and then nailed a 15-footer to cap off the fast break. Even the one ref who was a regular in this league had a big smile on his face after that move. I was able to contain mine, perhaps out of respect for Lape.

Aside from these small handful of leagues, there was one other form of organized hoops that I got to play in those first few years out of college

… namely, the prison games. I believe those were strictly the brainchild of Bill Clancy, a 1961 graduate of WHS who used to brag that he once "held" Rick Barry to 53 points in a high school game at Westfield when Barry starred for Roselle Park. Bill was a bit of a wild man and certified basketball nut who still loved to play and watch basketball at all levels. I remember him initially from the Washington School Saturday morning clinic and league where he helped out by refereeing some of the games there. Once I graduated from college, I started to see him regularly down at the Westfield Y. While I remember him as being quite a bit older than me and past his prime, he was actually just 11 years my senior and not exactly washed up.

I was only about a year out of college when Bill called and asked if I wanted to go play the prisoners. The first time he called it was about playing inside the Rahway State Penitentiary on a Friday night. The second time he called it was to go play the prisoners on a Saturday afternoon at the famous Sing Sing prison overlooking the Hudson River. The Rahway state prison, where I played twice, was particularly memorable. Bill had recruited eight players for the evening encounter. We were told to bring valid ID, like a driver's license, and nothing fake because it would be checked. I wasn't about to test the prison system by doing anything otherwise. We got there about 6:30 pm and after getting through the initial processing we were taken to a dark and dingy locker room where we put our gear on. The prison official then led us through about five check points and metal detectors before finally reaching the gym.

It was quite a sight and looked like a scene right out of a prison movie, only much more real. The gym itself was very long and old looking, with the court situated right in the middle, leaving maybe another 60 feet or so of space beyond each baseline. At one end was a boxing ring, and at the other end was a bunch of free weights for body building. There must have been several dozens of prisoners milling around the gym as if Friday night was their free period. There was a bunch of activity at each of those respective ends of the gym, with the remainder of prisoners more or less lining the court to check out this all-white team from outside that was about to take on the all-black prison team. We were told that the other prisoners didn't like the prisoner team out of jealousy, because the prison team got extra privileges. I suppose playing us that night was one of those privileges.

The timekeeper, another prisoner, told me we need to win because he had cigarettes bet on us.

The prison organizers, whoever they were, didn't mess around. No high school or college rules here. We were to play NBA rules. That meant four 12-minute quarters, and it would take six fouls to foul out. It would be the only time in my life we would play that except, of course, when we went to Sing Sing, where we would do the exact same thing. It must be in the prison manual or something. The zebras hired for the night were experienced referees who were used to working in this environment. In any event, we came prepared with a pretty good team. In addition to myself and Clancy, who was about 6-foot-3 and not afraid to mix it up, he brought along fellow old guy Lenny Braunstein, who was 15 years my senior but still a great shooting guard in Y pickup games, Scialabba, Blejwas, Kevin Maguire, a small lefty guard who was a good playground player, and Jerry Richards, a very good 6-foot-3 player who starred on the WHS team that won the '65 Union County Tournament along with my older brother Tom. Our eighth player that night was a big guy whose name I forget but had good size and muscle to help us on the boards against what would likely be a physical opponent.

The prisoners played hard but not dirty. The two officials kept everything under control. We managed to eke out a close win that first night but were not able to repeat that in our return trip there a few months later. The feeling that couldn't escape me, though, whether we were on the winning or losing end, was that for two hours we were their equals, competitors within the four lines on the court. Then, when it was all over, we would all go back to our separate worlds. During the postgame handshakes you could sense how much they appreciated us being there, giving them a brief respite from their otherwise very confined world.

Despite taking similarly strong teams up to Sing Sing, my record in those games was a miserable 0-4. Twice we played the prison team and twice we played other outside teams that were participating in a tournament that the prison was hosting. Needless to say, other teams that ventured into Sing Sing came well prepared and not undermanned. We did come very close in one of those losses, losing 125-123. With two seconds to go, I inbounded the ball, received a return pass, and then launched a 25-

footer that bounced off the rim. Before leaving the prison grounds that day, we posed for pictures on that blustery winter day with the wind whipping off the Hudson River and the giant prison wall in the background. Clancy was planning on including that in a basketball book he was working on at the time.

Before leaving the namesake town of Ossining, NY, we made our way into a local bar called *Close Encounters* to put a cap on the day's events. Aside from one other customer in the bar, we had the bar to ourselves along with the sweet and somewhat gorgeous blonde bartender. Initially we were ribbing Clancy, who had recently quit his successful corporate sales job, that he should spend some of his newly found free time on ball handling drills, a not-so-subtle reference to a couple of costly turnovers from earlier that afternoon. As the beers flowed, our attention gradually shifted from our lost game to our attractive server. We asked about whether she had any similarly attractive friends and whether they might come down to see any of our games back home. Her naturally sweet disposition probably unwittingly egged us on, and this was only compounded when she returned from the restroom with the buckle to her jeans not quite back where it should be. Unfortunately, Braunstein ruined our afternoon by announcing that he needed to get back for the Knicks game he was attending that night. The rest of us reluctantly departed the bar that afternoon sooner than we would have liked … there would be no happy ending in Ossining that day.

Between ages 24 and 28 those leagues would continue for the most part while I was also getting married and having the first two or our kids. By this time, I had to start negotiating for how many leagues or how many times a week basketball would be a permitted activity. I certainly wasn't playing very often on Saturday afternoon at the Westfield Y after playing three times during the week. All in all, Susan was very accommodating. She knew that basketball had been a staple in my life and wasn't about to make me go cold turkey.

Then came along a veritable death blow to those leagues – a job change at age 28 and a move to a new area where I knew no one. Two kids soon became three at age 30. I settled for pickup games at the local Y and one league in Phoenixville, PA in the vicinity of Valley Forge. For two years I also played in a summer version of the same league in the old civic center there, which was nothing more than an old, hot gym with little air circulation. One particularly hot, humid summer night I spent the entire halftime outside the gym trying to get my breath and cool off. After the game I changed into a new shirt as the game shirt was completely drenched. By the time I got home 15 minutes later the second shirt was also completely drenched. Talk about a good sweat!

At age 35 came another job change. This, of course, meant starting over again in terms of finding a place to play or a league to play in. I was fortunate to get a little help with that from our realtor. While we were scouting out new houses in one area of interest, I inquired about youth basketball and if there were any leagues available for them to play in. She replied that there were – in fact, the guy who started the league in the township where we were looking lived right down the street and he would often go jogging around the block with his son while each of them dribbled a basketball. My ears perked up when I heard that. I asked the realtor for his name and number and decided I would call him if we pursued this one house that happened to be a stone's throw from his. Sure enough, that house became our top choice, so within a day or two I called up the number my realtor had given me, the number for a James Natale.

Mr. Natale was kind enough to take my call and quickly provide a strong endorsement for the neighborhood. "It would take a scud missile to get me to move out of here", he proclaimed. In the wake of the Persian Gulf War, the reference to scud missiles was indeed an effective reference and powerful endorsement. He then went on to describe the youth league that he had formed a few years earlier when his son was about 6 years old (he was now 10, the same age our son David), and that it was both a boys and girls league, which was good news to us given that we also had three girls after David who were now 9, 7 and 1 years old. Finally, he started to tell me about the leagues that *he* still played in. Natale had played college hoops at Millersville University and, like me, had never stopped playing since then. Far from it, in fact. It seemed that I had stumbled upon another Bill Clancy – i.e., a true basketball fanatic! This was almost too good to be true. I didn't need to hear anymore to know that Natale would be a great neighbor if we got the house deal done. As soon as I got off the phone, I turned to Susan and said: "It sounds like a great league – I think we should buy the house."

Shortly thereafter in the spring of 1991 we did exactly that. Within months of that I was playing in a league with Natale. I was 37 years old by this time and he was 45. While the league was in fact a strong league with many former college players, it was an "over 30" league which was my first experience with an age-restricted league. I guess in hindsight that was inevitable. By eliminating the local twenty-something hoopsters from team rosters, it would give diehard forty-something players a chance to prolong their playing days against good competition, and thirty-something players like myself a chance to be the top dogs once again.

We managed to win the league title that year but then failed in the next three attempts as we got older, lost a player or two, and other teams seemingly got younger and/or stronger. I had now hit the big Four Zero age milestone. My wife even hung a big homemade sign from one of our windows stating: "Lordy Lordy, Stephen is Forty" for all the neighbors to see. My basketball opponents didn't need a sign. Not to worry, though, as Natale was already ahead of the age impediment. He got three of us entered into a local 3-on-3 tournament that was an NBA sponsored event at various locations around the country and which had various age divisions. Naturally, we were entered in the 40 and over division, just two months past my 40th birthday. We played respectably and managed a tight victory against one good team but lost to two other teams, thereby knocking us out. There are seemingly always better players than you out there, or players in better shape. Commuting to NYC every day, which I had now been doing for the past five years with a 1-hour and 45-minute door to door each way doesn't exactly lend itself to playing great basketball, but hey, that's life.

The "over-30" league came and went, but with a couple of years Natale recruited me into another league, this one played on Sunday nights at a local Jewish Community Center. While it wasn't age-restricted like the former one, this was generally had older players, like Jim and me, and was not as strong overall. That said, it did have a smattering of good younger players who could compete and beat you on any given night, so it did provide the competitive challenge that we older players still craved. Jim and I and our teammates managed a couple more league titles, for whatever they were worth.

Then something happened that makes you stop and think. It was just the second week of a new season at the community center when barely ten minutes into our game one of our opponents went down hard to the floor … untouched … and moments later is having convulsions. Someone called for paramedics. I ran out the door to go drive the short distance to the local rescue squad. Ten minutes later I was back at the gym, standing with Jim about 20 feet away from the player being worked on by the paramedics, seemingly trying to resuscitate him. After a few moments of silence Jim states: "That's how I want to go." Knowing Jim and how much he loved basketball, I couldn't help but think that he'd probably get his wish someday. A few minutes later the paramedics wheeled the player out on a stretcher. Moments later the rest of us slowly filed out of the gym. There would be no more hoops that night.

The following Saturday morning I saw Jim down at the Newtown Athletic Club, or the NAC as it was known locally. I asked him if the guy had died at our last game. He shook his head yes. He had been 53 years old. Jim was now 54 and I was 46. We weren't spring chickens anymore. The next time it might be one of us. You just never knew when your time might be up, when you might be playing your last game.

A few short months later I would play my last *league* game. It was the league championship game in early June, and for some strange reason the humidity or AC caused the gym floor to be extremely slippery. By the end of the game, we felt like we were ice skating our way around the court. It was terrible. It was dangerous. It wasn't worth it. It wasn't fun. It wasn't real basketball.

After that night I decided I'd had enough … no more leagues. First, it was just not having a school to play for. Now, a quarter of a century later, I would never have another team to play for. The next time I would lace up my sneakers and walked onto a court I'd be strictly playing for myself. It was time.

VIII.   Flying High (Jan 1 – Jan 30, 1972)

"Each and every victory was more and more fun.
Would we ever lose a game? Were we number one?"

from *A Team to Remember*, November 18, 2000

On Monday, Jan. 3, 1972, school resumed after a cherished 11-day break from classes and homework, not to mention the last second victory that kept our record perfect. All good things must come to an end, I suppose, but we weren't ready to give up status as an unbeaten team. It felt good, even though it was only six games. But we knew it was going to get harder, and quickly, as a very meaty part of the schedule was now upon us. The last thing we could afford to do was rest on our laurels for what was still a very young season. We were to play 3 games this week, on Tuesday, Thursday, and Saturday, the only week all season where that was the case. The first two figured to be games that we should win handily, with the third one against Colonia at their gym promised to be much tougher.

January 4, 1972

Something we never concerned ourselves with previously changed on this day. Tuesday was when the Newark *Star-Ledger* state rankings came out and, for the first time this season, Westfield showed up in the top 20. In retrospect, I suppose it shouldn't have been a surprise that we cracked the top 20 given our 6-0 start and having knocked off a very respectable Roselle Catholic team since the previous rankings had come out. But what was surely unexpected was that we claimed the No. 11 spot on that list. Clearly, we must have impressed the powers that be at the *Star-Ledger*. Of course, Horne would have preferred that none of us ever saw a newspaper, and knew full well that any ranking at this stage of the season was nothing to brag about and would only be a distraction and perhaps make us overconfident. Still, it was clear evidence that we were at least on the radar screen of those who scout out the competition throughout the state.

That afternoon we would make the five-minute bus ride for an afternoon game against Clark, a team we should probably beat ten out of ten times. They simply didn't have any weapons that should be able to hurt us, although they did have a promising up and coming sophomore in 6-foot-3 Greg Hurley. That said, they were 5-3 and had just beaten a strong Colonia team that we would play in just a few days, so we couldn't afford to take them lightly or just go through the motions.

We played sloppily that day and finished with a season high 23 turnovers. Fortunately for us, our defense and rebounding did not take the day off and gradually wore them down, forcing Clark into 30 turnovers themselves, while outrebounding them by 10. We also shot the ball well from the field at 51%. In a generally ugly game to watch, we managed a 13-0 run in the first half on the way to a 10-point halftime lead, which we then nursed on the way to somewhat methodical 59-44 victory. Goski led us in scoring with 17, while Pfeiffer and Novacek added 12 and 10 points, respectively. We were now 7-0.

January 6, 1972

Hillside was next up for a rare Thursday afternoon game at home. Hillside promised to be a tough opponent, and though only 3-2 at this stage, they had whipped Scotch Plains by 15 in their season opener, a much better result than we had obtained a couple of weeks earlier. Their main weapons were 6-foot-3 seniors Paul Yungst and Paul Losseff, and Horne had us focusing on these two the prior day in practice. But they also had a wild card in 6-3 sophomore Harvey Wooten, a wiry athletic kid who was still blossoming.

Both teams shot the ball well in a high scoring first half with WHS leading by 6 at the intermission, 39-33, with Pfeiffer leading the way with an impressive 16 points. In the second half we used pretty much the same formula to put Hillside away as we did with Clark two days earlier. For the second straight game our field goal percentage was slightly better than 50 percent, we outrebounded them by 12 with a 30-18 count, and force them into 10 more turnovers than we committed at 32-22. Again, that was a high number for us, certainly something to improve upon, but when you beat your opposition in those three major categories you are very likely to come out on top, which we did in an 80-56 victory. We also had balanced scoring with Goski leading with 18, Pfeiffer and Novacek had 16 apiece and I finished with 11. Steve Lee also had eight points as we pulled away in the fourth quarter.

January 8, 1972

Saturday promised to be our toughest test of the week, if not the season to date. We were to face Colonia at their gym in a rare (for us) Saturday night game. Though their record was somewhat mediocre thus far, we knew a couple of the players firsthand from Gumbert, specifically Steve Solop and Jon Franken, and knew these guys could play. They also boasted the tallest front court we had seen all year with their big three standing 6-foot-8, 6-6 and 6-4. All we had height-wise was Novacek at 6-4. Franken was another up-and-coming junior guard, like Ross Kindle from Roselle, who was physically very strong with massive thighs and already had a lot of experience playing against upperclassmen. We simply couldn't afford to look ahead to next week's foes, Thomas Jefferson, who was also unbeaten and ranked No. 1 in the state, and Cranford, our main Watchung Conference rival who only lost once this season.

Sometimes it's not enough to just come mentally ready to play. You still have to physically get the job done on the court, and sometimes the other team does the basic things better than you, like shooting or handling the ball well without turning it over. In the first period the game took on a very similar feel to the Roselle Catholic game and we found ourselves down by seven points at the end of one period and then the deficit became nine points at halftime with a score of 33-24, thanks largely to very poor shooting by us. We improved our shooting in the third period, narrowing our deficit to a single point at 43-42 when I hit a jumper with one second left in the period. We finally knotted the score at 46 early in the fourth period before Colonia responded with six straight points to again take the lead at 52-46. I hit jumpers on the next two possessions to again cut the deficit, this time to two points at 52-50 with only 2:43 remaining. Colonia scored again after running some time off the clock and then I did something I had not done in my previous 81 games playing for my school teams that past five years – I fouled out.

It happened with 1:11 remaining on an offensive foul, my third of the game. It had been a strange game for me as I had scored 18 points, my second highest tally of the season, but had gotten careless with the three charges and the five personal fouls. The last thing I wanted to do was take a seat on the bench. More importantly, though, was that we were down four points and Colonia had the ball with only 1:11 to play and without a shot clock to ensure we would even get the ball back. I reluctantly took my seat at the end of the bench where I would watch my replacement Mike Cooney and my other teammates try to save us from our first defeat.

Our defense the rest of the way was stifling. Larry Simmons intercepted a pass and hit Novacek down court who converted the basket underneath, cutting the deficit to 54-52. Moments later Larry intercepted another pass, but we returned the favor with a bad pass that was nabbed by Franken who breezed in for an uncontested layup. But Franken fouled Novacek on the subsequent inbound pass, stopping the clock at the 29-second mark. Scott converted both free throws to once again bring us within two. On the ensuing inbound pass, our guards trapped the ball and forced a pass that Novacek was able to knock down and recover, thanks in part to his huge wingspan. He then gave it up to Goski, who aggressively attacked the right side of the lane before pulling up from about 15 feet and banking it in with a line-drive shot. It was the kind of shot that Tim was adept at hitting back at Gumbert during summer nights when line-drive bank shots would help counteract difficult outdoor conditions. It was only Tim's sixth and seven points of the night, but they came when we needed them most, tying the score again at 56, now with just 16 seconds left.

Colonia was still in the driver's seat, though, and had a golden opportunity when we fouled them with 11 just seconds left, giving them a one and one free. Colonia missed, but we inexcusably got called for being over the line too soon, thereby giving the shooter another attempt at the one and one. Thankfully, he missed again. We had dodged another bullet. Now it was our chance to deliver the fatal blow. We pushed the ball up court quickly and Pfeiffer managed to draw a foul with just two seconds left, again yielding a one and one opportunity. But Tom was also unable to cash in, and as regulation time expired and we regrouped at the sideline, he was clearly miffed at himself for the blown opportunity.

Still, we had forced the overtime session which had looked like a bleak proposition just moments earlier, so there was no time to feel sorry for ourselves. There were still three more minutes of basketball to decide the winner of the night's contest, and Horne made sure that we refocused to capitalize on our successful second half comeback. Fortunately for us, the basketball gods must have still been on our side as the overtime went all our way as we shut out Colonia 8-0 to claim the 64-56 victory. Perhaps as a bit of redemption Pfeiffer scored five of our eight points during the overtime, including three foul shots.

Much like the Roselle Catholic game, we seemingly pulled a rabbit out of the hat to preserve our perfect record, fighting from behind most of the game but hanging in there until the deciding moments. Our first lead of the game did not come until we scored the first basket of the overtime session! Also, like Roselle Catholic, and all our prior games for the matter, we got contributions from so many players. Novacek and I both finished with 18 points, Pfeiffer added 11 points, Goski had hit the big game tying basket, Jester added five points and helped us control the boards again, and Cooney played crucial minutes down the stretch run. But Simmons was the real hero that night with an incredible 22 rebounds, helping us to 50-30 advantage off the boards despite their superior height, and four stolen passes in the crucial fourth quarter, including two in the last minute.

After returning to WHS on the bus that night, I headed over to Friendly's in neighboring Mountainside and bumped into Mr. Pfeiffer who was on his way out. "Nice game, Steve" he said in his distinctive and emphatic tone. I had already felt good about the evening's events, but getting the positive reinforcement from Tom's dad, perhaps the toughest critic in town, was like the cherry on top. The strawberry Fribble that followed tasted very good indeed.

Two days later we returned to the gym for practice right after school. There was no discussion of the Colonia game. That wasn't going to help us the next day when we would face Thomas Jefferson who now had an 8-0 record and was ranked No. 1 in the state. We had one day to prepare, and Horne wasn't going to waste one minute on what had happened Saturday night.

So, Horne did what he did best – he stuck to his routine. Once the regular season began, every practice consisted of three things: a) certain drills we would do almost every practice to keep developing individual skills, b) certain specific team concepts that might be employed in specific game scenarios, such as sideline out of bounds plays with 4 seconds left, or beating a full court man-to-man press after a made foul shot, and c) reviewing our next opponent's offense and other tendencies that Horne had learned of through scouting or other sources he had.

Figure 3 provides a good illustration of this. It shows Horne's prepared notes for our practice that day with specific segments of practice devoted to each of those three categories just described. The first four items, along with #9 and #13, all described drills designed to improve individual skills. The full court 1 on 1 drill was particularly appropriate this day as Horne expected us to be picked up full court all game long by their lightning quick guards, Monte Jones and Willie Hopson. In fact, this drill had been a staple at our practices all season long so that we could be as ready as possible for a foe like Jefferson. Items numbered 5, 8, and 10-12 addressed team-oriented concepts such as helping out on man-to-man defense, zone defense, and our delay game offense, which was designed to wear down an opponents by making cut after cut in an endless repeatable pattern until the defense faltered and let a cutter get widen open. Indeed, Horne had decided that we would start the Jefferson game with this offense, something he hadn't done all season, in the hopes that Jefferson would be slow getting over picks and give us some good scoring opportunities, presumably better opportunities that we might get out of our regular double stack offense. Finally, items #6 and #7 were specific to Jefferson. For #7, Horne had been so concerned with Jefferson's swarming defense that he devised this "Pass-Pivot" drill in which someone would receive a pass and then immediately get double teamed, at which point the player with the ball had to somehow pivot through the double team and pass the ball off despite the pressure. A good double team would make that difficult to do, which is why Horne had us prepare for it. Pivoting is such a basic fundamental basketball skill that is usually taken for granted, but against a swarming defense it could become the difference between a good offensive move and a turnover.

Figure 3

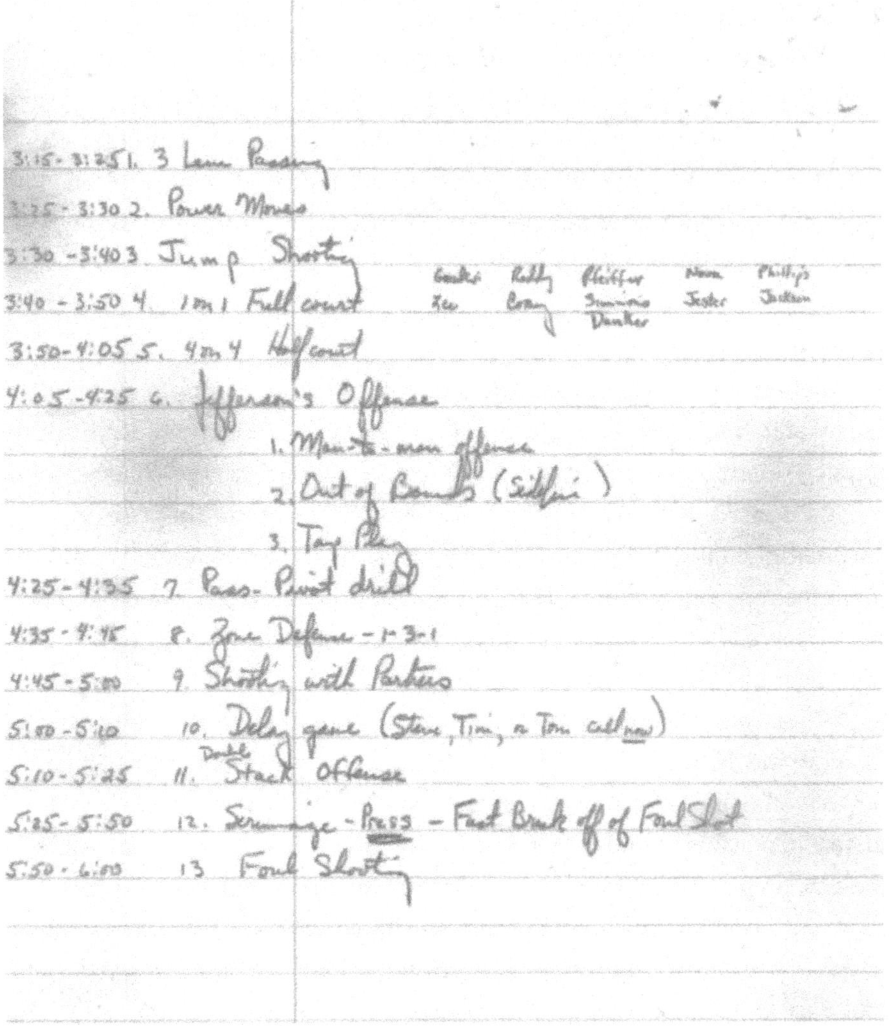

Horne announced one other thing in practice this day – that if Jefferson were to apply full court man-to-man pressure as anticipated, that the ball should go to me and everyone else clear out and head up court. You could tell that Tim was not exactly thrilled with this plan given no one could honestly make the case that I was our best ball handler, although I was pretty darn good. If anyone was the superior ball handler, it would have been Tim, especially against tough man-to-man defense. But Horne was a step ahead of all of us, anticipating a fast-paced hostile environment, and recognizing the temptation for Tim to get caught up in a personal challenge against the speedy Monte Jones and in the process lose focus on the offense we needed to run. It didn't matter if Horne was right or not, just that he decided it was a risk he didn't want to take. Besides, once the game started, he always could (and likely would) make adjustments on the fly if necessary. In less than 24 hours we would all find out how well Horne had prepared us, and more importantly how well we could execute things we had been working on all season.

January 11, 1972

Before we would ever take the court this Tuesday afternoon, the *Star-Ledger* state rankings came out that morning. Of course, it would have no impact on our game that day, but rather would serve to give some recognition to what had happened to that point in the season. Not surprisingly, on the strength of our three wins the prior week, we moved up in the rankings from No. 11 to No. 8, while Jefferson remained No. 1. We would have all of about eight hours to bask in the glory of our new higher rankings.

Those eight hours would pass quickly enough, and before you knew it, we were in Battin Gym in Elizabeth warming up for the big game. Between the lines it was like most gyms we would play in that year, at least in terms of court dimensions and backboards. The stands were smaller though, only going up four or five rows. It was standing room only by game time, with each of the corners of the gym lined with late arriving fans who had come to catch a glimpse of the action. Among the SRO crowd was a 6-foot-8 dude replete with a pink beret, none other than Jefferson and Gumbert alumnus John Shumate, who was currently making his impact at Notre Dame in South Bend, IN.

The crowd, while small in number, would make up for it with animus. As we finished our warmups and headed to our bench for the last-minute instructions from Horne, we began to feel the impact of not being in friendly territory. Several amongst the four rows of fans sitting behind our bench began trash talking the entire bench and trying to drown out our huddle with yelling, shouting, and various derogatory remarks. Some of them were racially oriented. One heckler told Simmons he was playing for the wrong team, an obvious reference to him being our lone black starter in contrast to Jefferson's all black starting five. There was no escaping that contrast in that moment, but we didn't care … but we were ready and we were focused … their shouting would not deter us. We broke the huddle and headed out on the court for the opening tap.

Novacek won the opening tap against the much taller Bruce Watson, and we immediately went into our delay game offense, which could be more aptly described as a continuous motion offense. Its purpose wasn't to stall, but rather to keep screening cutting and passing until an open cutter or easy shot emerged. As if Horne had a crystal ball, it worked to perfection in that first possession, which ended a mere 15 seconds later with me catching a pass from Simmons in the lane for an easy three-foot bank shot.

We then dug in for their first trip down court, but despite good defense they managed to bank in a shot from the foul line. The ball was then inbounded to Goski, who against his basketball instincts but dutifully following Horne's instructions, flipped the ball over to me and headed

Novacek cuts down the lane and I start across the area the just vacated

With Hopson (34) trailing, I pull in Simmons' pass with my right hand

I turn and hit the easy 3 foot bank shot before Watson (22) can react

down court. It was now just me and Hopson in the backcourt, and we were about to find out if Horne's confidence in me was justified. I methodically worked the ball up the court, keeping the ball behind me the whole way, essentially keeping my body between Hopson and the ball. I used three reverse dribbles on the way up court to keep the quicker Hopson at bay, but he forced me closer to the sideline than I should have been, so we were already out of our offense. But Goski bailed me out when he took a pass near the right sideline and then after two dribbles to his left hit a running bank shot from about 12 feet to put us up 4-2. The two teams then settled in for the rest of the quarter, which was marked by tough man-to-man defense and very few if any uncontested shots. We forced them into a couple of bad passes and made them work for every shot. When the first quarter ended, we held a 13-9 lead. We certainly had their attention.

The second quarter would bring more of the same – tough D on both sides leading to contested shots and lower than average shooting percentage. Jefferson started collapsing a bit on defense, clogging up the lane and more or less forcing us to accept mid-range jumpers. But nothing was easy for them either. Turnovers were about even between the teams. We clung to a narrow 25-22 lead at halftime.

To start the third quarter, Novacek won his third straight tip against Watson. That was big for us – in this game, it might come down to one possession, so every tip mattered. But then Jones stole a careless pass near half court and raced in for a layup. On the next possession, Watson finally grabbed an offensive rebound and put in a short one in the lane. We had shut him out in the first half but now he was on the board and we were down 1. The rest of the quarter the game opened up a bit and they got the better of it. Novacek kept it from being worse by hitting three midrange jumpers in that stretch, but Jefferson was now getting closer attempts and Watson got another put back off a missed shot while getting fouled himself, leading to a three-point play. By the time the third quarter ended, our three point halftime lead had turned into a six point deficit at 41-35. They had outscored us 19-10 in the period. In a low scoring game like this one, a six-point deficit felt much bigger. We were in trouble.

The fourth period would begin as the three previous ones, with Novacek outjumping the 6-foot-8 Watson and controlling the tap, and for the fourth straight time the tap came backward into the hands of Pfeiffer. Unfortunately, that possession ended with a turnover as I tried to hit Novacek cutting underneath the basket, but the pass got deflected off a Jeff defender and then off Scott and out of bounds. Jeff came right back and patiently worked the ball against our man-to-man defense, until Jones swished a 17-footer from the left side. It was now 43-35, our biggest deficit of the game.

We kept working our motion offense for the most part but were having trouble penetrating their defense or creating any easy baskets. Then, off a sideline out of bounds play, Goski received the ball just beyond the foul line on the left side. He faked the jump shot, and then with the defender leaping past him, Tim took one dribble closer and swished a 12-footer from just outside the lane. It was the kind of move and shot I had seen him make countless times down at Gumbert.

Goski nails a 12-footer from just outside the lane

It was now 43-37. We slid back into a 1-3-1 zone, which Horne occasionally liked to do to mix things up. It worked on this possession with a missed baseline jumper that we corralled. Next time down court our motion offense got the ball to a cutting Goski, but his short-range bank shot amid a sea of bodies came off the rim and got knocked out of bounds near the right sideline. It was our ball again for another sideline out of bounds play from the same spot as the previous possession. This time Novacek received the second pass on the left side of the foul line and rose right up for a 15-footer. Watson lunged toward Scott, but he was too late to affect the shot. The shot bounced off the front rim and then was hauled in by Jeff's Sandy Beasley, who saw Watson starting to race down court. Watson had a nice head start given his lunge at Nova's jumper, and Beasley laid the ball out there like a quarterback would for an open receiver. Watson caught it without breaking stride near the top of the key and, with Goski and me in hot pursuit, took one dribble with his long stride and proceeded to lay it in.

Jefferson's Watson on a breakaway drive towards the basket

The place erupted. The corner where John Shumate stood was now visibly excited. The scoreboard now read 45-37. I had gotten a good look at the shot, having been right behind Watson and then passing him as he rose up to the basket. As Watson released the ball, I was now looking up from just inside the baseline and got a good glimpse of what looked like a two-handed dunking motion as he pushed it through. I wasn't sure if the ref had seen it or would call it.

The moment of truth

I wouldn't have to wait long, though, as the ref's whistle came a split second later. Amidst all the bedlam he emphatically waived his arms. No basket, he signaled! Thankfully, the ref had seen the same thing I saw. Bruce Watson had dunked the ball with two hands, perhaps a barely visible dunk where his two hands made a slight downward motion forcing the ball downward after he had brought the ball to just above the rim's surface, but a dunk, nevertheless. Dunking was not permitted in high school games, a recent rule change that had been made at both the high school and collegiate levels, with the penalty being disallowance of the basket and a technical foul.

Goski made the technical foul shot, and the scoreboard now read 43-38, a three-point swing from what it had read moments earlier before the big call came. Novacek missed a baseline jumper our next time down while Jefferson then responded with another Jones 17-footer, this one swishing from the right side. It was now 45-38, with just under six minutes remaining. Jefferson continued their man-to-man pressure as I worked the ball up the court. As I got doubled right near half court, I hit Simmons in the frontcourt by the sideline, who fed it to Novacek at the top of the foul line, who then drove it down the lane for a short running banker. The scoreboard now read 45-40, with 5:35 remaining.

We dropped back into the 1-3-1 again, and Novacek promptly blocked a shot along the right baseline. They maintained possession, but after two more missed shots, Goski grabbed the loose ball and hit Simmons racing up court, who missed a contested runner down the lane. It's Jeff's ball again and we retreated back into man defense. I deflected a Hopson pass near the right sideline, forcing the turnover, but we gave it right back as Novacek was called for travelling along the left baseline. The clock read 4:07, and points were not coming easily.

We were back in man defense again, and Goski was dogging Jones as he crossed midcourt. Jones then attempted to hit Beasley who was near the top of the key, but Pfeiffer, in perfect denial position, used his extended left arm to bat the ball forward. He scooped it up, still on their side of midcourt, and raced downcourt with both Jones and Beasley on his tail. After four dribbles Tom went up for the layup, but the ball was swatted off the boards by the jumping jack Beasley who had timed it perfectly. The ball caromed straight out to Novacek who was just catching up with the play along with several others. Scott grabbed the rebound about eight feet out with his momentum still carrying him toward the basket and rose up for the short banker. Too hard. It hit the board, then the front rim, and then came off the left side of the rim. Pfeiffer, whose momentum had carried him well beyond the baseline on his layup attempt, had just gotten back in bounds and rose up from the left side to tap the ball in, just a fraction sooner than Beasley and Watson who were there to watch it go through. 45-42.

Pfeiffer makes a textbook steal at the top of the key

Jefferson's Beasley blocks Pfeiffer's driving layup off the backboard

A trailing Novacek hauls in the rebound and puts up a short bank shot

Pfeiffer, just back in bounds, rises up to tip in Novacek's missed shot

On their next possession we forced Jeff into an errant pass along the left baseline, but we failed to capitalize as Pfeiffer missed a driving shot along the left baseline that Watson might have gotten a piece of. There was now 2:50 showing on the clock. The next time down court our defense saved us again, with Simmons intercepting a short lob entry pass into Watson. We again resorted to our motion offense to generate something. Sure enough, Goski hits Simmons as he comes across the lane, who then rose up for a twisting 15-footer from just outside the left lane. Larry smartly headed back into the lane as his shot hit the front of the rim and came straight out to him now only 10 feet from the basket. He put it right back up and this time it circled the rim before draining through. It was now 45-44 with 2:09 remaining.

Larry Simmons nails this short jumper to pull Westfield with 1

After Watson missed a one and one free throw, we had a chance to take the lead, but Hopson picked Larry's pocket while dribbling near the top of the key. Jeff raced downcourt on a 2-on-1 break with Goski defending. As

Hopson came flying down the left side of the lane, he didn't quite get as close as he would have liked as Goski was right there alongside his right hip. The ball narrowly missed and came off the front of the rim and was snatched by the trailing Simmons. But Jeff also got their hands on the ball and forced a jump ball call. Just as Scott had won the prior four, Larry made sure he won this fifth one too. Simmons controlled the tap, and once we secured possession, we signaled for a timeout. Horne wanted to set something up, and we needed a basket. We were down 45-44 with 1:10 to go.

We came out of the timeout and set up a sideline out of bounds play, but with the ball being taken out about 10 feet or so behind the mid-court line on the left sideline. It was the kind of play that we had worked on several times in practice in those short segments that Horne incorporated into practice to prepare us for specific end-of-quarter or end-of-game scenarios. We set up in box, with half of the box set up in the front court and half in the back court. I was throwing the ball in. Novacek, who was furthest from me, took a couple of steps toward me and then headed downcourt toward our basket. He got a step on Watson, so I let it fly with a baseball pass, likely the only one I had thrown all year. Fortunately, the pass was hauled in by Scott just a few feet from the basket, who was then promptly fouled by Watson as he attempted to finish the play in the lane. Scott made one of two free throws to knot the score at 45. Jeff then called their last timeout with the clock now showing just 59 seconds left.

The first half of that last minute would be spent by Jefferson working the ball around looking for that first good shot without forcing one up, but a good shot never materialized. With 30 seconds left they took a contested 17-footer which came hard off the rim right to Pfeiffer, who then pushed the ball hard up court and, finding no resistance in the lane, took it straight down the lane and all the way to the basket for the crucial basket with 25 seconds left. We had finally regained the lead, 47-45. Jeff came right back and managed to get a decent shot off a few seconds later, only to miss again and have Novacek come up with the rebound this time, now with only seven seconds left.

Scott was immediately fouled and had a chance to ice the game with a one and one. With no three-point line he just needed to hit the first to more or less put the game out of reach. Scott came through and made the first, but then missed the second. The rest of us were already back ready to defend the other basket, but more specifically, we retreated with orders from Horne not to foul. Then Jefferson, without any timeouts remaining, rushed it down and made an uncontested layup with two seconds left, to make it 48-47. I grabbed the ball as it came through the net, clutched as I stepped across the baseline, and then hearing the buzzer go off, gave the ball a good fling towards the ceiling.

Within seconds we were in the locker room, which fortunately was situated near the end of the court where the game had ended. I remember hugging Pfeiffer as soon as we got in there, and how the excitement within the locker room reached another level compared to our previous wins. We could all feel it and sense it. There was lots of hand slapping but no high fives – those weren't invented yet. Even Horne allowed his normally stoic voice to show a hint of happiness as he reflected on what we had just done. We had knocked off the #1 ranked team in the state … in their gym. After they had outscored us 23-13 the first ten minutes of the second half, we managed to shut them out with a 10-0 run the final 5:50 of game until we let them score in the final two seconds. Fittingly, each of our five starters had made a key play during that stretch run as if to punctuate the total team victory.

We were on Cloud 9 as we left the locker and headed to our bus for the 20-minute ride home. But some of the Jefferson contingent weren't finished with their hospitality. A few of the hangers on jeered us as we boarded the bus. We then discovered that the bus windshield had been smashed, presumably some kind of parting gift. We didn't care. We had given them a gift of our own.

After we got back to WHS and dropped our bags back in our locker room, Goski and I decided to head over to the Burger King on Central Ave. As we waited in line, Tim proclaimed: "We did it, Redeye!" I responded with: "Damn straight, and now we can celebrate." We then celebrated with a Whopper. I guess one good whopper deserved another.

That night I thought about everything that had happened that season … and more specifically, how it had happened. Yes, we were now 10-0, but four of those of those ten wins had come by the slimmest of margins: four points, one point (on a buzzer beater), overtime, and one point again. In those four games we had overcome second half deficits of six, eight, nine, and eight points, respectively, not to mention fourth quarter deficits that were no fewer than six in each of those games. How many bullets were we going to dodge? How many could we? Someone up above certainly must have been watching over us. If I was dreaming, I most definitely did not want to wake up.

During homeroom class the next morning, the school principal Albert Bobal got on the intercom and congratulated our team for our big victory the previous afternoon. Now even non-hoops fans knew something about what our team had achieved thus far. Unfortunately, classes were not being cancelled that day to honor our victory. School would go on uninterrupted.

Not only would classes not skip a beat, but when third period came, I had to participate in gym class. There had been a school policy which excused varsity athletes from gym class, presumably on the theory they would get more than their share of physical exercise during the daily practice session. Apparently, that policy had been reversed recently – not sure why or how – but I had to participate that day in gym class. The subject matter that day happened to be none other than basketball. So, there I was, a mere 18 hours after playing against the top ranked team in the state, now playing against a bunch of non-athletes and guys who would probably never pick up a basketball unless they had to. Dutifully, I participated in one of the half court games. On one play the ball came to me at the foul line and I took one dribble straight down the lane for what should have been an easy layup. But something got in the way. It was the knee of John Hause, a prototypical non-athlete, better known to me as a "greaser." John's legs and knees were about three times as wide as mine, and rather than let me cruise past him down the lane, he decided he would stick his knee out directly into my path. Before I knew it, his knee caught me directly in the middle of my right thigh. As soon as I landed, I felt a surge of pain in my thigh. I had never been hit that hard or that flush in that area. I stopped for about two minutes to allow the pain to subside and so I could limp it off a bit. I eventually resumed playing without really playing, but mercifully class ended a few minutes later.

I had math class the next period. During the course of that period, I could feel the leg throbbing and stiffening. By the time that period ended, I was in extreme discomfort. I decided I needed to get back to the gym and find our trainer John D'Andrea to see what he could do about it. D'Andrea got me on the trainer's table and then gradually forced me to pull my right heel up to my right buttocks, thereby stretching out my quadriceps muscle that had been bruised. I was practically in tears at this point. The leg did not want to go there right then, but D'Andrea insisted that it had to. An ice bag then went on my thigh. I had a thigh contusion, also known as a Charley Horse. I had a bad one. I would stay there about another hour and then would gather my stuff from my locker. I was done for the day.

I would spend much of the rest of my day icing the thigh and keeping the leg stretched as D'Andrea had done. I would hear nothing more about our big victory the previous day. I now had to deal with my new problem. When I went to bed that night, I had to sleep with my heel pulled up to my buttocks, hardly the most comfortable or natural sleeping position. The alternative, though, was to have it stiffen up overnight and then not being able to bend it the next morning. If I wanted to return to the court soon, I would need to follow D'Andrea's instructions. Indeed, there was no time for basking in glory or delaying my recovery as we were to host Cranford in just two days, arguably our second toughest opponent of the year right behind Jefferson.

Meanwhile, back at school, the *Daily Journal* newspaper paid the school a visit that afternoon to do a feature article on our team's surprising success thus far in the season. The article appeared a day later with a picture of the other four starters along with Coach Horne. I guess when you beat the top ranked team in the state, not to mention being undefeated through ten games, a lot of people start to take notice. Of course, that would include our future opponents who would no doubt be gunning for us, wanting to take us down.

Another article appeared that day in the *Daily Journal*, this one focusing on our head coach. "Horne Sounds" was the title of the article written by Milt Farb. It started out with "The trumpets are blaring today for the 'horn man' at Westfield High School." Now our coach had a nickname, at least amongst his players. So "Horn Man" or "Horne Man" would be his new moniker, at least while things were going well. After all, everyone deserves a good nickname.

The next day I missed school, preferring to nurse my bruised thigh at home and keep up the ice treatment as much as possible, rather than hobble around school hallways all day and probably delay my recovery. By mid-afternoon I was already going stir crazy, so I headed over to school to watch practice and at least try to get myself mentally ready for Friday night's game assuming I would be able to physically play. Being injured is no fun. As soon as you have to sit on the sidelines and watch everyone else play, it doesn't take long to appreciate just being healthy enough to be out there playing. We had been lucky so far in our still young season, at least up until my injury in gym class. No other injury or illness had kept any player, starter or reserve, out of any of our first ten games. My plan now was to keep the thigh muscle stretched as much as possible, and then with heat treatment the muscle should loosen up enough to play the next night.

January 14, 1972

This day marked the first day that our school observed Martin Luther King Day. It had recently been proclaimed a national holiday, but it fell on a Saturday this year, and not been moved to the following Monday like it is today and has been for decades. This Friday school was closed to observe this new holiday, closed for classes at least. The school would be open at night for a little battle in the gymnasium between Cranford and Westfield.

We knew Cranford pretty well, at least their main guys. Norm Hobbie (aka "Stormin' Norman") and Richie Mazzella were fixtures down at Gumbert for much of the summer, so Tim, Mike, Jester and I knew their tendencies from our frequent encounters down there. Furthermore, all of our returning seniors had faced them the previous year when we managed to beat them twice in very close games. Hobbie, a junior, was their big scorer and had been a starter since his previous season as a sophomore, which was unusual in those days. Most varsity teams wouldn't even carry any sophomores on their rosters, let alone have one in their starting lineup. But the 6-foot Hobbie was a skilled guard with a polished jump shot with textbook technique, and a penchant for being able to get his shot off. Mazzella, on the other hand, relied on sheer quickness to beat you. He didn't have the textbook game that Hobbie had, but instead would be inclined to shoot running, off balanced floaters inside the lane after using his speed to gain an opening. He was also a pest on defense and would often pick off lazy passes if you weren't careful. Cranford also had a solid center in 6-foot-5 John Zebrowski, another guy frequently seen at Gumbert, and Charlie Pryor, an athletic forward who did much of their dirty work, i.e., their version of our Larry Simmons.

Pfeiffer and I were also familiar with their coach, Bill Martin, from having watched some of their games against my brothers' teams and more recently, our two games against them as juniors the prior year, including one where we upset them in their gym. Martin was bald and had the habit turning a bright red whenever he was mad at the refs or how the game was going. We had often joked about how great it would be to light up Bill Martin.

Of course, even more important than our players' familiarity with Cranford was Coach Horne's familiarity from scouting them in real game action. As with every opponent we would face, Horne would give us the scoop on Cranford's tendencies in one or two of the practices leading up to that game, as well as in the pre-game talk on game days.

I got a bit of a scare that afternoon when I heard that I may not be allowed to play. There was a school rule that said you couldn't play in school athletic contests if you didn't go to school that day, but I don't think that rule applied for a Saturday game if you missed school on a Friday. In this case it was a Friday game where I had missed school on Thursday and there were no Friday classes. Fortunately, logic prevailed and I was cleared to play not long after I heard about it.

The gym was buzzing that night as we took the court for only our second home night game of the year, and this time we came into the game with a totally unexpected 10-0 record, having just knocked off the #1 ranked team in the state, about to face one of our two arch rivals who was also having a great season up to that point at 8-1 overall and 6-0 in Watchung Conference games, averaging a very healthy 75 points a game. Could there be a better Friday night matchup than that?

In the hours leading up to the game I got plenty of heat treatment on my thigh and did lots of stretching to loosen up the muscle as much as possible. I would not be 100 percent, but I would be close enough and the adrenaline that was about to kick in would push me over the top and allow me to play that night. I wasn't going to miss this one.

The first half of the game played out in a somewhat similar manner to the Jefferson game earlier that week – in other words, a low scoring defensive battle where each team was seemingly feeling out the other despite the intimate knowledge of the other team's tendencies. After one quarter we led 8-6, and then we increased that lead just slightly to 20-14 by halftime. Sometimes good defense gets the better of good offense. Martin couldn't be very happy with Cranford's low offensive output, but it was still anybody's game. At this point, it seemed like we were destined for another second half battle that would go down to the wire again.

But then, early in the third period, something gave way. With the lead now at 25-18, we went on a 12-0 run to break the game open and take a commanding 37-18 lead, with Novacek getting six points during that stretch. We maintained our momentum through the end of that third period, outscoring them 25-8 to stretch our lead to 45-22.

Horne wasn't going to take the foot off the gas pedal though. Cranford was too good and this game was an aberration thus far. However, any concerns Horne might have had going into the fourth period were quickly dispelled as we picked up right where we left off. Early in the fourth period we began another run, this one a 10-0 run, and our reserves then took over the rest of the way. Martin quickly threw in the towel as well. As bad as the third period had been for Cranford, the fourth quarter was even worse. We outscored them 22-5 to reach a final score of 67-27, a 40-point blowout! Certainly no one saw that coming, and with a 20-14 halftime margin, the final margin would have been even more unpredictable. We had beaten our average offensive output by two points, while holding Cranford an astonishing 48 points below their average! What was going on here?

I hadn't played particularly well or contributed much offensively, scoring only four points. Horne limited my minutes seeing I wasn't quite 100 percent, but I didn't care. It was great to see everyone else picking up the slack and maintaining our balance, with Novacek and Pfeiffer scoring 14 each, Goski adding 13 points, and Jester getting eight points off the bench, while Simmons led the way on the boards again with nine rebounds. A look at the team stats revealed the extent of the all-out massacre. We had outrebounded them 47-27, outshot them from the field 38% to 22%, had only 16 turnovers to their 26, had 8 assists to their 2, and went to the foul line 28 times to their 9.

Right after the game ended, Pfeiffer, Goski and I did something at the spur of the moment. We went into their locker room to console the guys we knew well, specifically Hobbie and Mazzella, telling them something like "it wasn't your night" and "we know you're better than that." I think they were mostly embarrassed at their performance, and there wasn't anything that we could say that was going to make them feel better. Nevertheless, it seemed like the right thing to do at the time.

Monday would bring a new challenge for Horne. We had almost been too successful in our first 11 games, with the last one almost taking on fairy tale attributes. We had now played six of the seven teams in the Watchung Conference, with the exception of the weakest team in Rahway, and over the next three weeks would play them all again for a second time. There was the potential for a letdown after the big wins in our prior three games. Next on the schedule was Scotch Plains at their place in the afternoon. The first time we played them the date had been circled on the calendar and was arguably the biggest game of the year, or so it seemed going into the season. Scotch Plains had been our nemesis essentially our entire basketball careers. Now in the wake of recent events it seemed like just another game, but we couldn't afford to think like that. They were too good, regardless of their record. Besides, we had only beaten them by four at our gym and had to come from six points down in the last quarter to pull it out. Perhaps most importantly, they would be gunning for us. At 11-0, we were now the team that Scotch Plains and other opponents would be circling on their calendars.

Of course, none of this was lost on Horne, and he wasn't about to let overconfidence lead to sloppy practices or execution. That would be easier said than done, however. There was an air of cockiness that would start to emerge, particularly with Goski and Novacek, who were very confident coming into the season; naturally our team success made them even more self-assured going forward. The seniors were a bit more disciplined, and less likely to joke around at all during practice. That said, everyone was feeling good about where the team stood so it was only natural that some good-natured joking would rise to the surface during practice. Somewhat counteracting that was the ongoing natural tension between the starters and reserves who continued to battle for playing time, especially Cooney, Lee, and Jester. Even Phillips and Jackson, who were getting even less minutes of real game action, were still hyper competitive in practices and took pride in defending against the first team and battling everyone else on the boards. This led to lots of contact and explicit language during half court drills whenever Horne let the action continue long enough. Players might get testy when the defense went all out even when they knew what the offense was supposed to be running. Inevitably, someone would get caught cursing during the action or talking while Horne was explaining something during one of the many breaks in the action. Horne would immediately give the offending player one or more suicides to run at the end of practice. Horne would sometimes increase the penalty for any given infraction in any given practice depending on how he sensed practice was going and whether the team was fully engaged while he was teaching. Goski and Jester were often the biggest offenders, not necessarily from their lack of attention, but rather because curse words would often roll naturally off their tongues during the heat of battle. On this particular day, Jester and Novacek came away with four suicides each.

January 18, 1972

Tuesday morning meant new *Star-Ledger* statewide rankings would be revealed in their morning edition. Given our two big wins the prior week over previous unbeaten Jefferson and once beaten Cranford, we were bound to move up from our prior week's position at No. 8. You didn't need to buy a paper to find out. You couldn't avoid finding out even if you wanted to as the word would quickly spread. Now three Union County teams, Jefferson, Roselle, and Westfield, with only two losses between all three, would occupy three of the top five spots on the list. When we boarded the bus that afternoon for the short ride to Scotch Plains, we did it as the # 2-ranked team in New Jersey.

Still, that ranking would go out the window as soon as we stepped on the floor. There was no way of knowing which of our teams would show up, the one that showed up in the first half of the Cranford game or the second half? Furthermore, afternoon games were tricky ... the crowds tended to be smaller, there was no JV game immediately prior to the varsity game during which the adrenaline could build up, and less time, literally only one hour, to transition from the classroom to the opening tip at another school. The bottom line was that you had to overcome those various headwinds and be ready to play when the ball was tossed up.

We scored the first two that afternoon, but Scotch Plains responded by scoring seven straight. After trading baskets to make the score 9-4, our more dominant side showed up again to reel off 18 straight and take a 22-9 lead, with Goski scoring five during the stretch and Pfeiffer and Simmons adding four each. Scotch Plains, who was shorthanded this day without their center Al Holiday, wasn't about to concede, however, and fought back to within six by halftime when the score stood at 30-24. During the first half of the third quarter, we stretched the lead to nine at 42-33, and then the damn burst open over the next eight minutes as we went on another big run, this one a 20-1 outburst. With four minutes left in the game our lead had swelled to 62-34 as some of the momentum from the Cranford game seemingly carried over into this one. A few minutes later the final buzzer mercifully sounded with the scoreboard reading 69-46, and the Raiders walked off the court feeling a bit of the same sting that Cranford had felt a few nights earlier.

We had four players in double figures again, with Goski leading the way with a season-high 24 points, followed by Simmons with a season high 14, Novacek with 12, and Pfeiffer with 10. We outshot them 40 percent to 31 percent, outrebounded them 47-26, and forced 30 turnovers to our 15. It was another beatdown with shades of the Cranford blowout and totally different than our first encounter with them. Today we clearly looked like the better team. Were we that good? What had changed?

Aside from generally better execution on the offensive end, Goski was finally coming into his own and playing more like the guy we were familiar with from Gumbert. In contrast with the first few games where several of Tim's shots had been rushed or forced, Goski was now waiting for openings to arise in the context of the team offense and then seizing those openings when they came. The two Scotch Plains games epitomized how Tim's season had been going. In the first one Goski had scored 10 points but sat the final minutes of a tight game, with Horne presumably concerned about Tim forcing things down the stretch. In the second game Horne sat Tim midway through the fourth period for an entirely different reason - to keep him from embarrassing the badly beaten Raiders team. Sorry Ray Ray, Goski finally got the better of you in this one. In our last three wins, Goski had scored a total of 51 points while I had only scored 12 points, four in each game. In the first nine games, our offensive output had been much closer, with Goski averaging 12.9 and me averaging 11.4 points, but now we were going in opposite directions. I may not have been 100 percent with my Charley Horse still limiting my mobility and practice time, but the real truth was that Horne was gradually allowing Goski to run freer and utilize more of the offensive skills that he had been honing the past couple of summers. It was only natural that my offensive output would come down a bit as Tim's increased. I understood that. It didn't bother me. There was no way it was going to bother me as long as the team kept winning the way it was. We got back on the bus with a 12-0 record.

Our next game would be against Rahway, an easy one. They were by far the weakest team in the conference. I was still getting a lot of heat treatment for my thigh contusion which had occurred one week earlier and was still not fully participating in our practice sessions. Horne and I agreed that I might help the recovery by sitting the next one out. Our next game after that would be a full week later, so hopefully by then I'd be pretty close to 100 percent. Meanwhile I would continue the heat treatment and stretching exercises, including the nightly routine of sleeping with my right knee in a fully bent position.

January 21, 1972

What normally would have been a Friday night home game against Rahway turned into an afternoon game with a 3:45 pm start. Supposedly Rahway had some prohibition, perhaps self-imposed, against night games due to unruly fan behavior at some of their games in prior seasons. Consequently, we had two afternoon games scheduled with them, with the second one coming 12 days later. I didn't particularly care as I wouldn't be playing in this one.

I took my seat at the end of the bench as the team took the court and proceeded to put Rahway away in routine fashion, 83-53. While Goski and Novacek led with 19 and 15, respectively, several others got into the act as Lee scored nine, Cooney had seven, and Chip Danker had six in the backcourt, while Jester and Phillips each had eight filling in for the front court starters. I got to be a fan for one game and was just as happy missing this one and watching my teammates play.

The following week brought a brief lull in the schedule, with only one game scheduled on Friday night against Clark at home. Then the next week we would play Rahway again before travelling to Cranford for the rematch the following Friday night. It appeared we would get to enjoy our unbeaten status a bit longer without being seriously threatened.

Of course, that meant Horne would have to continue to watch out for complacency, overconfidence, and losing our competitive edge. One way he did this was to continually change things up in our practice schedules. He would keep changing the matchups in our one-on-one drills, and he would switch up the drills from one practice to the next. No two practices were alike. We started to do a bit more scrimmaging towards the end of practice, during which we would work on various things we needed to execute during game situations, like out of bounds plays or plays with the clock winding down. He would also call out plays to run while the action was going on, so it was scrimmaging with a purpose. We would also scrimmage against the JV on occasion, where they might be full court pressing us or playing certain zone defenses to see how we handled it. Finally, there was usually 20-30 minutes devoted to preparing for our next opponent's known tendencies. With four practices this week, there was more than enough time to prepare for anything that Clark might throw at us. While I wasn't quite back to 100 percent physically, I was now fully participating in practice again, and I needed it. I could already feel myself losing a bit of conditioning, so I needed the scrimmaging and any other drills that required some amount of physical exertion.

January 28, 1972

Our 14th game would be just our third Friday night home game. It started out in typical fashion with us leading by 12-10 after one quarter. Clark was shooting a high percentage to take the lead back at 20-19 midway through second period before we finished the quarter with an 11-0 run to lead by 10 at halftime. After that our defense and rebounding were too much for Clark to handle, and we gradually opened up a 24-point lead early in the fourth period. Clark would battle back to get within 66-52, but it was too little, too late. The final score read 74-56.

The stat line was not a lot different than it was for many of our victories. The scoring was very balanced with all five starters finishing in double figures, with Novacek leading the way with 16. As in almost all our games, we dominated the boards again with a 43-25 margin, with Simmons grabbing 14, while we also forced them into 30 turnovers compared with our 17. Clark did manage to shoot 55% from the field, but we were right behind them at 49%.

We sent the crowd home happy once again. We had surprised a lot of people thus far in the season, but we were no doubt starting to make believers out of many given some of our impressive wins to date against top notch competition. Football coaches Gary Kehler and Bob Martin had witnessed our home wins up close, taking their positions along the wall behind the baseline near our locker room entrance. I caught a glimpse of Martin during this game and wondered what he was thinking now. Was he happy with our success? Did he respect it? Or were basketball players still just second-class citizens in his mind? I didn't dwell on it long. As long as we were winning, I was going to be content regardless of what Bob Martin thought.

Two days later on Sunday evening I went down to the basement, grabbed one of our basketballs, and inflated it with more air. I then put on a heavy sweatshirt, sweatpants, and a beanie, jumped into the car, and made the short drive over to a place I hadn't been to in months – Gumbert. The temperature was just above freezing, there were no lights on, and, not surprisingly, I was the only one there, but thanks to a full moon the courts and baskets were plenty visible for my purpose. My objective was to get in some running and improve my conditioning a bit. My right thigh contusion, which had occurred 18 days earlier, was finally feeling quite good, but my conditioning was not quite what it had been immediately prior to the injury. I started dribbling up and down the court, taking layups at each end. I would dribble the ball up as if there were a defender guarding me and continue all the way to the basket for the layup, but sometimes pulling up from 15 to 17 feet for a jump shot. I stopped once to add a bit more air into the ball, but aside from that it was up and down the court pretty continuously for about 45 minutes. I then returned home feeling like the mission was accomplished.

When I went to bed that night, I thought about the season we were having. We were about to finish January still unbeaten, defying all the odds along the way, and now the victories were seemingly coming more easily than ever. Was it possible that we might go undefeated for the whole season? All I knew was that I didn't want to do anything to screw up the good thing we had going. That was why I had gone down to Gumbert earlier that evening in the dark and cold of winter. It was why I hadn't had a drop of alcohol since my misstep early in the season. It was why I had gone to Church that morning. Our season had just passed the halfway point, but I already had a lot to be thankful for. I fell asleep easily that night, feeling good about what the second half might bring.

IX.   We Got Next

In the summer of 2000, I was sitting in the waiting room of the dentist's office waiting to be called in. I grabbed a magazine, *The Atlantic*, from a nearby table and started flipping through it until I came to an article that caught my attention: ***The Best Pickup Basketball Player in America***. The article described a 51-year-old businessman who would play hoops three to four times a week, often at the Ridgewood YMCA in northern NJ, but also anywhere he could find a game in his various business travels around the country. He would seek out games in tough neighborhoods, like Harlem or the Bronx, and would often school much younger competition with a combination of skill, experience, savvy and toughness. I was intrigued as I started making my way through the article, in part because in many respects it appeared to be describing my neighbor Jim Natale who was a bit of a basketball zealot himself. That seemed especially so when the article described the subject's belief that "when you're tired of basketball, you're tired of life." I was also impressed by how the article so aptly described so many aspects of pickup basketball that I could easily relate to, certainly not something I expected to see in a magazine that I would normally never even pick up. When I finally got called inside for my dental appointment, I casually slipped the magazine into my briefcase...it was simply too good to not finish.

Of course, at the time I read this article, I already had plenty of experience playing pickup basketball and understood many of the nuances referenced in the article. Perhaps first and foremost is that it represents the purest form of basketball with the fewest constraints around it. Pickup basketball only requires a basket, a ball, and two or more players. There are no age restrictions. There are no gender restrictions. There are no particular levels of skill or experience required. You don't even need to know anyone. You just need to show up.

Pickup basketball sheds the burdens of having to get on a team or forming rosters, of having to get a coach or be a coach, of making up schedules or sticking to a schedule, to find refs, pay refs, or be subject to a ref's whistle. It usually requires no money either...once you've made it to the court, money is no object. It's strictly basketball stripped down to its core.

Pickup basketball can be a magnet for all sorts of people. It appeals to younger kids who wish to gain experience playing against older, stronger, physically more mature players. It appeals to older players who are past their prime but still have skills developed over a number of years, experience at using them, and perhaps most importantly a love of the game they are not ready to abandon. It can also appeal to the less skilled player who might not otherwise be chosen to play on a team. It may appeal to the highly skilled player who may want to show off his talents to the local crowd while refining his skills even further. It can even appeal to the best player in the world. That's right, Michael Jordan famously had a clause in his contract allowing him to play pickup basketball anywhere, anytime. Pickup basketball can offer the thrill of team competition, an unmatched workout, and perhaps most of all an equal opportunity to everyone who shows up to play on a given day at a given location. Oh, and one more thing, you won't find any parents at pickup games complaining about little Johnnie or Lizzie not getting enough playing time…in fact, there isn't even anyone they *could* complain to.

With pickup games, all you know is the court, the location, and what time others are likely to show up. In the summers at Gumbert, that meant 6 pm on weeknights – i.e., Monday through Thursday. If the courts happen to be popular, like Gumbert was when I was growing up, there would be more players than available courts. That's where the local rules and practices would come in, aided by self-appointed "commissioners" who might take it upon themselves to get the games organized and sometimes rule on disputes over who's turn it was to play.

The most universal rule of pickup basketball, whether it is a YMCA, Gumbert or any other playground, is that winners stay on and losers go to the back of the line. Games might be played to 11 or 15, with each field goal counting as 1 point, so free throws or 3 point shots are non-existent. It would often be sudden death, with no two point margin required, but that rule would vary widely from one location to the next. Given the absence of referees, players call their own fouls. This is where you need the courage of your convictions, otherwise you risk the wrath of an opposing player who openly questions your knowledge of basketball or your manhood, or both. Calling violations, like travelling, would be just the opposite – they would typically only get called by the opposing team and automatically honored unless overwhelmingly vetoed by everyone else on the court.

Even more significant than how the games are played is who gets to play each game. Yes, winners stay on and losers sit – but who gets to play in the first place? It might just come down to the first 10 who show up, and then in order of arrival after that. In other words, first come, first serve. But if there are more than 10 when the first game is organized, it may get decided by foul shots. In other words, it may be part equal opportunity, and part meritocracy. Things can get even trickier at courts where it's not automatically the next five in line. Some local practices will allow a group of 3 or 4 to claim the next game and then fill out their roster only after the current game is finished, at which point they might select a player from the losing team. The primary reason this would be done would be to improve a team's chance of winning, but it could also be done to improve an otherwise overmatched team or to make up for a shortage of height, or maybe just to team up with a friend. The local rules will dictate what's permissible in those situations.

Pickup basketball is the perfect opportunity to improve one's skills or, at the very least, to test them. You can make mistakes without worrying about a coach's critique. However, you can't play foolishly either as that would likely invite the wrath of your teammates and increase your chances of losing and sitting out multiple games at a crowded court. It's also a place where players can earn a reputation, good or bad. It was Tim Goski's growing presence at Gumbert even as a 9th grader that was brought to my attention when I was a sophomore before I had ever seen him play. Of course, the word gets around when a lot of people see someone do something special on the playground or at the Y, especially when they do it over and over.

Perhaps the best part of pickup basketball is that everyone does have a more or less equal chance to play and show what they can do on the court. It's a great melting pot for anyone who loves to play hoops. On its face, status goes out the window when you show up to play pickup ball. At the Westfield Y I remember a many a day and night when the diversity of players showing up would run the gamut – from young to old, from local guys to out of towners, from gym rats to college players, from guys known for the basketball prowess to guys who starred in other sports. One would regularly run into guys like Lennie Baumstein, who was about 15 years older but looked and played much younger, and Bill Clancy, a self-proclaimed basketball junkie who played for WHS and graduated in '61, Dickie Meyers, the All State guard who graduated in '62, Jeff Bauer, a great WHS baseball catcher who graduated in '65, Paul Byrne, one of WHS's great football running backs who graduated in '69, Craig Johnson (aka, CJ) a gym rat who was not quite varsity material but still had game and loved to hang out and play at the Y, and Jay Boyle, who was three years younger than me and would eventually play for Roselle Catholic and then Seton Hall in college. It didn't matter how much basketball might be on your resume, and like the song said: "It doesn't matter what you wear just as long as you are there". Everyone would get their chance to play, and those who played best and won would get to play the longest.

The lack of an age requirement is forgiving in one respect – it will get you onto the court and into the game. But it's unforgiving in another. At some point the greater speed, quickness and jumping ability of the younger player will start to get the better of a more experienced player who is now past his prime. Father Time can be cruel in this way, but it happens at such a gradual pace that you may not notice at first. Greater skill and experience may help offset or camouflage some of the physical advantage of the younger player. Sooner or later, however, the physical decline is undeniable. We see it all the time with professional athletes that face the same dilemma in full view of the public. But professional athletes are usually forced into retirement if they resist it for too long because an owner won't want to keep paying them beyond the point they can help the team win. The amateur hoopster can pretty much stay at it as long as their bodies will permit it. They may be content trying to replicate some of the moves of their younger self, however slow or unimpressive it might look to others.

I myself was able to remain pretty competitive in pickup games for a long time, but then physical ailments started to get the better of me. Pulled muscles during my forties were merely an annoyance compared to the arthritic left hip I developed a few years later and eventually had replaced at age 53. Then I began having meniscus issues in my right knee. Up until that point, my knees had never bothered me, but now Father Time was telling me that my number was up. My right knee was almost out of cartilage and would never feel quite right again. Doctors told me I should avoid impact activities; otherwise, I would just be accelerating the need for a knee replacement. After two arthroscopic surgeries on that knee, I no longer felt any desire to ignore their advice, at least on the basketball court. I hung up my sneakers for good at age 57. I had had a good run.

X. Crashing & Burning (Jan 31 – Feb 23, 1972)

"It wasn't supposed to happen; we came apart at the seams,
A painful unravelling of our basketball dreams."

from *A Team to Remember*, November 18, 2000

We started the new week with a 14-0 record, with the game schedule for the week being another odd one. This week's games would be played Wednesday and Friday, rather than the more customary Tuesday and Friday. The Wednesday game promised to be another laugher against Rahway, while the Friday game would be our highly anticipated rematch against Cranford at their place. Having two practices to prepare for Rahway and then only one for Cranford would be the last thing Horne would want if he had anything to say about it.

Not surprisingly, Monday's practice had a lot of cockiness being displayed with the associated chatter, and Coach Horne was on high alert for it. His notes for that day showed an above average number of suicides being dished out for verbal transgressions, with even the normally mild-mannered Phillips having to run four himself. Goski and Jester were also active that day. Horne continued to mix things up at practice to guard against complacency. That included almost an hour of scrimmaging that day, half of it versus the JV team. Scrimmaging was perhaps the best way for players to burn off energy, as well as preserve the competitive edge our team had going for it. However, it didn't necessarily stop any trash talking that might be going on at the same time.

The next day, Tuesday Feb. 1, brought about something that Horne probably both wanted and feared. Tuesday meant new Star-Ledger rankings, and before the start of practice that day the word had gotten around that Westfield now held the top spot in the statewide rankings. This wasn't particularly surprising since we had been in the No. 2 spot for two straight weeks and had several strong team performances in a row to our credit. But if Horne was pleased with the ranking, he wasn't about to show it. He was far more concerned with what overconfidence might do to us over the remainder of the season.

Figure 4

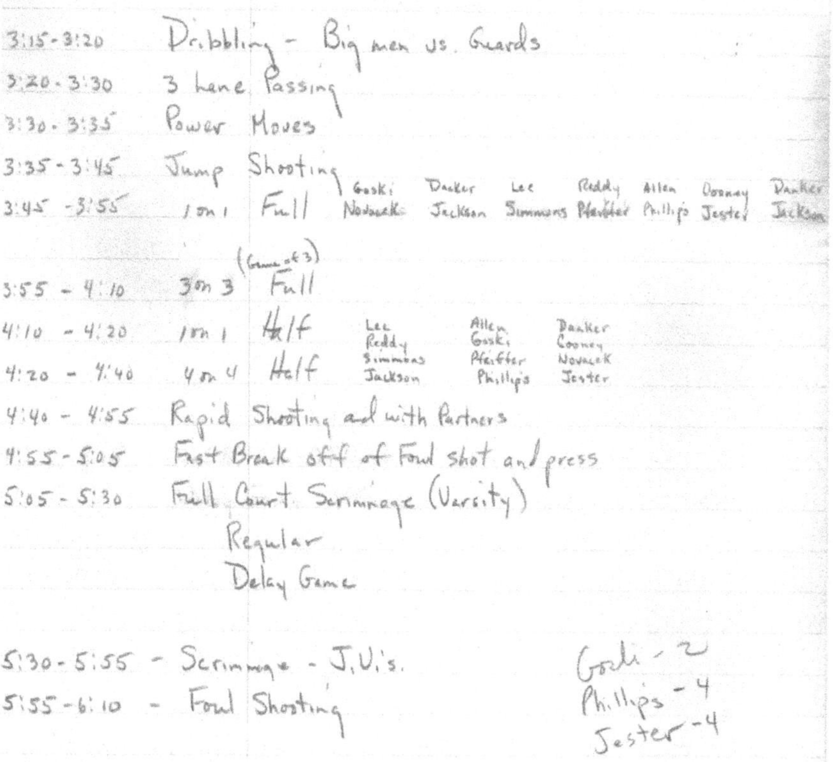

3:15-3:20   Dribbling - Big men vs. Guards

3:20-3:30   3 Lane Passing

3:30-3:35   Power Moves

3:35-3:45   Jump Shooting

3:45-3:55   1 on 1   Full   Goski   Danker   Lee   Reddy   Allen   Cooney   Danker
                                          Novacek   Jackson   Simmons   Pfeiffer   Phillips   Jester   Jackson

3:55 - 4:10   3 on 3   Full (Game of 3)

4:10 - 4:20   1 on 1   Half   Lee   Allen   Danker
                              Reddy   Goski   Cooney

4:20 - 4:40   4 on 4   Half   Simmons   Pfeiffer   Novacek
                              Jackson   Phillips   Jester

4:40 - 4:55   Rapid Shooting and with Partners

4:55 - 5:05   Fast Break off of Foul shot and press

5:05 - 5:30   Full Court Scrimmage (Varsity)
                  Regular
                  Delay Game

5:30 - 5:55 - Scrimmage - J.V.'s.   Goski - 2

5:55 - 6:10 - Foul Shooting   Phillips - 4
                                           Jester - 4

So, when practice started that afternoon, Horne seemed particularly edgy in contrast to the lighthearted and carefree demeanor that his players were showing. Horne would always be blowing his whistle throughout practice to point out this or that, how something was being done incorrectly, or what needed to be done better. But his patience seemed short this day … and he had rabbit ears as well. "What did you say?" Horne said to Jester, certain that he had heard BJ utter his favorite curse word - "bastard." But before Jester could respond, Goski, showing incredibly quick wit, interjected, "He said, 'Cut to the basket.'." I couldn't believe what I just heard, but still tried to keep a straight face knowing full well that Horne's initial suspicions were correct. For whatever reason, Horne let Jester slide in that moment ... practice resumed. Horne's whistles were more frequent than normal though, which left more opportunity for someone to be talking under someone's breath. Goski and Jester appeared to have some kind of running conversation going, which was likely their typical low-key trash talking that inevitably ended with somebody laughing. Well, somebody laughed at the wrong time and Horne had had enough. "That's it. Go home! Get out of here," he yelled in his loud and commanding voice. "You didn't come to play," he continued. "Go home and read about yourselves!" He then walked out of the gym.

It wasn't even 4:30 yet and suddenly practice was over. Everything got quiet immediately. There's nothing you can do at that point except do what the coach says. We all left the gym quietly and then proceeded to shower and dress to get out of there as quickly as we could. Some of us had to make calls or search for rides home because of the early departure.

After dinner that night I decided to head over the 7-Eleven in Mountainside to pick up a Star-Ledger. I suppose I was going over there to get my money's worth...if you're going to get thrown out of practice for wanting to read about yourself, you might as well go read about yourself. Unbeknownst to me, my convictions were about to be tested. As soon as I put the paper on the counter, into the store walks none other than my good buddy Bob Martin, who made sure to make the most of our chance encounter. "What are you doing here, Reddy? Gonna read about yourself?" My brain had already been trained to deal with that kind of incoming, so I was able to deflect it with a sheepish smile but not a single word. I couldn't believe my bad fortune though. It was almost as if Horne had called up Martin up after practice and asked him to follow me into the 7-Eleven so he could harass me in his own special way. So far being ranked No. 1 wasn't all that great. It seemed that it was more of a curse than an achievement. Once again, we were going to have to prove ourselves on the court.

February 2, 1972

By the time we were all dressed in the Rahway locker room the next afternoon, everyone was focused and determined to play hard to get back onto Horne's good side. You couldn't tell from Horne's pregame talk what had happened the day before. It was back to business now, and it didn't matter that it was a weak team we were about to take on. We needed to play the right way.

We did. We jumped out to an 11-0 lead and stretched it out to 56-34 by halftime. Rahway had no chance that day. Not only did we have them thoroughly outclassed, but we came to play to atone for the previous day's transgressions. The pummeling continued in the second half as we forced them into 40 turnovers for the game. Everyone was racking up points. Pfeiffer led with 21 points and I even managed 16 after a few low scoring games in a row. The starters were gone pretty early in the second half and our team had scored 85 points by the end of the third period. Halfway through the last period the lead stood at 98-57 when Horne called timeout. We were to run the delay game offense and not take any shots unless it was an absolutely uncontested layup. Horne decided we should not be getting any cheap thrills at Rahway's expense in their gym. I suppose their coach appreciated the move, but how good could he feel after a beat down of that magnitude? The final score read 98-59.

This game would be forgotten by the time our bus had returned us to our gym. In two short days we would have our rematch with Cranford.

Cranford was now 12-3. Despite their blowout loss to us, they were still averaging almost 74 points a game, so there was no disputing their offensive firepower. They were playing well again and would most definitely be gunning for us. They also had the home court this time. Their home court was known as the "Pit," a tiny old gym with a wall at the near end of the court just a few feet behind the baseline and bleachers just beyond the far baseline. There was also a balcony overlooking that far end of the court with some seating that made up for the relatively small bleachers along each sideline. There was no elbow room in the entire gym, with a feeling that the fans that were lucky enough to get seats were right on top of the court. This could be disconcerting for any player or team that hadn't played in that environment before.

We didn't need any additional incentive, but if we could beat Cranford this night, the win would tie the school record of 16 straight wins set a decade earlier. Frankly, we were more interested in staying unbeaten. That alone was a feeling worth fighting for. We knew one thing for certain: Cranford would not lay down for us like they had in the previous game. We would have to earn number 16.

February 4, 1972

At this point in the season, we had built up a pretty good following within the student body. Friday night games offered a perfect way to start the weekend, especially against one or our arch-rivals. When someone was hosting a party on a game night, that made it all the better.

On this particular day one of our grammar school classmates, Bill Weldon, was hosting such a party. Bill had been going to the Pingry School since the sixth grade but still lived in Westfield and still mingled with other Westfield kids since Pingry was an all-boys school. Bill's parents also had the perfect party house…in other words – huge; it even had two driveways leading out to different streets. Bill's party started early, to get people primed before they headed over to the Pit for the big game, and then it would resume after the game. We were hoping to join it after the game with another reason to celebrate.

On the bus on the way to the game Scott Novacek showed me a baggie with something that was hard to make out. Scott explained that it was hair clippings from his own head. It seems that Horne had been putting pressure on Scott to get a haircut to make his shoulder length hair a little more respectable. Scott had relented, but in his own unique way, and now was bringing proof that he had complied with his coach's request. A short time later inside our locker room in the Pit, I was standing nearby when Nova presented Horne with his evidence. Horne replied in his strong voice: "That's great, Scott", with his eyes moving back and forth between the baggie and Scott's head. There was no sarcasm in Horne's voice, but you could just sense what Horne was thinking: "That's great, Scott, but what about all the hair that's still on your head?"

Moments later we headed out of the locker room to watch the JV game that started at 6:30. There was only one problem - there were no seats left. I guess word had gotten around Cranford that the No. 1-ranked team in New Jersey was in the house, and it just so happened to be the same team that had whipped the hometown boys by 40 just three weeks earlier. They came early for this one. They wanted their seats. On top of that, they wanted revenge!

Their fans had rolled out the welcome mat for us. Greeting us upon our first steps out of the locker room was a large seven letter message hanging from the entire left side of the balcony at the far end of the court, with one poster sized paper used for each letter. R-E-V-E-N-G-E was the message that greeted us and reflected the mood of the crowd as we entered the Pit and tried to find a spot for the next 45 minutes until it was time to suit up.

We made our way down to the far end of the court and finally settled into the only "seats" that appeared to be available – literally right on the floor itself just a few feet beyond the far baseline and right next to several of the Cranford players. We barely acknowledged each other as we plopped our butts on the floor. A couple of minutes later Norm Hobbie, sitting just a few feet away from us, broke the tension by saying: "Guys, just don't beat us by 50 tonight." Naturally that brought a little bit of nervous laughter in response, but it was muted. No one was in a laughing mood, and the adrenaline was already kicking in and with tip off time quickly approaching. Still, the wait seemed endless, and nervous energy continued to build as the JV game played out.

Finally, it was time for the main event and our turn to take the court. There's no feeling quite like running out of the locker room into a packed gym with adrenaline pumping. People were there to see *you* play. The warmups and layup lines were a chance to burn off some of the nervous energy and get acclimated to the gym environment. In moments like this there was an extra bounce in your step, and you could get up a little higher off the floor. Your pent-up energy and adrenaline were hard to contain. Whatever nagging aches and pains you might have felt earlier were now gone.

Horne had instituted a practice where the starting five, after leaving the team huddle before the opening tap, would go to the foul line nearest our bench for a quick mini huddle of our own. The place was already loud with anticipation. "Let's fuck 'em up" we collectively said as we put our hands together and then headed for center court. It was game time.

Things didn't start well for us. Charlie Pryor, Cranford's version of Larry Simmons, tapped in a missed shot on their first possession. Then on our first possession against their 1-3-1 zone, I threw a lazy pass across court to Goski, but Richie Mazzella, with water bug-like quickness darted into the passing lane, intercepted the pass and easily raced down court for an uncontested layup. On their next possession Hobbie hit a jumper for 6-0 lead. We finally broke the ice with a bucket, but then a couple of more turnovers by us allowed them to stretch the lead to 16-6, before we went on an 8-2 run to close the gap to 18-14. But they were hitting their shots and showing the form that we hadn't seen in the first game but which we knew they had. They increased the lead again to 33-23, but then Goski and Novacek combined for the next six points on corner jump shots.

We hadn't seen that much zone defense during the season up until this point, especially the 1-3-1, but corner shots were there for the taking if you could get the ball there. Our biggest problem was stopping them at the other end of the court. Hobbie closed out the first half by making the first of two free throws, with John Zebrowski tapping in the missed second shot. Cranford led 36-29 at halftime.

Unfortunately, the intermission did nothing to change the course of the game as Cranford came out again playing up tempo and our defense wasn't doing enough to disrupt their rhythm. Mazzella liked playing at a helter-skelter pace, flying all over the court, while Hobbie played the role of assassin, working to get off his technically pure jump shot whenever he had the slightest opening. It was bad enough that those two were on their game, but making matter worse was that Pryor, who was missing in action during our first game, was seemingly omnipresent during this one, especially around the basket. He was both hurting us on the boards as well as knocking down shots from close range. Within a few minutes Cranford was breaking the game open and Horne signaled for a timeout. The scoreboard read 56-39. We managed to chip away at the lead by the end of the third period to make it 62-50, but we still weren't doing enough to slow Cranford's scoring down. Hobbie and Mazzella had eight points each in that quarter, while Pryor killed us with ten more of his own.

After the buzzer went off to signal the start of the fourth quarter, our five starters who had played the whole game instinctively went to the foul line to huddle one more time before our final push here. It was going to be now or never. In the 4th period we were clicking offensively with all five players contributing, but we were just matching baskets for the most part and Cranford was able to maintain the double-digit lead. With the score at 82-72., we finally made a run with just over a minute left. Novacek hit a short bank shot inside and then we got a steal that Goski was able to convert on a pull up jumper. We then forced another turnover at Cranford's end and Novacek was able to score again inside the lane on a short banker. But it was too little, too late as Cranford was able to inbound the ball, advance it, and run out the remaining seconds. The buzzer went off with the scoreboard reading 82-78. We walked off the court unbeaten no more.

The fans continued the celebrating that had already started before the final buzzer. As we left the court, I saw Goski take his sweatbands and throw them against the wall in disgust. Back in the locker room things were pretty quiet. I don't remember Horne's exact words, but he wasn't mad and didn't chew us out at all. He seemed surprisingly accepting of the loss, almost as if he felt our unbeaten status had been a bit of a burden and that getting rid of it might help us going forward. Besides that, it wasn't like we had played badly as much as Cranford had played an exceptional game, so perhaps Horne was just being pragmatic and taking the view that it was their night to shine.

Cranford had whipped us pretty good. The game was not as close as the final score might have suggested. A review of the stats shed light on what had just happened. They shot lights out at over 54 percent compared with the 22 percent egg they had laid in our gym, but we were right behind them at 52 percent. Cranford was only the second team to outrebound us all year, with a 30-25 advantage, pretty low numbers attributable to the high shooting percentage, but also to an effective zone defense that kept us spread out more and limited our offensive rebounding. Cranford also got to the foul line ten more times than we did, and we shot a lousy 6-for-14 from there which certainly didn't help our cause. We did take reasonable care of the ball with a 17-12 turnover advantage, but that simply was not enough. The bottom line was that we could not stop them from scoring, with their 82 points being 20 more than we had given up to any team all season. Offensively, we arguably had our best game as Novacek had put up a season-high 27 points and Goski added 21, and we were only one point away from everyone scoring in double figures, but Cranford trumped that with three of their players scoring 20 or more – Hobbie with 25, Mazzella with 20, and Pryor with an unexpected 23. We just found out what had made them the highest scoring team in the county.

While Horne may have been philosophical about the loss, that didn't make me feel any better about it. The less frequent the losses, the more they hurt. I somewhat tearfully apologized to Horne for what had happened earlier in the week, feeling like I should take responsibility for our less than perfect preparation, but he quickly replied: "It's ok, Steve. We'll be ok."

After we got off the bus back at our gym, Scott and I talked about going over to Weldon's party. The idea of us showing up at a party wasn't nearly as appealing as it was a few hours earlier. We drove over there as we mulled it over, and once there we sat in the car another five minutes debating whether to go inside. Scott, being philosophical, reasoned that we should go in: "Hey, it's not like we lost a war." I knew he was right, and he certainly had nothing to be ashamed of with his results. I just didn't want to be the focus of anyone's attention in that moment, but I also knew that you couldn't stop living just because you lost a game. We went inside and made the best of it, hoping it would help put the loss behind us.

The next morning, I got further confirmation that the world had not ended. At the Washington School clinic where our team helped out Saturday mornings, no one looked at us or acted any differently. It was naïve to even think that they might.

By Monday the sting of our first loss had started to abate from the passage of time alone. Having to go to class helped even more as you have no choice but to focus on other things. But most of all, unless your season is over, there is always a next game to prepare for, leaving you no real choice but to put the last one behind you. Going to practice was great therapy.

Rather than *thinking* about all the things that went wrong or what you could have done better in the last game, it felt a lot better to be out on the court actually playing.

Horne was also in no mood to revisit the Cranford loss any further. We never watched any film of that game even though we often did have film sessions. There was always a lot of mistakes that Horne could point out during those sessions, and there were always a few plays that we looked forward to seeing replays of or got good laughs from, like a Simmons jump shot off the side of the backboard, or the "Nova Shuffle," or Goski expressing his displeasure after a run by the other team. No, mercifully there would be no rewatching of Hobbie drilling jump shots or Mazzella stealing lazy passes.

This week had us scheduled to play Berkeley Heights, an easy one, and then Linden, a tough one by any measure. They were both home games, our last two home games of the season, with only county and state tournament games to follow.

February 8, 1972

Berkeley Heights had the misfortune of having to play us right after our first loss of the season. We had methodically taken them apart in our first game, particularly with stifling defense and overwhelming rebounding. We were chomping at the bit to get back into the win column and punish whoever we were facing. While no one was talking about rankings at this point, we were anxious to get back on the winning track. As it turned out, the Star-Ledger had indeed taken us out of the top spot down to #5. We couldn't wait to get back out onto the court and start working our way back up.

We got off to a fast start with a 10-0 run after they scored on the opening possession. We continued to throttle them the remainder of the first period as we played textbook basketball, smothering them on the defensive end and moving the ball well on the offensive end. We led by 23-8 after the first eight minutes with Goski leading the way with eight points. The lead remained 15 at halftime before we again widened the lead in the third period, stretching it to 25 points. Just like in the first game, we were overwhelming them on the boards at both ends of the court, ultimately winning that battle by 48-27. We also shot the ball well all game, hitting 48 percent of our field goal attempts. However, we were very sloppy with the ball, especially in the last period. Instead of pulling away down the stretch, Berkeley gained ground that last period to make the final score 71-54. The stat sheet showed we had an embarrassing 31 turnovers, 16 of them on bad passes. Unfortunately, Horne would make us watch film of this game and all those bad passes.

With the regular season winding down, the anticipation of the Union County Tournament, which was scheduled to start the following week, was beginning to build with the seedings still yet to be announced. Union County was loaded this year, with Westfield, Jefferson, and Roselle all highly rated with only one loss each so far, two of them being to each other. There was also Cranford, Linden, Roselle Catholic and St. Patrick in the mix. A No. 1 seeding would be particularly important in this year's tournament as the Nos. 2 and 3 teams might have to beat two of the teams with only one loss to win the title. We were hoping that our loss to Cranford hadn't cost us the top seed that we otherwise would have had locked up. We were also looking forward to a potential rematch with Jefferson to prove that our first win over them was not a fluke. I'm quite certain Jefferson was looking forward to that too. On Thursday the seedings were announced and we got the good news we had hoped for: Westfield - 1, Jefferson – 2, Roselle – 3, Cranford – 4, Linden – 5, Roselle Catholic – 6, St. Patrick – 7, Holy Trinity – 8. But that was next week's business. In the meantime, we had a date with Linden on Friday night.

Having played Linden a lot since the eighth grade, we were quite familiar with them. Pfeiffer and I had had some success against them during our junior high years, but they still had gotten the better of us overall, especially the last two years. During our JV season Linden had spoiled our surprise run to the finals of the Union County tournament by beating us by about 10 to win the whole thing, and then beaten us twice more during our junior year. In one of those games, they had whupped us 104-71 at their place, giving their fans the 100-point thrill that Horne had denied us against Rahway this season. Linden had lost good players to graduation, but they still had tough, quick guards in Eddie Ciemniecki, who was also one of the top sprinters in the state, and Freddie Short. Their front line consisted of Tom Woytowicz, Al Mehalik, and Mike LaPrete, who was a rising star and their only non-senior starter. We knew all these guys to some degree from either in season games, playground games, summer camps, or summer leagues. Linden entered the game with a 14-5 record, but that was deceiving as three of those losses had been to Jefferson and another one to Cranford. We knew it would take everything we had to beat them.

February 11, 1972

The fans filled the gym for what would be our fourth and final Friday night home game of the season. While we boasted an impressive 16-1 record coming into the game, we knew the visitors would present a serious challenge on this night. It didn't get any better than this for the hometown fans.

The game was nip and tuck throughout and neither team could sustain a lead of any size. Linden led throughout most of the first period which ended at 21-18 in their favor. It stayed close through the second period, although things didn't look too good when Goski picked up his third foul only two minutes into that period. He would sit the rest of the half, but we didn't skip a beat as our bench helped us match Linden basket for basket. We were down 29-28 when we scored five straight to take a 33-29 lead, but then Linden closed out the half with three straight field goals to lead 35-33 at halftime.

The second half was a see-saw affair that would bring about a few mini runs and more lead changes along with them. We jumped out first on a 12-4 run with Goski back in the game, putting us in front 45-39. We still clung to a 47-44 lead when the third quarter ended. After we scored the first point of the last quarter, Linden then went on an 8-1 run, which gave them the lead at 52-49. We stopped the bleeding when I caught a pass underneath and put it in, and then we recaptured the lead when Pfeiffer came up with a steal and then fed Goski who hit a short jumper to make it 53-52. Linden then tied it once again with a single free throw. With just over two minutes to go, Goski was fouled while shooting. He hit the first but missed the second. We managed to stop Linden on the next possession and then went into our delay game offense, clinging to a one-point lead while trying to run the clock down.

Linden finally fouled me with 59 seconds to go. I knocked down the first shot but missed the bonus attempt. Fortunately, Jester came up huge by grabbing the offensive rebound and putting it right back up and in for a 57-53 lead. On the next possession, we fouled Ciemniecki intentionally with 36 seconds left as they were not shooting one and one yet. Ciemniecki made the sole free throw to make our lead 57-54. We attempted to stall but turned it over with a travelling violation, only to have Linden capitalize on the turnover with a jumper by LaPrete with 27 seconds left to cut our lead to one again. Our next attempt at playing keep away turned out much better as we were able to run the clock down to two seconds left when Novacek was finally fouled. For the third straight trip to the foul line, we only managed to convert only the first of two shots. But it still proved to be enough, as Linden's desperation heave from half court fell short and sealed a hard fought 58-56 win for us.

We all knew we were fortunate to come away with a W. The stat sheet bore out how close this one was, with 16 lead changes perhaps being the best indicator of all. We did have a slight edge in rebounding and turnovers, but the biggest difference was that we went to line 22 times compared with their 15, making two more free throws than they did, which proved to be the difference. Once again, our balance served us well with Goski scoring 15, Novacek 12, and Pfeiffer and me adding 11 each, while Novacek and Simmons also grabbed 15 and 14 rebounds, respectively.

We breathed a sigh of relief when we left the gym that night. Our home season was now over. We were now 9-0 in our gym and it was going to stay that way. Unfortunately, you don't win any titles for great home records. To achieve our goals, we would have to win the rest of our games on the road.

We still had one regular season game remaining against Hillside, but that wouldn't happen until after the Union County Tournament, or "UCT," which was slated to start in five days on the following Wednesday. The UCT was a tournament we all looked forward to and indeed a tough one to win. The winner would have to best 15 of the other strongest teams from Union County, traditionally one of the strongest counties in New Jersey. The UCT had been played 35 consecutive years, with Jefferson leading the way with 8 titles over that span. Westfield had done reasonably well over that period with three UCT titles, all in the past 13 years, with the last one coming in 1965 when my brother Tom's team, along with Bob Felter, Jerry Richards & company, pulled off a big upset of Cranford in the finals.

We had gotten the No. 1 seed we had hoped for, which pitted us against 16th-seeded Kenilworth in Wednesday's first game. If we got by that, we would then face the winner of the first-round matchup between No. 8 Holy Trinity and No. 9 Hillside. It was hard for us not to get excited about a potential second-round game against our much smaller intra-town neighbor Holy Trinity. Holy Trinity should have no business beating a much larger Westfield as that would be like a filly taking on the colts in the Kentucky Derby and beating them. But Holy Trinity did exactly that two years earlier. Holy Trinity came into our gym and whupped our varsity team 77-67, primarily on the strength of super sophomore Joe Cullinan who poured in 32 points that night, along with help from fellow sophomore Jack Steimel who contributed 13. There was even another Goski in Holy Trinity's lineup that night, John Goski, who scored 7. But now John's kid brother Tim had jumped ship to try to make his mark at the much bigger school just down the street from the little Catholic school. Goski would love the chance to prove himself against his old school and would-be teammates that he had left behind two years earlier. In fact, Tim later admitted that he left Holy Trinity to escape the shadow of Joe Cullinan and improve his own chances to play and realize his potential. Quite frankly, we were all looking forward to that chance to show Cullinan and company who the better Westfield team really was.

But first things first. We had to take care of business with Kenilworth in round 1. By all accounts Kenilworth had one very good player in 6-foot-3 junior Tom Lavan, but only had a 9-12 record against weaker opposition that we had faced this season. We would have no business losing to these guys. With 18 games under our belt, we were still exhibiting great depth in addition to our 17-1 record. We had four players who had been the high scorers in at least one of our previous games, with Goski and Novacek each averaging about 15, Pfeiffer more than 11, myself right at 10, and Simmons at 7 ppg. We still had to play the game and get it done on the court, however. Winning on paper counts for nothing.

February 16, 1972

The tournament organizers put together a nice program with pictures, rosters and feature articles about a few of the teams and coaches in the tournament. Unfortunately for me, the photographer who took all the team photos had come to our school the day I had gotten hurt in gym class and left school early. I guess that's called adding insult to injury. Goski was now getting a little more ink at this point in the season, and he was one of the individual players highlighted in the tournament program. After a somewhat slow start when Tim had averaged a more modest 13 points a game the first nine games of the season, the last nine games he had increased his output to 18 ppg. After failing to be our high scorer in any of our first five games, he had now led us in scoring in nine of our last thirteen games.

The game against Kenilworth took place in Hillside's gym, with big bleachers along one side and a wall immediately behind each bench. Kenilworth started out strong and managed a 9-8 lead part way through the first period, but then we went into a full court press which began to rattle them. Kenilworth was missing one of their starting guards due to illness, so our press was all the more effective. We scored 12 straight to end the first quarter with a 20-9 lead. Still, Kenilworth battled throughout the second period to keep the game reasonably close at halftime with a score of 41-28.

Then in the second half we finally overwhelmed Kenilworth with a 22-8 blitz that put the game away. We were moving the ball well and everybody was contributing. The final scoreboard showed WHS winning by an 81-48 margin, and while Goski had an off night with only six points, we had four other players in double figures, including Mike Cooney with 10 points. Jester also added seven points off the bench. We had our usual rebounding advantage (29-15) and turnover advantage (28-16) to help make the difference. Lavan had a very respectable 29 points for Kenilworth, but he obviously needed more help. We got back on the bus that night with an 18-1, and now waited to see whom we would play on Saturday.

Holy Trinity did not get the job done against Hillside, so the matchup we had hoped for would not happen. We would have to shift our focus to Hillside for round two on Saturday afternoon in Clark. We beat them early in the season by 24 at home, but Hillside had talent and they had now had two wins over Scotch Plains and a win over Cranford, so this game would be no gimme.

On Friday, the day before the Hillside game, we got more news that was going to make the game even tougher. Something had happened the day before that got Cooney and Novacek suspended for one day which was also making them ineligible for Saturday's game. In fact, they weren't at school Friday when we all learned of the incident as they were already serving their suspension. The rest of the players were only given spotty information about what had happened.

It was only later that we would hear more details from Mike and Scott and their stories were very consistent. Essentially, they left school to go home for lunch. What made it worse was that Mike's parents were away and he had driven their VW to school despite not having a driver's license. Scott was hitching a ride with Mike even though Scott's house was just a few short blocks away. Ironically, everything probably would have been fine except for the actions of the third person in the car, Bob Swab. According to both Mike and Scott, a cop was coming in the other direction and Swab, who was sitting in the back seat, ducked to avoid detection. Instead, the opposite happened and the cop turned around to pursue the runaway lunchers. Mike was able to temporarily get away from the cop, at which point Scott jumped out of the car and ran into someone's back yard to escape detection. He waited a bit in a patch of woods and then finally reemerged, but unfortunately the cop had not given up and was there to nab him. Still, Scott thought everything was fine when the cop asked him for his name and then dropped him back off at the high school. In Scott's words, "I thought it was all good because I frequently went home for lunch. Big deal. I did nothing wrong." Unfortunately, the school didn't see it the same way. The next morning both he and Mike were summoned to Principal Bobal's office to face the music for leaving school grounds without permission – a one day, and more importantly, a one *game* suspension.

Horne gave us the official word at practice on Friday and started to prepare accordingly for the next day's game. Jester would start in Novacek's place, and Steve Lee would be the first guard off the bench in place of Cooney. Jester had already been seeing a lot of action and we had no doubt that he was up to the task, and while Cooney had generally been the first guard off the bench, the fight for that third spot had been very competitive all season. Cooney might have had a slight edge on the offensive end, with a bit more size and maybe a little better jump shot, but Lee (aka "Rat") was quicker and the better defender. There were several heated battles between the two during practices, which one day boiled over to the point where Horne threw them both out of practice. You could hear the scuffling still going on in the locker room hallway until (Football) Coach Pete Lima jumped in to diffuse the situation. Lee had played well in the minutes he had gotten this year, so perhaps this was the break that he needed.

February 19, 1972

We were to be at the gym at 12:30 for 15 minutes of foul shooting before we would board the bus at 1 pm for the short ride over to Clark, the neutral site for our game against Hillside. Our foul shooting had been a weak link for us and was something that might make or break us in any tight game over the remainder of the season. Horne had devoted time virtually every single practice for foul shooting, but we didn't have much to show for it, at least in terms of our overall shooting percentage which now stood at just a shade over 62 percent during games. I don't know what percentage might have been in practice, but there could be no denying that it needed to be higher. In previous years my brothers had put our foul shooting to shame, at least during practices. My older brother Tom held what I suspect is still the gym record of 106 made free throws in a row, while Mark wasn't too bad himself, three times having streaks of 50 or higher during practices.

Scott and Mike joined the rest of us on board the bus, minus their uniforms and sneakers. When we all got up to de-board the bus in Clark a few minutes later, Goski, who had been sitting right behind Cooney and Novacek, directed a barb right at them: "Players off first! Suspended pussies off second!" He didn't just blurt it out, but rather he said it with a scowl and condescending tone while looking down at his still seated teammates. It immediately reminded me a bit of the famous fight scene with Cassius Clay looking down on and scowling at a knocked-out Sonny Liston. The comment was uniquely Goski, both in the language used and the manner in which it was delivered. It was both funny and puzzling at the same time. What motive could Tim have in publicly scolding and embarrassing his teammates for their actions? I guess it was just Tim showing how he was annoyed at Mike and Scott letting the team down. Novacek, who by almost any measure had been our most consistent and valuable player thus far, looked like a scolded puppy as he remained seated in the bus seat, absolutely speechless. Scott was always quick with a quip or a good comeback line, but not in this case. There was nothing he could say that would help the situation. Mike and Scott probably didn't deserve it...besides, none of us were saints to be perfectly honest ... but Goski certainly put his own stamp on the whole situation.

We would start this game in a 1-3-1 zone defense. We had played the 1-3-1 on occasion in various games, but never started in it. Presumably Horne was concerned about us getting into foul trouble while already starting the game without two of our top players, and Horne knew that Paul Yungst and Paul Lossef were solid players capable of getting us into foul trouble if we got sloppy. But that strategy could backfire as well, with less pressure on the ball and more time for Hillside to seek a good shot. Hillside took advantage early and took an 11-5 lead. Then we got going with 11 straight points, including five by Goski, to close out the first quarter with a 16-11 lead. Hillside fought back in the second period with six straight to tie it at 18 all, and then it was nip and tuck the rest of the second quarter until Lee hit a jumper to close at the half to give us a 28-26 lead.

At halftime Horne decided we needed to ramp up the pressure and go to full court man-to-man defense. Hillside was getting too many easy uncontested shots and had hardly any turnovers in the first half. The strategy worked as the pace of the game picked up. Goski again led the way in the period with 10 points as we outscored them 21-12 and finally forced a few turnovers. Simmons and Jester were also controlling the boards on their missed shots. Still, we were not able to pull away from Hillside in the fourth but played well enough to win by a 65-56 margin. Goski finished with 18 points while Jester scored 15 points on 6-for-8 shooting. Pfeiffer and Simmons also had 11 and 10 points, respectively.

All in all, we had played well enough to get the W, and left Clark's gym with a 19-1 record and a semi-final date with the winner of the Linden and Cranford game. Cooney and Novacek breathed a sigh of relief knowing that their suspension didn't cost us the game. Unfortunately for them, however, they weren't spared a lecture from Tim's dad Sig during the game, so they got two Goski scoldings for the price of one! Like son, like father, I suppose.

Linden, the fifth seed, would be our next opponent in the UCT semis as they had knocked off fourth-seeded Cranford 65-49. Meanwhile, Jefferson and Roselle were to face off in the other semifinal game as expected. This week was also our mid-winter break, meaning no school all week, or at least no classes. Basketball heaven once again, hoops without the burden of going to classes or doing homework.

Cooney and Novacek couldn't wait to get back out on the court in practice and get their suspensions completely behind them. They wouldn't have to take any more crap from Goski now, at least not without responding in kind. While Tim wasn't shy about speaking his mind, Scott knew how to respond, between his unorthodox but effective play on the court and his short but witty retorts. One minute we'd be battling intensely and the next you'd have Tim or BJ cracking up for something Scott said under his breath. Boys will be boys, after all. It was Horne's job to figure out how much to roll with and how much to punish. The past few games it seemed like the suicides were being doled out at a higher rate, our 19-1 record be damned.

We were to play Linden on Wednesday afternoon. There would be no surprises at this point of the season – we knew them and they knew us. Our first game with them just 12 days earlier had been a dog fight, in our gym no less, and could have gone either way. The stakes were even higher now. We would need to play better if we wanted to get to that rematch with Jefferson.

February 23, 1972

The Linden game was another afternoon game in nearby Clark. Fans showed up in big numbers despite it being an away game for both teams, being a weekday afternoon game, and taking place when the schools had no classes all week. The people who showed up were real basketball fans who knew the importance of this game for each team. Of course, some were just loyal students who wanted to be there to support their classmates on the court. Besides, by Wednesday afternoon they had probably run out of things to do during their week off from classes.

The number of fans in the stands didn't matter, though. What mattered was which team got it done on the court. We got off to a great start for a change and jumped out to a quick 9-0 lead following two Novacek jumpers from the left baseline and one from the right. Linden started in a zone and thus far our shots were falling. Linden called timeout to stop the bleeding. I remember feeling a little sorry for them as I walked past them back to our bench. Not a very smart thing to do for a team as good as Linden. They finally broke the ice with a just over four minutes left, but then we traded baskets until the end of the quarter when we still held on to a 15-9 lead.

In the second quarter we stretched the lead to 18-9 before Linden went on a 9-1 run with four of their guys hitting field goals in that stretch while we only managed a single foul shot. Suddenly our lead was gone, and the game started to take on the same tone as our previous battle with them. During that stretch, Linden's Mike LaPrete went down with a leg or ankle injury that seemed pretty severe. The game was stopped for several minutes as they tended to him an eventually helped him off the court. It looked like a possible broken leg ... in any event, there was no way he was returning to this game. So even while our lead had dissipated, we had gained a personnel advantage going forward.

We finished out the half clinging to a 25-22 lead. After a quick exchange of baskets to open the second half, Linden scored six straight to take the lead for the first time at 30-27, spurred on by Freddie Short's steal and driving layup during that stretch. We responded in kind with a 7-0 run to take the lead back at 34-30 on field goals by Goski, Pfeiffer and me, along with a Pfeiffer free throw. During our run the speedy Eddie Ciemniecki went down with what appeared to be a head injury, apparently banging his head against the floor after a loose ball scramble. He was also helped off the floor and back into the Linden locker room. Meanwhile, his teammates kept clawing away until they tied the score at 39 all. Pfeiffer then gave us the lead again on the last basket of the third quarter.

Ciemniecki made a surprisingly quick return to the court for the start of the fourth period. The concussion protocols weren't quite as strict in those days, if they existed at all, so as soon as the cobwebs had cleared, Ciemniecki was back out on the floor. Linden then seized the lead right back at 42-41 when Mehalik made one free throw and then Woytowicz grabbed the missed second shot and put it right back in. Horne then called timeout and it paid off as we came back with a press that caught them off guard and another mini run of six straight points. Novacek knocked down a 15-footer and made a driving layup, and Pfeiffer caught a nice feed from Goski underneath and laid it in to give us the biggest lead of the second half, 47-42.

But Linden refused to buckle. Woytowicz knocked in a 10-footer, and after a missed free throw by LaPrete's replacement Joe Kuchar, Mehalik made a driving layup to make it 47-46. I drew a charge on Mehalik on the play, but his basket still counted. I managed to knock down both ends of the one and one at the other end to make our lead 49-46.

Then we got sloppy at the worst possible time. First, we committed a travelling violation, which Freddie Short followed up with two free throws to narrow our lead to one point. The next time down court, still trying to penetrate Linden's formidable zone, we forced the ball again trying to dribble through it and were called for walking again. Linden responded with another Woytowicz basket inside after a nice feed from Mehalik, giving them their third lead of the game at 50-49 with just over two and a half minutes left. The next time down we were more patient and worked the ball around for a good shot. Finally, with 1:45 left I rose up from just above the right side of the foul lane for a nice wide-open 17-footer. In my peripheral vision, I saw Novacek open in the lane about ten feet in front of me, and at the last second, I aborted the jump shot in favor of dumping down to Scott for a shot in close. Immediately I wished I could take it back, as Scott had already started spinning away from me to get into rebounding position while Ciemniecki darted into the lane to snatch the misguided pass. Eddie may have intercepted it even if Scott hadn't turned away.

Linden now had the ball and the lead and was attempting to just run the clock out. They were succeeding until we fouled Kuchar with 53 seconds left. Kuchar missed the one and one attempt, but then when the ball caromed hard off the back of the rim, Kuchar grabbed his own miss in the lane and then rose right back up to bank it in. 52-49. That was a killer, the second put-back after a missed foul shot that quarter! We came back down and worked the ball around until Simmons was able to take and make a short jumper to pull us back with one point and now just 22 seconds left. As soon as they got the ball inbounds we had to foul, but it still took seven seconds off the clock. Short would shoot the one and one shot and he was already 5-for-5 this game. The darn kid knocked 'em both down again. 54-51. Without a three-point line to save us, we rushed the ball downcourt, but one missed shot and a Linden rebound sealed our fate. Our desperation foul with only two seconds left only delayed the inevitable for a few more seconds.

We left the court stunned. It had all gone wrong so quickly. We had been leading for the entire game except for maybe three minutes and change. Then three straight turnovers in the last three minutes killed us, not to mention failing to box out the foul shooter in that critical last minute. I felt terrible about my bad pass down the stretch. If I had just taken and made that open 17-foot jumper, we'd have had the lead again and it could have ended the way it should have. Instead, we walked back into the locker room defeated.

It only got worse from there. It would not be the same Coach Horne who consoled us after our first loss against Cranford. Instead, he ripped into us as soon as we got back there. He didn't mince any words either. Horne was not one to use any curse words in the course of our practices or other team gatherings, but on this day he broke from that practice in a big way. He berated us for not playing the right way, for playing selfishly, for trying to dribble through their zone, for failing to box out on foul shots. He minced no words and said we got what we deserved and that our practice habits finally caught up with us. He specifically excluded Pfeiffer from his criticism as Tom had played an exceptional game with 18 points and without some of the critical errors that sunk us, but the rest of us weren't spared any criticism whatsoever. It only compounded the miserable feeling

I had when entering the locker room a few minutes earlier. Horne ended his tirade by announcing that practice would be at 10 the next morning. The locker room then became very quiet and somber as we showered and dressed to get out of there as quickly as possible.

There's nothing like a crushing loss to ruin what is normally one of the best weeks of the year – namely, a week off from school during the school year. How could I even think about enjoying something else? I felt like we had just blown the whole season. That all the big wins we had achieved up to this point were now just going by the wayside. We really hadn't achieved anything. When my father returned from his daily commute to Manhattan, I had to give him the bad news. I slumped down in our living room chair as I tearfully delivered the news, wallowing in self-pity as I could barely stand to think about or talk about what had happened just three hours earlier.

A few minutes later I got a telephone call from Peter Demarest, a classmate that I knew pretty well but didn't hang out with much at all. He was having a couple of other guys over to his house that night and invited me to join them. The thought of socializing with anyone that night wasn't that appealing, but then I quickly realized the alternative would likely be worse. I decided that anything that could prevent me from reliving today's game over and over again would be worth it. I accepted the invitation.

I drove over to Peter's house right after dinner. I was only halfway through his front door when he asks in a somewhat disbelieving tone: "I heard you guys lost today? What happened?" I shamefully acknowledged it and then tried to switch the topic as quickly as possible. Demarest was a captain of Westfield's always stellar swim team, and we were joined that evening by Dave Johnson and Jed Beardsley, a couple of guys who played on the golf team who I had known since junior high. Not exactly basketball types or guys that I would normally hang around with, but on this particular night that all suited me just fine. Anything to keep me from thinking about basketball. It turned out that the activity of the evening would be roulette, and for money, no less. I don't remember who played the role of the bank … all I remember is that I cleaned up to the tune of five dollars and thirty-eight cents. More importantly was that over those next couple of hours I was able to completely block out our basketball loss while getting fully immersed in a game of roulette with guys I had never really hung out with before. I even went so far as to laugh and enjoy myself.

As I was leaving that night around 11 o'clock, I remember how surprised I was that I was somehow able to enjoy myself while another part of my brain was telling me I should still feel miserable. I wasn't sure how it was even possible that I could be laughing after the terrible thing that had happened just a few hours earlier. Then I remembered the ending of *It's a Mad, Mad, Mad, Mad World* when Spencer Tracy, after having lost everything in his life of any value, said he only hoped he could find something to laugh at over the next 10 or 20 years, and then moments later he does a big belly laugh when Ethel Merman storms in and slips on a banana peel. That scene seemed similar to what I was going through at the moment. Maybe the body is always looking for some natural therapy to help itself heal. Bewildered though I was, I was thankful for those good therapeutic feelings that had engulfed me that evening. As evidenced here, I would never forget that brief evening out for the rest of my life.

I retired to bed shortly after returning home that night. As I laid in bed one part of my brain struggled to retain the happy feelings that arose from the ashes at Pete Demarest's house. Another part tried to pull me back to reality and to snuff out those good feelings. I suppose in the end it was a bit of a stalemate, or perhaps a compromise of sorts. I would put off reality for a few more hours and drift off to sleep somewhat at peace with myself and the world. Tomorrow I would face the music.

XI.   The Parent Trap

Every parent wants the best for their kid. We all know it. We've all seen it when it comes to sports. It manifests itself in any of three ways. First, the parents might cheer on their kids from the sidelines. Second, they might play the role of coach of their kid's team. Third, they might tell the coach of their kid's team how the coach is underutilizing their kid to the detriment of both the kid and the team.

It's unfortunate because basketball is such a simple game that doesn't need the conflicts that parents bring to the table. Nowhere is this clearer on the playground or down at the local Y where pickup basketball games are played with great regularity. The playground or the local Y is the last place you'd see a parent hang out to watch their kid play hoops. Kids certainly don't need any hand holding in these places…what they really need is some good ball handling. What's so great about hoops games played at these venues is that you don't need a parent, or anyone for that matter, to weigh in on who's playing well and who isn't. These games are self-grading tests. When the game is over, you don't need an outsider to come in and interpret what just happened. It's already known without any words being spoken.

It's unrealistic, though, to think that games played at playgrounds, YMCAs, or someone's driveway could ever be sufficient. Parents want more opportunity for their kids, so they create more games that they can be a part of. If conflicts of interest arise as a result, so be it. The parent-coach is the classic example of a conflict of interest, but don't hold your breath waiting for a parent-coach to recuse themselves before a big game because of that conflict.

It's hard to blame any parent for this. They've created youth recreation leagues, in this case youth basketball leagues, so their kids could have organized games where they could further develop their skills under the watchful eyes of their parents. Of course, organized youth leagues don't run by themselves. They need volunteers to get them organized and to help them function properly. Since parents are the ones with the greatest vested interest in their kids' development, they are invariably the volunteers that these youth leagues ultimately get and depend on.

Volunteers aren't needed to just organize the leagues. They are needed to play the role of coaches. They need people to teach the kids how to play, and how to play the right way. So, the first order of business is to find coaches. The next is to find coaches who actually know how to play the right way. It's a bonus if your league or your team can find the latter. Yet even if they are so lucky, it's more likely than not that it will be a parental coach with the aforementioned conflict of interest. That coach now has to figure out how to coach his kid relative to the other kids so as not show any favoritism or bias that might draw attention or, worse still, get under the skin of any of the other parents with a kid on the team. That's been proven to be a nearly impossible task.

It's not such a big deal when the kids are still in grammar school and the leagues are less competitive. At this stage most parents just want their kids to get a taste of the sport and a chance to run around with their friends for an hour. Unfortunately, things start to get very competitive once they get out of grammar school ... sometimes even before that. Nowhere is this more evident than in AAU basketball. I've seen it firsthand with my daughter's teams between the ages of 10 and 17. I don't know if it starts any younger than that, but it wouldn't surprise me if it did. I'm pretty sure the parental issues are more or less the same on the boy's side as well.

Making matters worse is that the stakes are higher with AAU basketball. It's where developing kids can find the best competition in their formative years, providing the best path for kids to make their high school teams and excel on them. It's also where college recruiters spend a lot of time doing their scouting and de facto recruiting since AAU basketball provides a platform for kids to compete against others outside their school conferences, thereby allowing for a more comprehensive evaluation of talent than local high school competition alone can provide. So, it's no exaggeration to say that college scholarships may be on the line with many of these AAU tournaments and games. There's also lots of time, travel and expense involved to allow their kids to participate on AAU teams. Parents may have to give up entire weekends, drive several hours, and spend money on hotel rooms to allow their kids to be part of tournaments that take place all over the country.

Given the investments that parents make in their kids and the potential returns on those investments, it's understandable that parents want to ensure that their kids get a fair shake. That's all the more reason that these teams will end up with parent-coaches rather than independent coaches. For every team that has one, that's two less parents that have to worry about their kid getting a fair shake. But it also means that the team may or may not have a coach that knows the game well and who will do right by all the kids on the team. The lucky ones will get a coach that has plenty of basketball experience, and hopefully not just experience gained on the family room couch in front of the TV. The even luckier ones will get one that have the desired hoops experience and can also treat all the kids as if they were their own. The luckiest of all will get a coach without their own kid on the team at all. This almost assuredly means that the coach knows hoops and enjoys coaching for coaching's sake since he lacks the inherent bias that all parental coaches bring to the table despite their best intentions.

I got my own dose of parental coaching in the 1993-94 season. I had volunteered to coach a 13-year-old travel team in the neighboring township, and I even knew the guy running the whole thing. I had some competition though. Another parent also wanted the spot, and his kid was arguably the best player in this age group at the time, while my son David was borderline to make this team. First, I found out that I lost out on the coaching spot. Then a few days later, my son became the last cut on the team, which obviously would not have happened had I gotten the coaching nod.

Then something strange happened. While I was still smarting from the double snub, the league organizer had the audacity to ask me if would coach the 12-year-old travel team that was loaded with talent but currently lacking a coach and desperately in need of one. Not only was I not in the right frame of mind to consider such a request, but I was also in my second year of a demanding job in midtown Manhattan, 70 miles away from my home in Bucks County, PA, which required an hour and 45-minute commute each day each way … and those were on the easy days when I wasn't flying somewhere halfway across the country. This team was to play in two competitive leagues, that included night games during the week, and there would be practices to organize and run as well.

It was hard to justify the time that would be required for such a commitment, and I had every excuse I needed to decline the offer. But something was pulling me in the other direction. Subconsciously I was putting value on what the kids and their parents would get out of it – i.e., an unbiased, non-parental coach with lots of basketball experience. I suppose something in the back of my brain was telling me that for once in my life I should be a *real* coach, and not just a nominal one who had to be there anyway because I had a kid on the team. It would be a real sacrifice, and almost certainly one that I would only make once in my life. I accepted the offer and became a coach to 10 kids I had never seen or heard of before.

Over the next four months I gave it everything I had. We would play 34 games and have 16 practices. I had to secure a nice nearby church gym to augment the meager amount of practice time that the township itself had secured for each team playing within its borders. Schmoozing was not something I was good at or liked, but I did what I needed to do in this case for the benefit of our team. The parents were for the most part very appreciative, realizing the good fortune that had come their way for the benefit of their kids. After all, who were the parents to second guess me? I'm sure the word got around of my basketball resume, including that I had played college ball for Jimmy V. The net result was that they had all managed to avoid the parent trap waiting to snag one or more of them.

The league organizer who had recruited me had not misled me when he said the team was loaded. It was hard for me to know for sure as these were just seventh graders who were still growing quickly and weren't physically mature yet by any means. We even had one kid who was playing up in age and more than holding his own against the rest of the kids on our team. But the kids clearly had basketball skills and athleticism, and it showed over the course of the season as they compiled a strong record against good competition within the region. We managed to beat a couple of the stronger teams we would face all year, but also lost a couple of close ones along the way too. With only ten kids on our roster, I had to push all the parents to get their kids to all of our practices so we could go 5-on-5 for portions of them. I ended up being the 10th player out of necessity in several practices, but I did what I needed to do. When it was all said and done, everybody learned something and experienced the ups and downs associated with any season. We concluded with a barbeque at our house with parents and kids to mark the official end to our unlikely yet rewarding journey together.

I suppose it wasn't until five years later when I realized how talented my group of kids was. Matt Verbit, the sixth grader who played up for our team, was now starting for Council Rock High School in Newtown, PA, as a junior. Scott Hausknecht was their sixth man and had become a nice 3-point shooter, while Scott Kernan and Brian Townsend were also on that Council Rock squad and got material minutes. Kevin Wise, whose father had been my assistant coach, had become a starting guard at Notre Dame High School in Lawrenceville, NJ, where my daughter would later play. Grant Holdren, who was our big guy five years earlier, was the starting center for Holy Ghost Prep in Bensalem, PA, a perennial force in Eastern PA high school hoops. Those were the just the ones that I was aware of...it's very possible that others were exceling somewhere as well.

As trying as it may have been, I never regretted the commitment I made that winter, or the time spent fulfilling it. Sometimes we are just too busy with our daily routines to even think about helping others, but the experience proved to me that it can indeed be very rewarding. I once heard a saying that the best way to forget about your own problems is to help someone else with theirs. My small contribution to those 10 boys did nothing to dispel that notion. Perhaps my reward for that was that five years later my middle daughter Jackie would have the opportunity to play on a very competitive AAU team that was also being coached by a non-parental coach with lots of relevant basketball experience. In other words, another parent trap avoided.

As I watched each of my kids go through their own youth league experiences from one season to the next, there was one thought that kept coming back into my head. It was the thought of how lucky I had been to avoid a parental coach throughout my junior high and high school years, and to avoid the whole AAU scene entirely. Instead, I had had Gumbert, where you could learn to play the game while parents, if they were there at all, would stand off to the side and merely watch. None were needed to coach. None were needed to referee. None were needed to organize the games.

For better or worse, it's almost impossible for any kid to play organized hoops today without parents being involved. This means that kids will often be coached by the parent of a teammate, and depending on the circumstances, this may end up being a blessing or a curse. The parent coach, biased though he or she may be, is simply trying to do right by their child, so it's hard to fault either their participation or their presence. Still, at the end of the day, basketball comes down to 10 players, four lines, two baskets and a ball, and parents can't step inside those four lines. Only players get to do that. That rectangular court inside those lines is a safe zone, relatively free from the impact that parents might bring one way or another. Parents can only take their kids so far, but that's the way it should be. After all, basketball is a kid's game, so it's only fitting that parents be relegated to the sidelines once the opening tip goes up. Kids are quite capable of doing the rest.

XII. Redemption (Feb 24 – Mar 15, 1972)

"Now Jefferson was waiting, it was our day of reckoning;
The loser would go home for good, the winner would be king."

from *A Team to Remember*, November 18, 2000

I got up about 8:30 on Thursday morning. Normally I would be in homeroom at this time, getting ready to kick off another day at school. But there was no school today or all week, for that matter, and I got to sleep in. I had my customary two bowls of Kellogg's Frosted Flakes and then after moping around a bit proceeded to get dressed and get my stuff together. It was time to face the music.

I left the house about 9:30 and drove over to the high school. After getting my gear on and sneakers laced up, I left the locker room toward the sound of the bouncing balls. Our team managers – Mike King, Brad Chazottte, and Paul Leifer – would consistently get there early so that the basketball rack with a dozen balls would be waiting near center court when the first player arrived on the scene. I walked over to the rack and grabbed one. Despite the painful loss of the prior day, the ball felt good in my hands. The leather pressed up against the palm of my hands felt familiar. It felt natural. Nobody was talking but you could hear the subtle squeaks of sneakers starting to permeate the air as the clock inched towards 10 am. The sound of bouncing balls began to become more pronounced, and then a voice finally cracked the air, and then a little chatter, almost as if we hadn't blown our season the day before. Maybe this was just the calm before the storm. Our 6-foot-5 head coach was the last to take the court, with whistle around his neck and clipboard in hand. Then the clock struck ten and the whistle blew.

"Everyone on the baseline," Horne said in his normal commanding tone. "Have a seat." This was unusual. We had never started out a practice this way. Horne then apologized for his profanity-laced tirade the previous afternoon ... the profanity part, that is. I guess he felt he had overdone it in his post-game rant and was now holding himself to the same standard as he held us to everyday. Once he got that out of the way, he recounted the various things that went wrong the previous day, like failing to box out on foul shots and trying to beat a zone by dribbling through it. Poor execution of so many things we had worked on all season. Horne made it clear that we had gotten sloppy ... and that it reflected the deterioration of our focus and discipline in recent practices. But his most important message he saved for last, and that was that we weren't going to play the string out. He was determined that we would play up to our potential the remainder of the season, however many games that might be. He wasn't about to let that Linden game define our season. It wasn't so much about wins and losses. It was more about making sure we played the right way from there on out. The last thing he wanted was a long summer to dwell upon how we had blown the great opportunity that we had collectively created for ourselves, only to see it vanish down the drain with undisciplined play during crunch time.

Our next game would be in two days on Saturday night against Hillside in Hillside. As fate would have it, the game we had hoped to be part of, namely the UCT finals, would be played in the same Hillside gym just a few hours earlier on Saturday afternoon. Jefferson and Linden would be going at it for that title, as Jefferson had vanquished Roselle for the second time this season, Roselle's only blemishes on an otherwise perfect record. Fortunately, our game on Saturday night also carried extra significance as we needed the victory to claim the Watchung Conference title. Our conference record stood at 10-1, losing only to Cranford. Cranford's record, meanwhile, stood at 10-2, having lost to us and to Hillside. So, while it wasn't the title we had hoped to be chasing that night, it was still a title worth going after and gave us some extra incentive.

Our pursuit of redemption had begun. We probably had our best practice of the whole season that day. Everyone was all business with no joking around. Everybody was going all out. Horne continued to hand out suicides for cursing. In fact, he upped it on this day to three suicides per infraction detected. Even with the stiffer punishments, Jester and Goski were incapable of refraining from it, especially on days when things were hyper-competitive. "Fuck!" Goski blurted out at one point, mad at himself on one play. "That's three," Horne stated matter-of-factly. "Damn, it's worth it!" Goski would reply right back, not directing it to Horne but rather to his own alter ego. "That's three more," Horne would reply without missing a beat. I eagerly anticipated the next utterance that might be coming from my backcourt mate, but even the temperamental Goski was smart enough to quit while he was behind. Shortly after that I even got nailed for a quick three for a barely audible "Damn" that Horne's rabbit ears somehow picked up. I'm quite certain we set the season record that day for the most suicides racked up in one practice.

Thursday's practice clearly demonstrated that the best way to get over a tough loss was to get back out on the court and get ready for the next game. Thank God there was a next game. That's why season ending losses are all the more difficult to put behind you as the wait for that next game is months rather than days and might not even involve the same players. But our wait was only two days. Friday's practice was just as focused and competitive, and the team embraced Horne's attitude as to how we should approach the remainder of our season. We then got our instructions to be at the high school at 5 pm the next day for our bus ride over to Hillside.

February 26, 1972

Hillside's record stood at 14-7 as we walked into their gym on Saturday night. We had handled them twice already this season, including once without the suspended Novacek and Cooney. But they had very good scorers in Paul Yungst and Paul Loesseff and had already knocked off Cranford, and now we had to play them in their own gym for the first time with the stakes being even higher. We could win the Watchung Conference title for the first time in four years when my brother Mark's team had won it and for only the third time in school history. We could not afford to play badly on this night.

The game had a similar start to the last time we had played in this gym ten days earlier against Kenilworth. We traded baskets with Hillside for much of the first period until the score was knotted at 13. Then we closed out the quarter with five straight to take an 18-13. They scored first to open the second quarter, but we responded with six straight for a 24-15 lead. We had a good rhythm going at this point with every player getting in on the scoring. After one more basket by Hillside, we continued to pour it on with solid play at the defensive end and good ball movement and shooting at our end. Goski was torrid the whole first half, but especially in the second quarter when he scored 14 of his 20 first half points. We outscored Hillside 24-6, taking a comfortable 37-19 lead late in the second quarter. The halftime score was 41-23.

We were in no mood to let up the pressure in the second half, and we were able to extend our lead in the third quarter to 67-41 on strength of a few fast breaks and good passing. I racked up five assists during the third quarter and Larry Simmons scored eight points on his way to 13 points and a perfect 5-for-5 from the floor. Horne then emptied the bench in the last period and we coasted to a 75-58 win. Goski led us again with 24 points on 9-of-15 shooting from the field. The rest of the team shot almost as well as we ended up shooting 56 percent for the game, our best showing of the season with the exception of the one Rahway blowout. We also moved the ball well with 18 assists, four above our team average, and maintained our usual dominance on the boards with a 32-17 margin.

We left the Hillside gym that night feeling pretty good about our effort and that now we had finally won a title that we could take home with us, helping to at least partially erase the sting of the Linden loss just three days earlier. The Linden vs Jefferson contest for the UCT crown that had played out in the same Hillside gym just four hours earlier resulted in Jefferson knocking Linden off for the fourth straight time this season to claim the coveted UCT title. Jefferson now stood at 21-1, having won 13 straight games since we upset them in early January. In the back of our minds, we all hoped we might see them again.

Our regular season was now officially over. We finished it with a 20-2 record as the Watchung Conference champions. We had failed in our Union County Tournament bid. There was only one thing left remaining in our season – the state tournament.

The State Tournament

The NJSIAA conducted the state tournament by Groups. Group IV schools would compete in one group against each other, Group III schools against each other and so on down to the parochial schools. Group IV contained all the largest public schools in the state by student body population. You also needed a winning record to even get into the tournament, at least in Group IV during 1972, and I'm not even sure that was sufficient. When the brackets came out, there were just 32 teams entered into the Group IV bracket, with eight teams in each of the four sections within Group IV. Our section was North Section II. The other three sections were called North Section 1, Central Jersey, and South Jersey. Within our section would be familiar foes of Jefferson, Linden and Cranford. However, our first-round matchup was against Parsippany Hills, a school I had never heard of.

The state tournament was single elimination – lose and your season was over. Westfield had never won the state tournament, although 10 years earlier they had come very close with their all-county stars 6-11 center Bob King and 5-9 guard Dickie Meyers, losing in the finals to Weequahic by 3 points and finishing with a record of 23-3. Earlier in the season we even got to see some film clips of that team with the towering King. It seemed like a different era. But Bob King and the 1962 team were the furthest things from our mind right now. It was our time now. Our one shot.

Our first-round game was scheduled for Wednesday at the County College of Morris in Randolph. Parsippany Hills carried a record of 16-7, but more notable was the height of their front court, which included 6-9 Dennis Vail, 6-7 Bruce Scherer, and 6-5 Ed Hood. It would be the tallest front court we had faced all year. As with all our opponents, Horne had found time to scout them in the days leading up to the game, so in practice on Monday and Tuesday we would walk through their triple stack offense and out of bounds plays, with Jester, Phillips and Jackson playing the role of their front-line guys. Knowing their tendencies could only help, especially against a team you had never seen before. Horne must have felt good about our chances as we wrapped up practice early on Tuesday with foul shooting at 5:30, about 30 minutes earlier than normal.

March 1, 1972

There was only a half day of school today for some reason, with classes ending just after noon. Horne had scheduled a film session for 12:30 during which we could watch one of our earlier home games while Horne would highlight mistakes or poor execution. We had no films of Parsippany Hills to watch, so Horne went over their personnel again to better prepare us for who we'd be facing that night. We walked out of there feeling good about our chances. They may have had the height advantage on us, but we probably had enough of everything else going for us that should more than offset that. We would find out for sure in a few hours.

The half day gave us a couple of extra hours to kill that we wouldn't normally have on a game day in the middle of the week. Those extra hours were fortuitous. Judy Smith had just had an emergency appendectomy a few days prior and was now home recuperating. I saw her best friend Laura Saunders in the school hallway that morning and asked if Judy were visitable. She replied "Very." The past two months I'd been relegating her to the back of my mind so I wouldn't go through any more heartache in the midst of our season, but I had no excuses now. It was an opportunity being presented on a silver platter. I had to visit her that afternoon.

Fittingly, it was a gorgeous March 1 day with the temperature already 73 degrees and still climbing by the time I got the nerve to leave the house for the short drive over to Judy's. Of course, being the social wimp that I was, I slowed the car down as I approached her house and momentarily pausing as I saw two people sitting outside on her front porch. For an instant I thought I might escape undetected, but it was too late. I pulled the car forward, parked and got out to find Judy and Paul Leifer sitting on the front steps basking in the unusually warm March sun. I didn't know Paul much other than that he was easy going, upbeat, and very likeable as one of our team managers. While I was initially embarrassed to have to walk up there with both of them already sitting there watching me approach, Paul's presence helped break the ice and relax me. Judy was in short sleeves on this beautiful afternoon, revealing a bit of weight loss from her already skinny frame due to her recent surgery. But she was on her way back already and would be back at school within a few days. The three of us spent the next 45 minutes chatting about petty stuff, mostly just passing the time. By 4 pm it was time for me to get home to an early pre-game dinner. I knew Judy couldn't be at our game later, but her last words as I was parting were: "You better win tonight."

We boarded the bus for the 45-minute ride to Randolph. I don't think any of us knew where this was, other than that it was a neutral site for our game. The gym was newish looking with taller bleachers than your typical high school gym. The court may have been a touch longer than what had been seeing all year as well. But it still had two sidelines, two baselines, and two 10-foot high baskets, which is all that would matter at the end of the day.

Parsippany Hills scored first but then we came back with 13 straight points, seven by Pfeiffer and six by Goski, before they would score again about five minutes later. Horne had us pressing full court the entire game, in part because he believed that their guards were not that strong and also because the big front line was pretty slow and would not like the up-tempo pace. The constant pressure much worked as planned and we forced them into five turnovers the first quarter as we went on to take a 21-10 lead. When Novacek and Simmons then combined for eight straight points to open the second quarter, we had pretty much broken them down with a 29-10 lead. The rout was on as we continued full court pressure and were having our way at the offensive end as well. By halftime we had stretched our lead to 43-20 as we were dominating in almost every aspect of the game. We also shot a torrid 67% in that first half.

The second half brought more of the same, and it didn't matter who was on the floor for us. We kept outscoring them at a two to one pace throughout the entire game as our entire roster got into the act. We had five players scoring in double figures, including Cooney with 10. Jester led us in rebounding with 11 boards as we dominated their giants with a rebounding margin of 43-28. Goski and I had six assists apiece while our team racked up a season high 26 assists for the game. We did that while only committing 14 turnovers while forcing Parsippany into 25 turnovers with our pressure D. On top of all that we shot 57 percent from the field while limiting them to 28 percent shooting. The final score read 88-43. We played like one of the best teams in the state that night, and there was not much that Horne could be critical of. Our spirits were a bit higher as we boarded the bus for the ride home. Our record now stood at 21-2.

We had passed our first test with flying colors, but the challenges still ahead would be much larger than Parsippany Hills had presented us. We would be matched against arch-rival Cranford in the next round, while Linden and Jefferson, both winners in their first-round games, would square off for the fifth time this season in the other sectional semifinal game. It was almost like the UCT semis all over again, minus Roselle who was competing in Group I. There would be no easy path to win our section – we would have to beat Cranford, one of our conquerors, and then either beat Linden, our other conqueror, or Jefferson, who was now 22-1 and back up to #2 in the *Star-Ledger* rankings with 14 straight wins and arguably currently playing better than anyone else in the state.

Our game with Cranford would not be until the following Tuesday, six days after our Parsippany Hills game. The tournament organizers were able to space out the games a bit more, essentially two games per week for the advancing teams, so that the finals for all the Group tournaments could be played on Saturday, March 18. We certainly didn't need that much time to prepare for Cranford. We knew them as well as anybody, and they knew us. But it did give us the chance to spend more time on situational strategies – e.g., what we might do with only a few seconds left in the game or any given quarter and the ball in a certain spot. That also applied to all sorts of defenses or presses we might see. Horne's goal was to make sure we would be ready for anything we might see or any situation that might arise in the game.

The slight break in the schedule meant it would be our first weekend since New Year's without a game being played, thus allowing a little extra time for socializing. Since my regrettable night back in early December I had generally not been hanging out with the juniors on the team, in part to avoid anything remotely resembling a repeat of my antics on that fateful night and in part because the ones I knew best had steady girlfriends at this point. Tim Goski and Nancy McDowell had been going steady since before the season began, while Scott Novacek had been seeing Ellen Cooney, Mike's older sister, pretty regularly as well. Almost as if on cue my mom inserted herself into my social life and arranged a blind date with Pat Gentino, daughter of one of my father's good friends in town, Ward Gentino. I didn't know anything about Pat, who was a sophomore, other than that she was the younger sister of Steve, a high school and Bucknell classmate of my brother Mark. I agreed to it in part because I didn't have much to lose and my social calendar wasn't exactly jammed, but also because Tom Pfeiffer and I agreed to make a double date out of it along with his girlfriend Lori Winer.

On Saturday night we drove to a bar on Staten Island where the drinking age was 18. I would break my vow that night to not have any alcohol before the season ended, although I did it with the knowledge that it would only be a couple of beers and that with Tom in charge things would not get out of hand. A couple of hours later Tom would drop Pat and I back at my house where I no doubt acted quite juvenile the rest of the evening on the living room couch. My actions proved that night that you don't need to be a sophomore to act sophomoric. I would never see or talk to Pat after that evening. I can only hope that I didn't diminish any love of basketball that she may have had before that evening.

Basketball, of course, would again be the cure for my shortcomings on the social scene, at least in the short run. Tuesday would be here soon enough. It was now crunch time in our season. There would be no tomorrows to fall back on anymore. One bad game and it would all end abruptly. It was now or never.

March 7, 1972

Our rubber match with Cranford would take place at a fitting neutral site – the gym of our other closest rival, Scotch Plains. Scotch Plains had a nice new gym that had opened just a year earlier. The court was beautiful but had stands on only one side with surprisingly small seating capacity. Our previous trip to this gym was a very successful one when we thumped Scotch Plains in mid-season right on the heels of our big Jefferson and Cranford wins. More importantly, our third matchup with Cranford would likely define our season. No one could have predicted the 40 point blowout in our first matchup, or how they came back to avenge that embarrassing loss just three weeks later. But those earlier margins of victory meant nothing now. It would all come down to this third encounter, the winner of which would have all the bragging rights, not to mention the right to keep playing.

The early stages of the game were quite different than our previous encounters with Cranford but had a striking resemblance to our two previous battles with Linden. We jumped out to a quick 9-1 advantage as Goski got off to a quick start. Then after trading a couple of baskets, Cranford started to climb back in it from the foul line as we started to rack up personal fouls. They narrowed the gap to 13-11 before the quarter ended with us leading 17-13. We managed to stretch out the lead again to 28-20 during the second quarter, largely on the strength of Goski's 14 first-half points, but we also continued to foul on defense and Cranford was knocking down their foul shots. Pryor hit two field goals and Hobbie scored six points late in the second quarter to tie up the game at 34, including four foul shots in the last five seconds. To make matters worse, Novacek and Simmons went into the locker room at halftime with three fouls each.

The pace picked up in the third quarter as the teams traded early baskets. Then Cranford took their first lead at 40-38 before we tied it up again and then surged ahead by six with a run of eight straight points to make it 46-40. Mazzella and Zebrowski were having poor shooting nights, but Hobbie was playing very well and keeping Cranford close. Meanwhile, Simmons picked up his fourth foul midway through the third quarter, forcing Jester to fill in for him. We nursed our lead to the end of the period when the scoreboard read 51-46.

After trading baskets to open the last quarter, Cranford scored five straight to knot the score again at 53. They did it on a three-point play by Hobbie which drew Simmons' fifth foul, sending him to the bench for good. Jester came back in to replace him with just under five minutes left. Novacek put us back on top on the next possession and we managed a stop on Cranford's next possession. Then we turned it over on a bad pass and Cranford's Tom Isaac fed Hobbie for a layup to tie it up again with just under 3 minutes remaining.

Goski, who had been quiet in the second half, gave us a much-needed boost with a baseline drive and score giving us the lead once again at 57-55. Then with just over a minute left I managed to knock the ball from Isaac near half court, dive on it and call a quick timeout before getting tied up. On the ensuing play Goski drove towards the basket and fed Novacek inside the lane who powered it in to put us up by 59-55. Cranford pushed the ball right back and Hobbie, still playing aggressively with the hot hand, drove to the hoop and got fouled in the act. He knocked down two more foul shots and now was 7 for 8 for the game. With about 45 seconds to go, Martin called for his team to foul and Pfeiffer was then fouled a few seconds later. Tom had had an excellent game up to that point, scoring 17 points to go along with Goski's 18. His only shortfall was 1-for-4 shooting from the foul line. Tom then missed the front end of the one and one and Pryor

Larry Simmons gets up to defend against Cranford's Charlie Pryor

grabbed the rebound for Cranford. Not surprisingly, the ball made its way to Hobbie, who then drove and pulled up for a short jumper, nailing it again! Hobbie's 26th and 27th points had tied it once more with 33 seconds left, 59-59. We called timeout with 28 seconds left to set up a last shot.

The play, which had a double screen being set down along the foul lane, didn't quite work as planned, but Jester, sensing the clock winding down, took a turnaround jump shot along the left baseline with about eight seconds left. It caromed off the rim and into the outstretched arms of Novacek right in front of the basket, who went right back up with the ball and banked it home with four seconds remaining. Cranford alertly called a timeout which stopped the clock with just :03 seconds on the scoreboard. Cranford then did a smart thing on the inbounds play, which was to fire the ball to someone near midcourt who immediately called another timeout, utilizing their last remaining timeout. That play only took one second off the clock, leaving two seconds in which to execute a final scoring play, but now from only half court rather than the full length of the court.

After the timeout, I was guarding Isaac who was about to inbound the ball along the left sideline. He fired the ball down along the sideline towards the left corner. I turned to see where the ball was headed, and I saw it wind up in the hands of Hobbie after a lunging Pfeiffer had narrowly missed a steal or deflection. Hobbie, after catching the ball, then pivoted, squared up to the basket and rose up all in one motion. Meanwhile, Pfeiffer had not given up on the play. After narrowly missing the steal on the inbound pass, Tom turned back towards Hobbie just as Hobbie was corralling the ball for his last second attempt. Pfeiffer, being the great athlete that he was, was able to time it perfectly and reach over Hobbie's shoulder to get a bit of his hand right on top of the ball, deflecting it harmlessly to the ground. The buzzer then sounded giving us the win just as the Cranford bench and players were erupting with claims that Hobbie had been fouled on the shot. I had a perfect angle and line of sight on the play and there was no doubt in my mind that Tom had blocked the shot cleanly. Fortunately, the refs agreed and no call ever came…we had beaten Cranford again!

The game had been remarkably similar to the first Linden game, which had also been a real dogfight the entire game with several tie scores and neither team being able to build up any kind of sizable lead or maintain the momentum. Rebounding and turnovers had been remarkably close for each team. While we outshot Cranford from the field by a margin of 43 percent to 35 percent, thanks largely to a off-nights for Mazzella (6 for 22) and Zebrowski (2 for 12), we continued to underperform from the foul line and were very lucky that it hadn't cost us the game. We had shot a pitiful 9-for-19 from the foul line while Cranford had shot a very respectable 15-for-18. We had been dodging bullets all year with our subpar foul shooting which had been hovering right around 60 percent for the season, but tonight we were very fortunate it had not cost us the game. I was happy for Pfeiffer, though, who more than made up for his missed free throws with 17 points and maybe the biggest defensive play of the year with just one second left.

On the bright side we had put together another strong team effort. While Goski and Pfeiffer led us in scoring, Novacek added 12 along with the game winner and Jester filled in nicely for Simmons. There's no question that our defense accounted for part of their poor shooting percentage, and in a game like this every rebound mattered. Novacek, as he was in most games, was a force on the boards, leading our team with 13 rebounds. He obviously impressed Cranford's head coach Bill Martin, who was quoted the next day in the papers saying: "He's my kind of ball player. He's tough and not afraid of contact." Scott had been a remarkably consistent scorer as well. While he had been averaging just over 14 points a game in the 23 games he had played in this season, and had led us in scoring just eight times, he had scored in double figures in all 23 games! Contrast that with Goski who had been coming on strong as the season went on and had led us in scoring 11 times, but four times had games in single digits.

We left Scotch Plains that night with the hard-fought W that we came for. It may not have been the prettiest win, but the bottom line was that we had now beaten our one of our two main rivals in the rubber match for the season and, more importantly, we'd be advancing in the tournament while Cranford was going home. The next time we'd see those guys would likely be down at Gumbert in the summer. On the short bus ride home that night we were anxious to hear of the outcome of the Linden/Jefferson game that ironically was being played back in our gym at the same time as our game with Cranford. We got our answer just minutes later when we walked back into our building. Jefferson had made it a clean sweep of Linden, vanquishing them for the fifth time this season while winning their 15th straight game and setting up the rematch that we all secretly wanted. In the case of Jefferson fans, they made it no so secret when towards the end of the game they erupted in a loud rhythmic chant: "WE-WANT-WEST-FIELD ... WE-WANT-WEST-FIELD", according to a straggling fan who had just witnessed it. On Saturday, they would get their wish ... and we would get ours.

The next morning the papers said that our rematch with Jefferson would be played on Friday night, but by the time we got to practice later that day Horne informed us that the game would take place Saturday afternoon at Roselle Catholic. That was good news all the way around, as far as I was concerned. We'd get an extra day to prepare for Jeff and Saturday afternoon seemed like the perfect time for a game of this magnitude, a time when anyone who wanted to see it should be able to. I also couldn't have asked for a better neutral location than the site of my game winning buzzer beater in late December, not to mention other good memories from games in that gym.

As far as the game itself, we viewed this as our state championship game. I don't think any of us even knew or cared about who might be in the other Group IV sections. If we could win this game, we would be state champs for our section, something that only the '62 team had ever done in WHS history. Even more than that, however, was the feeling that we had to validate our earlier victory over Jefferson. It was the only blemish on their 23-1 record, and there were no doubt many disbelievers throughout the state that felt that win was a fluke. There would be only one way to convince those people, and that was to do it again. We all felt that we could, but no one thought it was going to be easy – to the contrary, it would probably take our very best game.

Horne reverted once again to the formula that had served us well all season. Our practices leading up to our biggest game of the season would focus on both fundamentals (dribbling, passing, shooting, and defense) and the tendencies of our upcoming opponent and what specific offenses, defenses and plays we would run against them. On top of that we would simulate certain game situations that might arise that would call for a very specific play. As with our first game with Jefferson, Horne wanted us to run a delay game offense whenever they were in a man-to-man defense, not to stall or run the clock down, but to force them to stay in constant motion and hope that mental lapses on their part would lead to open shots within 15

Figure 5

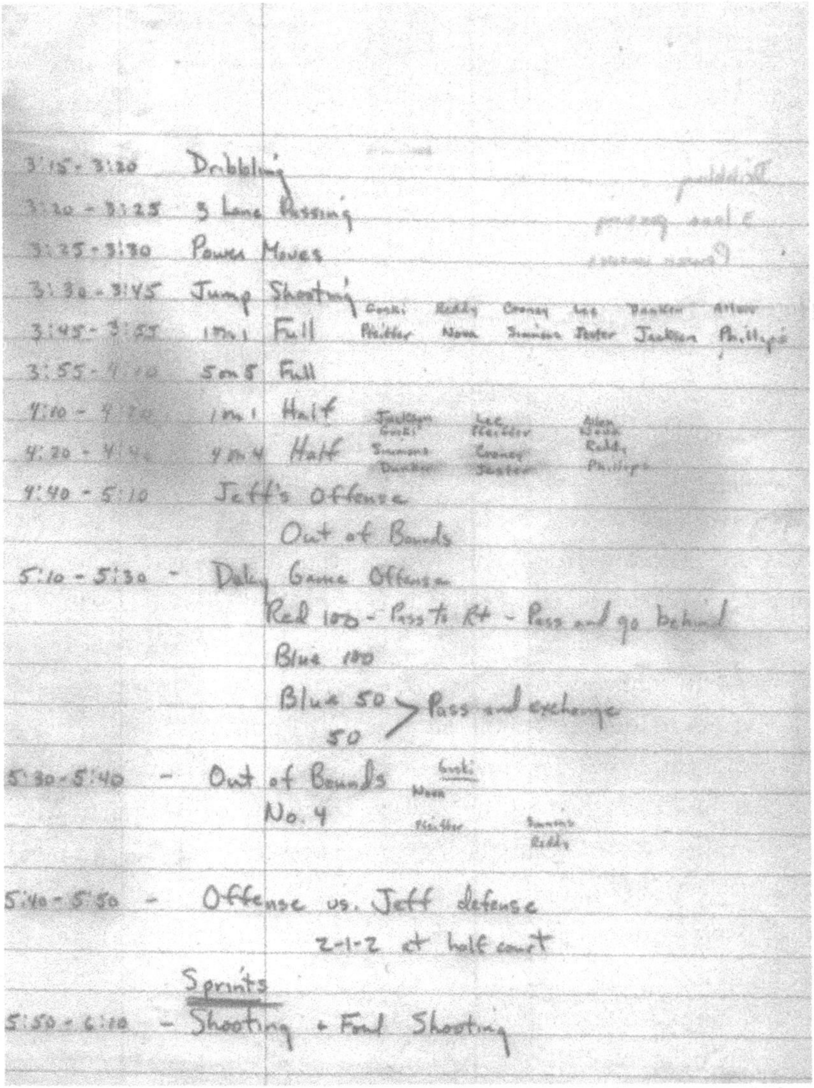

feet or so from the basket. We also had two or three plays that we could call while running the delay game offense, which would deviate from the repetitive screens and cuts that are normally made and might catch their defense off guard. One change that Horne had decided upon, however, was that Tim was free to bring the ball up court against Jeff's full court man-to-man defense. Whereas Horne may have been concerned earlier in the season that Goski may have reverted to playground ball in that situation, he now felt that Tim was playing with more maturity and control and would handle the pressure appropriately.

Horne's notes for our March 9 practice are shown in Figure 5 above. As with every practice, we would finish up with foul shooting, and our first 24 games were clear evidence that we still needed it as much as ever. Hopefully poor foul shooting would not be our downfall in what promised to be a hard-fought game.

March 11, 1972

We assembled at 12:45 in the lobby just outside our gym as we prepared to depart for Roselle Catholic. Just before we left the building, Kevin McGlynn, one of the better players on the prior year's team who had graduated in '71, walked in. I'm not sure what he was doing there, and he may have been wondering the same thing about us. It was a bit of an awkward encounter for Kevin, who appeared surprised to learn that we were 22-2 and still playing well into March. Who would have thought that possible just 12 months earlier? Nevertheless, he wished us well as we departed the lobby to board the bus.

We got to Roselle Catholic shortly after 1 pm. After getting dressed we spent about 20 minutes reviewing everything we had worked on in practice the past three days. By 1:40, there was nothing left to do but to take the court for warmups. Roselle Catholic's gym was pretty long, with tall end zone bleachers at each end of the court. Supposedly the gym held 2,200 fans, and while every seat was not taken, it was a pretty full house and undoubtedly the biggest crowd we had seen all year, and for good reason. Over the next several minutes we got loose and burned off some of that nervous energy that was inevitable before any game, but especially a big one like today's. By about 1:50, we noticed that something was wrong – Jefferson had yet to take the floor. There was no sign of them. It was just a couple minutes later that Horne called us over to let us know that Jefferson's bus had broken down and their team still wasn't here yet. Supposedly they were taking taxis to get to the game.

It wasn't clear where they were exactly or when they were due to arrive, so we just resumed our warmups as if nothing were wrong. After another ten minutes with no sign of Jefferson, Horne summoned us back to the locker room. It was now just past 2 pm, the scheduled game time. Horne wanted us to just sit and relax as there was nothing more for us to talk about at this point, and conserving our energy was probably the wisest thing we could do in this unusual situation. This was easier said than done, however. Just 20 minutes earlier we had taken the court with adrenaline pumping like never before in anticipation of our biggest game of the year. I laid down on one of the long narrow benches while staring up at the ceiling. I tried closing my eyes but it was of no use. There was too much nervous energy all throughout the locker room. After about ten minutes Horne let us back out on the court to shoot around and stay loose while we waited it out. Another 10 minutes later everyone got the welcome sight of the Jefferson players filing into the gym with their gym bags in hand as the surprisingly patient crowd expressed its approval. A minute or so later Horne summoned us back into the locker room once more for a reboot of our pregame routine. Five minutes later, we would take the court for the third time and restarted our layup lines at just after 2:30 pm. It would be another five minutes still before Jefferson would finally take the court for their warmups as the buzz in the crowd now amped up to another level. A few minutes later the national anthem was played with a color guard at center court, and then at 2:45 the opening tipoff had finally arrived!

Meanwhile, it appeared that there had been some discussion over the proceeding 45 minutes as to whether the game would start with technical fouls, but it was not to be. The game would start with the usual jump ball, just 45 minutes later than scheduled.

Watson won the opening tip, in contrast to our previous meeting when Novacek won all four jump balls at the start of each quarter. The defense was scrappy at both ends and we got a few early fouls called on us. Jefferson had a 5-0 lead before we finally broke the ice after three minutes on a couple of Goski baskets. Jefferson stretched the lead to 9-4 before we closed out the first period with two field goals and a free throw to knot it up at 9. Tim made his third jumper of the period and then hit me on a nice back door feed for a layup in that stretch.

Pfieffer picked up three quick fouls with just over two minutes left in that opening period. Jester was off the bench shortly after to take his spot. Also, troubling was that we had racked up six first-quarter turnovers. If we kept that up things were not going to end well. Fortunately, our defense was keeping us in the game, as did four missed Jefferson free throws.

Both teams settled in a bit in the second quarter and started to trade baskets, but the score would remain close throughout the period. The turnovers continued to mount though, and with five minutes left we had already hit the double-digit mark. Fortunately, our defense was making it tough for them as well. At one point Jones, their super-quick point guard, missed four straight driving layups over the course of several minutes, no doubt owing to the presence of Simmons and Novacek inside the lane. Goski kept us going on the offensive end with a running bank shot, his second of the game. That was then followed by Simmons and Novacek jumpers in the lane. Watson then put them up again with a short jump shot, but Goski hit me again with a beautiful back door pass off our motion offense for another layup inside before the 6-foot-8 Watson could react to the play. Beasley put Jeff ahead again with a short jumper, but once again Goski was able to tie up at 20 with his fifth field goal of the half, this one a 15-footer off the glass. Tim was working the ball against Jones' tight man-to-man defense and often resorting to the bank shot that was more accommodating of the very low arc on his shots. After a stop down at our end Novacek was able to knock down his second jumper of the period to give us our first lead at 22-20 with just under 30 seconds left. Jeff countered that by getting the ball into Beasley inside the lane who powered it up for a layup in traffic. Goski's last second attempt missed the mark as the buzzer sounded as we headed for the locker room tied at 22.

As bad as the turnovers were in the first quarter, it got worse in the second quarter with eight more for a total of 14 for the half. Thankfully, good defense and a handful of Jeff turnovers was helping to offset that. Horne implored us to take better care of the ball and to be more patient in the second half and not rush our shots.

The opening tip of the second half went our way for the first time this day, and Novacek knocked down a jumper to give us the lead again. A minute later Pfeiffer added a foul shot for a 25-22 lead, but on the next possession he committed his fourth personal foul and had to sit again. Over the next couple of minutes Jefferson could only manage a couple of free throws, while Novacek hit Goski for a fast break layup and then I hit a baseline jumper to give us a 30-25 lead with just under four minutes left. Shortly after that Jones, who had been playing aggressive man-to-man defense trying to contain Goski, committed his fourth foul while trying to draw a charge. On the next possession Novacek was fouled, made the front end of a one and one, and then Simmons grabbed the rebound and put it back in, giving us our biggest lead of the game at 33-26.

But Jefferson fought back. Novacek fouled Watson and he made both free throws. Then Porter made a short jumper to close the gap to 33-30. We were being more patient on offense, but again they forced a turnover and the previously cold Hopson knocked down a 20-footer to make it a one-point game. Goski then had a chance to stop the bleeding with a one and one from the foul line but missed the front end, and Jeff responded with a Beasley field goal from inside the lane. After missing everything earlier in the quarter, Jefferson was now making everything and had taken the lead back at 34-33 with just over a minute left.

We finally broke their streak as I made the first of a one and one, but missed the bonus shot. Jeff came right back, with Hopson drilling another 20-footer, and they now led 36-34. With 30 seconds left in the quarter, Goski took an opening down the lane and dumped the ball off to Jester down low, but Bob was then called for an offensive foul as he tried to power the ball up. It was Jester's fourth foul as well. Making matters worse, Jefferson came back on the next possession and with eight seconds left Porter hit a jumper from the left side for a 38-34 lead. That's how the third period ended - our seven point lead had turned into a four point deficit in less than four minutes.

Horne had put us in a zone defense for a portion of that third period to protect us from further foul trouble, but Jefferson had been taking full advantage of it by taking fewer contested shots and starting to knock down more of them. Horne had seen enough of that and knew it was now or never. He put Pfeiffer back in with his four fouls to start the last period and switched us back to man-to-man defense. The move paid immediate dividends as Novacek won the tap directing it to Pfeiffer, who secured the ball and then streaked down court for a contested layup, pulling us back within two. But we failed to score the next two possessions while Jefferson scored twice, giving Jeff their biggest lead of the day at six points. The second basket was another outside shot by Hopson who was also fouled by Goski during the shot. Hopson, who was being very aggressive offensively with Jones sitting out with four fouls, failed to convert the three-point play, and Novacek, after hauling in the rebound, fired up court to a streaking Pfeiffer for a layup at the other end. Jeff's lead was back to four points, 42-38.

After a missed Jefferson one and one attempt, I made the front end of a one and one opportunity at the other end. Porter then missed on Jeff's next possession, which Pfeiffer rebounded, drove down court and then hit Novacek coming down the lane for a short banker. We were now within one at 42-41. At the other end Hopson launched another one from long range, and an alert Beasley scooped up the short rebound and laid it to make it in to make it 44-41 with just over four minutes remaining. We now had half a quarter left to save our season.

On the next possession Pfeiffer missed a 15-footer but then came up with a stolen pass at the other end, and after pushing the ball down court, again found Novacek flashing down the lane. Novacek converted at short range to pull us within a point, 44-43. Our defense tightened up and forced another turnover on a deflected pass and now we had a chance to grab the lead back. We were running our motion offense when I got the ball in to Novacek in the low post on the right side of the lane. Novacek rose for a short jumper but the 6'8" Watson went up with him and partially blocked the attempt. The ball fell right into Watson's lap, who then looked to make the outlet pass up the left side of the court. We were all retreating back up court when Novacek, who was still waving his arms around Watson, somehow batted the outlet pass down, quickly scooped it up in the lane, and banked in the short layup over the startled Watson. We had seen Scott attempt his one man press many times before – we called it the "Nova Press" – and Horne had often chided him for it, but Scott had just deployed it now to pull off the biggest play of the game thus far. It was also his 15th point of the game, and sixth in the fourth period.

Jeff now appeared to be slightly rattled, and who wouldn't be? We capitalized again, this time with Goski's on the ball defensive pressure forcing a bad pass, giving us the ball back with a 45-44 lead and 2:12 left on the clock. Horne called for a timeout.

The next sequence worked like a dream. We were still running our motion offense, out of which a lot of good shots could arise for any player. Not surprisingly, it came down to Goski making a move from the top of the key, first heading left and then quickly changing direction and darting down the right side of the lane. Hopson had been guarding me along the right baseline but turned to step towards the oncoming Goski. I immediately headed for the basket and a split second later a pinpoint Goski pass was in my hands and then up and off the glass for an easy two pointer before Watson could get his big arms in my way. My third back door layup of the game! All on perfect feeds from Goski. Tim could be tough to play with at times, but if I was cutting to the basket and had an opening while he was driving or rising up for a jumper in the lane, he would always get it to me. His peripheral vision was good, but his basketball skills and ability to deliver the ball in those situations were exceptional.

Jefferson's coach Ron Kelly then called a timeout to regroup, with his team trailing by 47-44 after six straight points by us. We had been successful in keeping the ball out of Watson's hands down in the low post, but it was hard to keep him off the boards with his size and agility. On Jeff's next possession Watson rebounded a missed jump shot and tipped it back in from very close range. We now clung to a 47-46 lead with 1:32 left. Goski continued to do a lot of the heavy lifting by bringing the ball up court with Jones dogging him the whole time. After crossing half court, we settled right into our motion offense again, which meant lots of cutting, screening, and short passes while looking for an opening in the defense. Tim found one again, which he seized by driving down the lane looking to attack the basket. Moments later it was deva' vu as I made another back door cut, another slick pass from Goski hit me in the hands, and then I got the ball up off the glass and through the hoop from short range! Less than a minute after a strikingly similar play, Goski and I had pulled it off again!

But wait…no basket, the referee signaled. That beautiful sight was being nullified by the referee's whistle and a foul call away from the play. The points came off the board, and instead Simmons would be heading to the line for a one and one with 1:13 showing on the clock and one-point lead for us. Our foul shooting on this day, 7-for-12 thus far, pretty much reflected our foul shooting all season, which was somewhere between mediocre and poor. Larry was one of our weaker foul shooters, shooting right around 50 percent for the year. He was certainly the weakest in terms of confidence. In one practice Horne had to implore Larry to keep shooting them. Larry replied "What's the point? I can't make 'em anyway." Horne encouraged Simmons to get up and keep shooting free throws with these words: "Larry, someday we're going to need you to make those free throws." Well, that day turned out to be this day, and somehow Larry put his lack of confidence aside, stepped up to the line and knocked down two free throws! We now led 49-46.

With time getting short and trailing by three, Jefferson was now in attack mode. Hopson, who had been their offensive aggressor all day, continued his ways by driving down the lane and missing an attempt in traffic. Porter grabbed the rebound and fed it back out to a retreating Hopson. Hopson launched another 20-footer and nailed this one to bring Jeff back to within one with 51 seconds left. We quickly inbounded the ball and passed it up to an open Simmons near half court, who was then deliberately fouled by Watson with a blatant shove with 46 seconds left. That worked to our advantage as Simmons would now get two shots instead of a one and one, taking a bit of pressure off that first shot. Other than that, it was essentially a repeat of the situation that we just had moments earlier. Then, almost defying the odds, Larry stepped up again and knocked down two more free throws while the crowd was in a frenzy! Now *that* was a beautiful sight!

We still were applying full court pressure after a made foul shot, which made it difficult for Watson to inbound the ball and caused him to call Jeff's last timeout. Coach Kelly wasn't exactly thrilled, but they did what they had to do. Coming out of the timeout, Jeff was determined to get the ball in to Watson in the low post, which we had been preventing for most of the second half. They got it into him this time, though, and he hit a short jumper inside the lane to close the gap again at 51-50 with just 32 seconds left. We advanced the ball against their pressure, which we had handled much better in the second half, but on this possession Goski was thwarted by a collapsing defense as he drove from the top of the key and his pass towards the perimeter was deflected and then recovered by Beasley with 25 seconds remaining.

The clock continued to wind down, as Jones advanced the ball into the front court and hit Porter, who then hit Hopson in the right corner. I saw Hopson about to rise up for the jumper with about nine seconds left as I lunged toward him. I feared watching the ball go through the hoop and our basketball dreams get dashed all in one second. I spun around just in time to see the ball graze the rim on the short side and come straight down to Simmons, who had inside position. But he couldn't secure it cleanly - Porter also got his hands on it, leading to a jump ball was with just six seconds left. We had just dodged a bullet but still had at least one more to dodge.

Porter and Simmons were each 6-2 and both were good leapers. The jump ball could decide everything. If we could win it, they would have to foul us and send the ball to the other end with about four seconds remaining and no timeouts for them to set up a play. But if they could win it, they'd already be in shooting range with plenty of time to get a decent shot off and maybe get fouled in the process. The remaining eight players all took a spot on the circle and braced for the tip. Sometimes it was the receiver rather than the tipper who was the key to winning a jump ball, and now eight potential receivers were ready and waiting. The ball went up. Simmons and Porter went up, but Simmons' hand got on the ball first and directed it back to 7 o'clock on the circle, where Novacek had planted himself. Scott seized the ball with two hands and pulled it in as a swarm of hands rushed in to grab at the ball and quickly foul him. Four seconds left, and we were now one big step closer.

We walked to the other end of the court where Novacek would get a one and one with a chance to clinch it. Horne was barking out instructions as Scott was getting ready to step to the line. Goski and I were at halfcourt while Pfeiffer and Simmons took a spot on the foul lane. "No fouls," Horne commanded from the sideline. The crowd was going nuts as Scott was handed the ball, took one dribble, and then swished the shot! We led 52-50.

Horne then signaled for our last timeout. "No fouls," again he implored. Even if Scott missed the next foul shot, all we needed to do was make it a little difficult for them to go the length of the court for a tying shot.

We returned to the court for Scott's next shot. This one he missed and was grabbed by Jeff's Don Harris, who had just replaced Jones who fouled out on the previous play. But Harris then threw the ball away in his haste to advance it quickly! Two seconds left. We rushed back down to that end of the court where we would get to inbound it along the baseline. The ref handed the ball to Goski, who spotted Simmons in the corner and got him the ball. A Jeff player then fouled him, but it came too late as the buzzer sounded at the same time. We had beaten Jefferson again!!

We went nuts when the buzzer sounded, and fans came out on the floor to celebrate the moment with us. You dream about those kinds of moments, and when they actually happen it's like a tidal wave of good emotions that sweep you off the court. The rush of euphoria I felt at that moment was further enhanced by the sudden realization that we had just achieved one of our big goals, even though moments earlier everything was hanging in the balance with Hopson's final shot and the jump ball that followed. Roselle Catholic's gym continued to be a magical place for me, with our fourth quarter comeback occurring at the same end of the gym as my game winning buzzer beater back in December.

Back in the locker room the celebration and hugs and hand slapping continued, and even Horne couldn't hide his happiness in that moment. The only similar scene all season had been our first victory over Jefferson back in early January, but while that game played out in remarkably similar fashion, this one had a little something extra on the line. That something extra was the state North II Group IV sectional championship! That wasn't all though. We would get to keep playing. Horne announced that our next game would be against Hackensack Wednesday night in Princeton's new Jadwin Gym. We cheered our approval! Who the heck was Hackensack? We didn't know or care at that moment. There was too much to cherish from this game first.

We were now officially Jefferson's nemesis, having beaten them twice and ending their season at 23-2 after they had beaten several topflight teams along the way. We had just completed our fifth successful fourth quarter comeback of six points or more this season. Simmons was nothing short of heroic with eight points, nine rebounds, four clutch foul shots down the stretch, and the biggest jump ball tap of the season! Novacek had led all scorers with 16 points, including six straight and a huge steal during our late comeback. Goski added 12 points and five assists and proved his mettle against the tenacious Jefferson guards who were hounding him all day. Tim made me look good with three beautiful back door assists plus a fourth one that got waved off, leading to a 4-for-4 shooting day for me. Pfeiffer didn't have his best day with the early foul trouble that plagued him for the first three quarters, but he rose to the occasion in the fourth with five points, two steals and two assists, all while he played with 4 fouls. Jester had played big minutes this day too and helped keep us in the game during the middle two quarters when Pfeiffer had to sit.

The stats confirmed the even battle that had just taken place. Jeff had the rebounding edge at 33-27, only the third team to outrebound us all year. They also had the turnover edge at 19-16, although we tightened that up during the second half. We had outplayed them at the offensive end though, with a 15-8 assist advantage, and a 49 to 38 percent shooting percentage edge from the field. This no doubt reflected our patience and better execution in the half-court offense that led to easier shots than they got at their end. Then came foul shooting, where we finally had the slight edge that helped push us over the top. Jeff was only 10-for-20 on the day, while we shot 12-for-18, including 5-for-6 in crunch time. Horne had indeed been prophetic earlier in the season when he warned Simmons about the day we would need him to come through from the foul line. Thank God for Larry – confidence or no confidence, he did what we needed him to do on this day!

Right after the game Horne got pulled into a quick radio interview for a station that had just broadcast the game. We didn't get to hear that until sometime later, but Horne had summed it all up perfectly when the announcers were wrapping up the interview and offered a final congratulations, to which he responded: "Thanks, but it was a team effort all the way."

The next morning seemed liked one of those times when it actually would be ok to read about ourselves. Who wouldn't want to see what the papers had to say about our repeat victory over higher ranked Jefferson? The Sunday morning papers would provide the perfect opportunity to do so. One headline read: "**Westfield Stuns No. 2 Jeffs**". Another read: "**Westfield does it again!**", while a third one said "**Starless Westfield Won't Crack; Upsets Jeff For Sectional Title**".

Once you got into the articles, you got more evidence as to what others had seen in our big win: The *Courier-News* wrote: "*Westfield High's faceless five have done it again. The Blue Devil cage squad had no big man, no great shooters and no legitimate star. The Devils are noteworthy only because they keep winning.*" Gene Picker of the *Daily Journal* wrote that Westfield "*again based its winning formula on a balanced performance, tenacious defense and a refusal to lose its cool when the tide turned.*" The *Star-Ledger* said our victory "*was no fluke*" despite having "*no real individual stars*", but rather "*a quintet which knows how to handle the ball and run plays well despite some close guarding...*" Even Horne gave his own take on it when he was quoted saying: "*We did the same thing we've been doing all year. Everybody did his thing. Larry Simmons and Scott Novacek rebounded. Tim Goski and Steve Reddy handled the ball well and Tom Pfeiffer gave us the clutch baskets.*"

Yes, there was a lot to feel good about, and by this time we had made a believer of my father who just three months earlier had scoffed at the suggestion that our team would eclipse the accomplishments of my older brothers' teams. Still, there was no feeling of "I told you so" that ran through me. Instead, it was just a sense of accomplishment, that we had done what we set out to do in the beginning. But there was another, much stronger feeling that began to consume me. We still had some work to do. Our season was not over. As good as the big win over Jefferson felt, this was no time to be satisfied with what we had already accomplished. Yes, we had just won the second state sectional title in WHS history, but now we would have a once in a lifetime chance to win the whole darn thing. All we had to do now was win two more games.

By the time practice rolled around on Monday, a lot of the euphoria from Saturday's big win had worn off, making it easier to focus on our next opponent Hackensack. Horne was going to see to it that we weren't distracted by anything else. As fate would have it, we got a chance to be distracted right away when the baseball team took to the gym because of rain. There we were inside the four lines of the basketball court while the baseball team was warming up with guys having a catch right alongside our court, guys like John Havas and Steve Tebbetts. It was sort of a strange sight for all of us. We had never caught a glimpse of any or their practices, and they had never seen a WHS hoops team playing this late into March.

We stuck to our usual routine by doing-many of the various drills we had been doing all season long, before reviewing various offenses and defenses that we might use against Hackensack. Not surprisingly, Horne found time to go see Hackensack play the previous Friday night, the night before our Jefferson win. He gave us the scoop, which was a high scoring backcourt in Kirk Scott who was averaging just under 20 points a game, and Bob Sefcik who was averaging 17. While their frontcourt wasn't particularly tall, it did feature Skip Johnson, one of the state's best high jumpers who had cleared 6 feet, 6 inches in a high school track meet.

Hackensack was coming into the game with a 24-3 record, so they were clearly a very good team that was going to make us earn it. At the same time, we were very confident at this stage and felt that we were the better team and could handle whatever they might throw at us. They might have had a slick guard in Scott and a great high jumper in Johnson, but we had Goski to challenge their backcourt and Pfeiffer, Simmons and Novacek to give them fits on the boards. I wondered what their coach was telling his players about us. If he read Gene Picker's pre-game writeup in the Daily Journal, he would know that Scott Novacek was Westfield's "Mr. Big", the caption right below Scott's picture in that article. We welcomed Scott's new moniker, and quickly adopted it despite the very late stage of our season. He had earned it throughout the course of the season. We could only hope that Mr. Big would live up to his name the rest of the way.

We finished up practicing with 20 minutes of scrimmaging, followed by 15 minutes of foul shooting. Scrimmaging during practice always felt like a bit of a treat. You got to play real basketball and put all the things you'd been working on to the test, instead of just standing and listening and constantly reviewing various game situations. Of course, that also meant that trash talking could erupt at any time. In those 20 minutes Novacek and Phillips picked up six suicides each while Goski earned a more pedestrian three for his outbursts. Jester somehow managed to avoid punishment that day and was shooting fouls with the rest of us while those guys were running.

March 15, 1972

Princeton's Jadwin Gym was a new modern looking structure that had just opened in 1969, replacing the older and more ordinary looking Dillon Gymnasium that Bill Bradley, Geoff Petrie and my brother Tom had played in. I had been to Dillon Gym the night that Dartmouth had upset Petrie's Princeton team, but I had never seen Jadwin Gym. The New Jersey state finals had been held in Atlantic City in recent years, but Jadwin's new state of the art structure earned it the right to host the event going forward.

Any high school player who walks out on the court for the first time might have some difficulty given how spacious and airy it feels. The arched ceiling was so high compared to a typical high school gym that you felt like you were outside. The walls and ceilings that would normally help give you more depth perception weren't there, so you had to rely strictly on the backboard and rim while launching shots from any distance, and while it may have felt like you were playing outside, there would be no wind to contend with. The Jadwin court was perhaps a little extra bit of challenge for each team to overcome, but it certainly didn't favor one team or another. The place held about 6,500 fans, so it was capable of handling any size crowd that a high school game might draw.

Our 7 pm game with Hackensack was the first of two games that night, with Trenton Central and Triton Regional to follow. The two winners would meet on Saturday for the Group IV title. We took the court about 6:40, giving us a few extra minutes to get loose and get comfortable with our surroundings. The place was buzzing with excitement. Many fans for the second game came early to catch our game as well, just as would typically happen at a regional NCAA tournament venue. Once again, the scoreboard read 0-0; as with our prior three games, it was another win or go home situation.

Goski hit the first basket of the game with a 17-footer, but then Hackensack reeled off nine straight over the first four minutes with Scott and Sefcik scoring seven of the nine points. We battled back to keep the lead from getting any larger and finally ended the first period trailing by 13-8.

Goski was off to a good start as well, going three for three from the field and assisting on our only other field goal.

Scott continued to hurt us in the second period with three more field goals in the early going, but we were able to match those and now trailed 19-15. We were now moving the ball better and settling in a bit more on offense. The result was three straight layups, two by Pfeiffer and one by me off a nice feed from Goski. We now had our first lead at 21-19. Two possessions later Scott was flying down the left side of the court on a fast break with the ball. I retreated on defense and made a split-second decision to try to draw the charge. I quickly moved another step over to my right and right into Scott's path. The shifty Scott tried to pull up just as he was landing on my right foot, and I began to fall backwards trying to draw the charge. Even though Scott's weight was only on my foot for a split second, my foot wasn't able to follow the rest of my body to floor in a normal manner. The result was what felt like a sprained ankle, and maybe a pretty bad one. I got up and tried to walk it off, but it was already hurting badly. However, anyone who's played basketball and experienced sprained ankles knows they can hurt like hell that first minute only to have the pain subside pretty quickly with the player often being able to resume playing right away with just some mild discomfort.

Unfortunately, that wasn't the case for me. I was forced to take a seat on the bench and have our trainer John D'Andrea tend to it. I didn't get the charging call I was hoping for, but Scott was called for travelling on the play which was just as good and a tiny bit of consolation for incurring the injury. The scoreboard still read 21-19 in our favor with three and a half minutes remaining. Horne put Jester in for me and moved Pfeiffer to the backcourt.

After examining my ankle for another minute on the bench, D'Andrea took me back to the locker room to get a thorough tape job. He had determined that the only way I was going to be able to return to the game was with the extra support of tape all around the ankle. I had never needed or had a tape job in the past, but now I had an urgent need for one. Meanwhile, back on the court our team fought to maintain our slight lead and a few minutes later they joined me in the locker room with the scoreboard reading 26-24 in our favor.

While Horne was addressing the team D'Andrea finished taping my ankle. Regardless of the injury I had just sustained, the heavy tape around my ankle and foot felt awful. It was wrapped tight around the top and bottom of the foot as well as around the entire ankle area. How was I supposed to run on this? It felt like I already had a small cast on my foot. I guess the idea was to make the ankle so rigid that you couldn't possibly turn it again if you tried to. Unfortunately, what the tape job couldn't do was stop the pain. I put my socks and sneaker back on over my bandaged foot and laced up the sneaker, got off the table, and took a few steps. As expected, it felt weird as I could feel the tape around the bottom of my foot as I walked on it. More importantly though, it was still hurting too much to put my full weight on it and push off it in any significant way. It became a fairly quick decision. I didn't even need to get out on the court to test it. As my teammates left the locker room for the second half, in some ways their night was just beginning, but my night was already over. I spent the rest of the game at the end of the bench with my ankle propped up on another chair and an ice bag laying on top of it.

Horne made a tactical decision to start Lee in my place instead of Jester, presumably to match up better with their backcourt and Scott in particular. Steve gave up a couple of inches to the 6'0" Scott but was quick enough to make him work harder on the offensive end where he had been hurting us. Meanwhile, Novacek and Simmons were holding their own on the boards, so we didn't necessarily need Jester's help there. The first half of the third quarter started out well enough, but we more or less traded baskets until we managed our biggest lead of the game at 36-32. Lee had scored a field goal in that stretch which no doubt helped his confidence in this tight game. Hackensack was hanging tough, though, and would go on a mini run the rest of the third period, taking back the lead 39-38 by the time the buzzer sounded. In the huddle, Horne calmly implored us to be more patient at the offensive end, clearly not liking the shots we had gotten the last few minutes.

Scott opened up the fourth quarter scoring with a bomb that put them ahead 41-38. After we made a single free throw, Scott came back with two of his own to give them a four-point lead at 43-39. Pfeiffer then scored on a fast break drive off a nice feed from Goski, but on our next possession an errant pass was intercepted by Hackensack's point guard Bruce Basile who took in all the way home for a layup and a 45-41 lead.

Hackensack had been playing man-to-man defense all game, which was always tempting for Goski to attack, thinking that he could beat his defender off the dribble and get off a good shot or drive to the basket. At this stage of the season Tim was being more prudent in picking his spots and not just resorting to playground ball. In a tight game like this, we needed that little edge he could provide at the offensive end when open shots were not coming easily. During our next possession Goski was able to beat his man off the dribble for a mid-range jumper to cut their lead back to two.

Goski pulls up for a short jumper

After a missed shot by Hackensack, we came back with a big play at our end. This time Lee was driving with the ball and a beaten Scott reached in and fouled him. Steve came up big and knocked down both ends of the one and one, tying the score at 45. Perhaps equally important was that Scott had picked up his fourth foul on the play. There was 4:58 left in the game.

Hackensack came back and broke the tie on a Sefcik jumper. Sefcik, Hackensack's other big scorer along with Scott, was having a cold shooting night, but gave them a 47-45 lead on this shot. Hackensack now dropped back into a zone for the first time and Horne called for a timeout with 4:11 left. He again reminded us to be disciplined, look for our cutters, and wait for a good shot. Right after the timeout Simmons was able to hit Pfeiffer sliding through their zone for an easy deuce inside. We then stopped Hackensack at their end which ignited a fast break for us. Pfeiffer took the outlet pass and drove to the basket but missed the contested layup as the high jumping Johnson defended the play. Johnson rebounded the miss and looked to make the outlet pass, but in a split-second Pfeiffer snuck up from behind him, stripped him of the ball and quickly laid it up and in. It was like shades of the "Nova press". Just like in the big Jeff game a few days earlier, this huge steal and layup gave us the lead at 49-47 in the waning minutes of the game. Tom was one of those rare players with the quickness, strength and agility to pull off that steal and score all in one quick motion against a tough player.

We stopped Hackensack again the next trip down court, forcing them to retreat back in man-to-man defense trailing by two. We reverted to our motion offense to both run more clock down and look for open cutters. Most of our points on this night had come at very close range, perhaps helping to offset the airy environment of Jadwin Gym. Goski, once again sensing the need to seize any opening, worked his way into the lane and nailed a short jumper for a 51-47 lead with a little more than two minutes remaining. Skip Johnson wasted little time on Hackensack's next possession, cutting our lead in half with a turnaround J. After running about 20 more seconds off the clock, Novacek got fouled at our end, but was only able to knock down one of two for a 52-49 lead with 1:26 left on the clock.

Our defense came through again and forced a turnover. We then got right back into our motion offense at the other end, determined to take more time off and force them to defend one cutter after another. As had happened so many times before, Goski saw an opening and attacked the basket. His driving layup would come off the front rim where Novacek was positioned to attempt the put back, but his attempt would also come off the front rim. Simmons was there to clean it up though, and his tip in gave us a 53-48 lead and a little more breathing room with just 36 seconds left. Basile responded with two made free throws with 30 seconds left, but we were able to quickly inbound and advance the ball against their full court pressure until they were forced to foul Goski with 23 seconds left. Tim, who was our best percentage foul shooter on the season at about 78%, calmly stepped to the line and knocked down both for the 56-51 lead.

We were able to run the clock out from there. Scott fouled out in the waning seconds, leaving the game with 26 points. The kid could certainly shoot, knocking down 8 of 18 field goals and 10 of 11 from the foul line. But he alone wasn't enough to match the one-two punch from Goski and Pfeiffer. Tim netted 20 points on 8-for-14 shooting, while Pfeiffer was right behind him with 17 points on 7 of 12 shooting. Goski and Pfeiffer were also a combined 7-for-7 from the foul line. We were fortunate that those guys were on because Novacek had his first real off night at the offensive end, failing to score in double figures for the first time all year. Scott was still a force, however, contributing seven points and 13 rebounds to our cause. Simmons also grabbed 11 rebounds and added five assists. Finally, Lee was huge for us in the second half, scoring four points and making life difficult for Scott who went scoreless in the final five minutes of the game.

I felt good for Steve. He had complained to me part way through the season that he felt he should be the third guard ahead of Mike Cooney in the rotation. Steve confided to me years later that he had confronted Horne late in the season, trying to convince our coach that Steve could help the team, especially at the defensive end. Despite his disappointment in how that was playing out, he never dogged it in practice or acted in any kind of disgruntled manner. On top of that, Steve bore the brunt of a lot of "Rat" jokes during the season that he would just shrug off. While they may have generally originated with the juniors who didn't know him that well, I was no doubt guilty of laughing along with them. This was a guy who just two years earlier was our lead guard and one of our top two scorers along with Pfeiffer, so Steve could definitely play. What probably hurt him more than anything was that he had grown very little since our JV year while everyone else had. Compounding all this for Steve was his parent's recent breakup, causing Steve to have to split time between his dad's place in Plainfield and his mom's at the north end of Westfield. Regardless of how he may have felt about lower position in the depth chart and all the other headwinds he had faced, Steve was able put it all aside and stayed ready to play all season. Perhaps Horne got more confidence in Lee during the county tournament when Cooney had been suspended for one game. Maybe Steve had finally convinced Horne that he deserved to be the first one off the bench. Whatever the reason, Lee got the call today and it paid off. He deserved the game ball as much as or more than anybody. While our balance had been one of our big strengths all season, Steve proved on this day that our depth was as well.

It was our sixth fourth-quarter comeback win of the year. While we only had to come back from four down in this one, we still managed to execute well down the stretch which had been one of our trademarks all year. Like our two games with Jefferson, this game was also marked by mini runs. In fact, even more so. After Hackensack has scored nine straight at the outset of the game, we came back with a 9-2 run in the second to take back the lead. Hackensack then seized the momentum back midway through the third with a 9-2 run of its own. Fortunately, there was enough time left for one more momentum shift, which we used to take back the game with a final 13-4 burst. Hackensack was one of the few teams to outrebound us all year with a slight 30-27 edge, but we eclipsed them in most other areas. We had only 14 turnovers to their 21, while dishing out 13 assists to their 5. We also shot 45 percent from the field compared to their 36 percent. We even came through at the foul line, making 12 out of 15 attempts. We had indeed adapted well to the Jadwin Gym environment.

It was the second time this year I had to watch our team pull out a close game while sitting on the bench. I suppose my injury may have dampened my mood a little bit, but that still couldn't diminish what had just happened. We had just made it to the state finals! We had just beaten another very good team and now we're just one victory away from winning the whole thing. Horne announced in the locker room that the team bus wouldn't be heading home until later. We would all stick around to watch the second game so we could see who we'd be playing on Saturday. All except me, that is. I had to head back to Westfield to get X-rays that evening at an orthopedic group on Broad Street, where the athletic department had connections with some of the doctors to get them to open their doors at night. It was an uncomfortable ride back with an ice pack on my throbbing ankle the entire way, but the thrill of our victory made the ride much more bearable than it otherwise would have been. Thankfully, X-rays showed no fracture. Just a sprain, albeit a bad one, that would require more "ice and elevate" in the enduring words of Trainer D'Andrea.

Meanwhile, back in Princeton, my teammates got treated to a real thriller that I wouldn't hear about until later the next day. It was going all one way for a while, with Trenton Central blowing out Triton Regional 51-33 early in the third quarter before Triton put on a furious rally to close the gap to 56-54. Still, Trenton was able to maintain a 61-54 lead going into the last period. Another burst by Triton put them ahead 62-61 early in the fourth, before both teams traded baskets the rest of the way. Trailing by 70-69 in the last minute, Trenton had a chance to grab the lead again but missed two free throws. Triton did not miss when they were fouled and that sealed a three-point victory for them. The Trenton fans apparently didn't take it well, and a post-game scuffle involving about 20 fans, which some people described as a mini riot, landed three Triton fans in the hospital. The star of the Triton team that led their comeback was a rather short and stocky guard named Bruce Leonetti who torched Trenton for 25 points. According to the Daily Journal, "his shooting, ball handling, and defensive steals completely rattled the Trenton team."

Our team now had a date with Bruce Leonetti on Saturday.

XIII. Like Father, Like Daughter

When my daughter Jackie was barely 5 years old, she took violin lessons for a brief period at her nursery school that was located on the small campus of Cabrini College in Radnor, PA. One day Jackie was asked to play Twinkle Twinkle Little Star for her classmates. The shy little girl reluctantly did so…but only while standing out in the hallway so no one could see her play. Ten years later she would return to the exact spot, where the nursery school used to be and where a nice new gymnasium now stood, as a member of one of the best girls basketball team in the country for her age group – the Philadelphia Belles. She had come full circle.

Like any parent, I wanted my kids to have the opportunity to participate and hopefully excel at team sports. Of course, I had a bias towards basketball given my experience, and presumably could teach my kids a thing or two along the way that other coaches may not be able to. I knew from an early age that Jackie was very athletic. During our first trip to Myrtle Beach when she was 7 and her older brother and sister were 11 and 9 respectively, they raced one night on a flat stretch of hard sand that was maybe 60 or 70 yards long. It was hard to tell who won. Jackie could also throw a baseball more like a guy than a girl, and whenever she got on our backyard trampoline, she would scare the heck out of us when she would do somersaults effortlessly.

Thanks to my neighbor Jim Natale, who had founded the youth basketball league in Washington Crossing for both boys and girls a few years before we moved in, Jackie had a place where she could play in organized games that first year when she was only 7. When she was 10 she got invited to play on an 11-year-old AAU team. The next year I decided to coach her AAU team for 11-year-olds.

I knew Jackie could be something special based on one play that occurred during that season. We were down in Virginia Beach at a Boo Williams tournament where our team would play four games that weekend, two each day. Our team was seriously outmatched in the first game against a bigger inner-city team from somewhere in Maryland. It was a 56-9 drubbing that we absorbed at their hands, a very forgettable game, but still there was one play that remains etched in my mind. The opposing team was coming down the court on yet another fast break while Jackie was back and retreating on defense. A big black girl who easily had a few inches and 30 or more pounds on Jackie was streaking down the left on her way to a fast break layup. But Jackie wasn't conceding the basket ... instead, she went up with the girl and with her left arm swatted the ball way behind the baseline, right into a big blue curtain about 10 feet behind the baseline that separated our court from another one just on the other side of the curtain. The swatted ball went into the curtain on the fly! It was the kind of play you might have expected from the team that scored 56 that day, not the team that scored 9. I knew right then that Jackie had a good basketball future ahead of her.

Not only did Jackie have natural athleticism, but she also showed good basketball instincts at a very young age. She was very efficient with her dribble, only using it when necessary, with the minimum number of dribbles to get from A to B. She would make good quick decisions and never hesitate out on the court. Jackie also tended to keep the whole court in her vision, always keeping her head and eyes up, rather than just seeing the defender in front of her – an uncanny ability for a young player. When Jackie was 12 she won the Founder's trophy as the best player in the girl's league still run by my neighbor. Natale, who had a sharper basketball eye than I did, even commented on Jackie's floor presence and how well she kept her head up. A couple of years later, when Jackie was playing CYO basketball, the head coach at Notre Dame High School, where her older sister was already enrolled, came to watch her play. I met the coach for the first time after the game and her very first comment was, "She sees the floor so well." Who says that about an eighth grader? Someone who understands the game, as far as I was concerned. A few months later Jackie would join her older sister at Notre Dame.

Jackie also caught the eye of another coach that same winter while playing in a weekend tournament. Tom Nerney, an insurance company president who just happened to have been a 1,000-point scorer at Cabrini College back in the mid-'70s, was coaching the opposing team one Saturday afternoon, after which he asked my wife Susan if Jackie might like to come play for his AAU team in the spring. Susan relayed the message to me later that day. It turned out it wasn't just any AAU team...no, this was the Philadelphia Belles, a perennial power in girls AAU hoops for the Mid-Atlantic region.

Herein came the dilemma that parents are constantly faced with these days – trying to figure out which team or teams are best for their kids. Jackie, in addition to basketball, had also been playing on a competitive travel soccer team for three or four years at this point, and also played softball, although that was already getting crowded out. Joining the Belles would mean a greater commitment to basketball, and likely having to give up travel soccer as well. While she may have favored basketball, or perhaps been better at that than she was at the other sports, she liked them all and to have to give them up would be a sacrifice. It's easy for a kid to be happy with the variety and freshness of playing multiple sports, and to try to specialize in one sport at the expense of others could backfire. Your kid may be unhappy in the end. He or she may regret missing out on the sports that were sacrificed, and the ones that were chosen may not ultimately work out the way either the kid or the parents had hoped for in the beginning.

It was no different for Jackie. Giving up her competitive soccer team would not be easy. After all, it's the reason we had a dog. When Jackie was 12 she had been asking for a dog for some time, but we had never been that close to getting one. One Saturday morning, perhaps in a moment of weakness, I told Jackie that if she scored a goal that day, I would get her one. I said it knowing that we were playing the toughest team of the year, a team we had never beaten. Furthermore, Jackie normally played on the defensive end of the field, so I thought I was safe. Sure enough, Jackie scored a goal in a 2-1 upset victory and we went right to the pet store and brought home Blackjack, who went on to become the greatest dog who ever lived.

Another consideration, even at 14, was college scholarships. This was especially true on the girls' side as Title IX of the Education Amendments of 1972 had essentially demanded that colleges offer up equal scholarship money in several sports even though female participation was not as high as on the boys' side. But that was quickly changing as parents saw an opportunity to use sports as their kids' ticket to colleges that had become off-the-charts expensive, and more so every year. In recognition of this dynamic, Jackie's travel soccer team had hired a very qualified coach, Kevin

Rooney, to take over the team from the current parental coach, who probably didn't know much more than the next parent on the sideline. This change was made "to take the team to the next level", and no doubt there were dollar signs in the minds of several parents associated with that team. Rooney would even openly talk about the opportunity for college scholarships, and these girls hadn't even entered the ninth grade! But he also said that they would have to work hard at it and that it wasn't a given. He was willing to give up his time and get paid very little to help the girls attain something big over time. It was a very good situation and opportunity for all the girls to be part of.

I was not focused on college scholarship money at this point – it was too early, and my income was high enough at the time that I felt I could afford the bill if it came to that. Besides, I didn't want to force my daughter's choice one way or another because of the possibility a college scholarship years down the road. I didn't ever want Jackie to be a pawn in her own life where we were making key selections for her when they naturally should have been her choices.

So that spring, after talking it through with Jackie, we decided to give the Philadelphia Belles a trial run before she would give up her spot on Rooney's team, because there was going to be some major conflicts between the two as the year progressed. AAU basketball tournaments would run from early March through the end of May at a minimum, and if the team did well, it could run through late July with the national tournament being held in midsummer. That year it was scheduled to be held at Disney World.

The trial run worked well enough. Jackie was quickly accepted by her new teammates onto what was essentially an all-star team of girls from the greater Philadelphia area. While Jackie was 14 at this point, officially this was the 13 year old Belles team, with every girl being 13 or less as of January 1. The team had practices twice a week in the new gym at Cabrini College, Nerney's Alma Mater, just down the road from Villanova University and about 50 minutes from our home. Nerney knew his basketball, was extremely well organized, and was a great teacher and communicator. While the girls were all talented players for their age group, they were still young teenage girls who got along great together and liked other things in addition to basketball. In many ways, it seemed like the perfect situation for Jackie at that time.

The team did quite well in its tournaments that spring, and well enough in the all-important regionals did to qualify for the National tournament to be held at Disney World, after not qualifying the previous year. While Jackie wasn't starting, she was getting significant minutes as either a shooting guard or small forward. It was early in the summer that I made the call to Rooney to let him know that Jackie's schedule, and more specifically her commitment to basketball, wouldn't permit her to continue with his soccer team. Rooney totally understood, as he was often on the other side of that conflict where a girl would choose soccer in favor of another sport. While that brought with it a little bit of sadness, it also bought back a little bit of time for Jackie so that pursuit of multiple sports would not consume her calendar or threaten burnout at an early age.

While Jackie had always displayed great instincts for the game and was never a fan of getting personal instruction from me, there was now even less need for that as she was getting great instruction from her new coach, not to mention the great facilities where the team practiced. This realization was further reinforced when the Belles came back from Disney World that summer with a fifth place finish out of 88 teams. The girls had made a very good showing and it was no fluke. It was pretty clear that the Belles were right up there with the best girls' teams in the country for their age group.

A few weeks later Jackie entered Notre Dame as a freshman and promptly joined their soccer team. She started as a fullback and it gave Jackie a nice break from basketball which had been going on for eight months straight between the CYO ball and the AAU tournaments. Of course, no sooner would that season end than basketball would begin. In a preseason scrimmage it became clear that Jackie would be a big asset to Notre Dame's team. A few days later she would start in her first game as a freshman, showing right away that she had a promising high school career right in front of her.

The next four seasons would be more than any parent could wish for their kid. With the lone exception of yielding to a senior on Senior Day, Jackie started 99 out of 100 games. No injuries or illnesses would keep her out of a single game. Notre Dame went 83-17 those four years, including 68-

8 the last three years. Notre Dame had an exceptional team her junior year, going 26-0 before finally dropping a 53-52 heartbreaker to a powerhouse Red Bank Catholic team that only had one loss going into that state championship game. That season brought back memories of my senior year when our team was chasing titles all season. Jackie showed incredible consistency during that whole period, no doubt better prepared for high school competition as a result of seven seasons of AAU basketball.

While it wasn't something she particularly worked at, she turned into quite an amazing 3-point shooter. She made a remarkable 189 shots from beyond the arc, over her four years at Notre Dame, including 68 her senior year. I kept informal stats of her 3-point shooting her last three years and had her making an impressive 44% of her shots from beyond the arc. She had several games where she made five or six threes in a game, and then went 7 for 10 from beyond the arc in a state tournament game that would be-the final game of her career. Perhaps even more admirable was that there was hardly a bad shot taken throughout her career. Jackie was probably the furthest thing from a gunner that you could have. Instead, she took the shot when it was there, but would never force it if it wasn't. As if to compliment her impeccable shot selection, her release was also as quick as you would ever see with any player. It was just one more aspect of her very efficient game with no wasted motion.

Not only was it hard to find something to criticize about her game play, Jackie had no interest in hearing about it anyway. She would just take the games in stride and not make them out to be more important than just games. She couldn't have cared less about stats and wouldn't have been able to tell you what her scoring average was, or any other stat for that matter. It was almost as if she was fulfilling her duty to play the games, so once they were over there was no need or desire to talk about them.

Jackie's career at Notre Dame was a combination of team success and individual success. Jackie certainly had some skilled teammates to play with, especially her junior year when they had a chance to be the top ranked team in NJ. They were ranked as high as #3 and I believe finished 5th that year after their one defeat at the hands of the #2 ranked team. Jackie was an important cog in that machine and all the ND teams she was a part of, averaging double figures the last three years and finishing with 1,113 points. It was the type of career any parent would dream of for their child, or that any kid would dream of for that matter.

But then it was over.

Jackie had done everything right along the way. She had played for the Philadelphia Belles for three seasons and certainly helped make them a better team, including 5th, 7th, and 2nd place finishes in the national tournament those three years. Still, the whole Belles experience was no picnic between the long travel to practices, many weekend tournaments that were even further away, and having to fight for playing time on a very competitive team.

After her second season there, Warren Buffet's Berkshire Hathaway acquired the small insurer that Nerney presided over. In their first meeting, which lasted six hours, Nerney and Buffet spent 45 minutes talking about girls basketball and Buffet promised to fly the Belles to their national tournament the next season if they won their regional tournament. The Belles responded by pulling that off for the first time under Nerney and Buffet made good on his promise and flew the girls down to Amarillo, TX, in one of his private jets. The girls went 10-2 that week, almost winning the whole thing before falling in overtime. Nerney updated Buffet daily on the team's progress, and one night the girls got to have a conference call with their famous benefactor. At one point, Buffet half-jokingly inquired of Nerney: "Do you think there is any way you could rename the team the Berkshire Belles?" Talk about having a good situation. Most kids are lucky to have their local car dealership sponsor their team, while my kid had the world's most famous investor and one-time richest man in the world as her team's sponsor. Buffet sent the team a letter congratulating them on their great run and explaining that no, he wasn't related to Jimmy Buffet – that was just a ploy to get into his will!

But all that success came with a price. AAU required dedication, and essentially that meant eight months in a row of basketball between your school team and AAU team. All the away tournaments meant that a big part of the girl's social life was hanging out with other girls on the team between games. That gets old after a while, even under the best of circumstances. Lack of playing time can make that even less tolerable, even on a team loaded with talent. It's human nature – everyone wants to play, and it can be a blow to your self-esteem when others are chosen ahead of you. Furthermore, while Nerney was a very good teacher with a ton of basketball experience, he could also be very critical of the girls at times. Over a three-year period, sometimes that criticism wouldn't be well received. There was one tournament in Virginia Beach where Jackie got benched for making one turnover. She was naturally upset and who could blame her? It all made for a recipe for some very long drives home.

Then there was issue of college scholarships, the issue that perhaps most of the parents, if not the girls, had in mind all along. In many cases that was their reason for being there, and who could blame them? Just as it had for girls soccer, Title IX had also created valuable scholarship opportunities for girls playing hoops by essentially requiring an equal number of male and female scholarships to be offered, despite the fact that male sports, primarily college football and basketball, were bringing in substantially all the revenue. Title IX had rendered that moot and leveled the playing field in a very important way. It created a powerful incentive for girls to devote large chunks of time pursuing various sports that they might not otherwise have been inclined to pursue. Given how expensive almost any college education is these days, it's very easy to justify the time and effort it takes to earn one of those scholarships, particularly on the female side.

All that assumes, of course, that the girl actually wants to play the sport and put in the required time and effort and has the athletic capacity to achieve the goal in mind. In Jackie's case this was a difficult issue for me to deal with. She had the golden opportunity to earn a scholarship, and all her AAU experience under Nerney helped make that more of a probability than just a possibility. But two things were also working against that.

First, I had already been earning a nice income for several years with my Manhattan based job and could afford those big tuition bills. Not that I liked paying them, but I didn't think it right to use finances as a motivation for Jackie to keep pursuing basketball. I thought about different ways to incentivize her without being pushy. One was to essentially share half the college tuition savings with her if she were to get a scholarship, but that would essentially be making her a professional athlete as a teenager. A more modest way would be to offer her a car, even a used one, if she got the scholarship, perhaps a more acceptable form of motivation and bribery. It would still save me a lot of money without appearing to be an egregious form of child labor. But no matter how I approached it, there would also be the issue of how her siblings would view any form of compensation that Jackie might get. Would they resent it? It seemed that that was a strong possibility, even though I was already paying their full way through college and had even gotten them cars to drive along the way, albeit not the cars of their choice.

Second, and perhaps more importantly, Jackie just didn't show a passion for the sport or a desire to play it at a higher level. The lack of positive feedback from her made it even more difficult for me to conjure up any form of financial incentive to motivate her. In the end, despite her capacity to play and even excel at the next level, I decided that it should be her choice as to how long to keep playing, and that a college scholarship should not even be a factor in that decision.

Not surprisingly, most of the letters that Jackie got from major colleges expressing interest in her future basketball services went unanswered. That still didn't stop me from making a 15-minute highlight tape from several of her games from both junior and senior year. I had taken video of a few games, while the school had videos of a couple more. Unfortunately, the video I took of her last game when she knocked down seven 3-pointers wasn't very good quality, so I decided to call the coach of Red Bank Catholic, thinking he might have a better tape of that game. Coach Joe Montano was gracious enough to make a copy for me and quickly offered to go even further. He said that, while he was sure that ND Coach Anne DeMille was pitching Jackie to any college coach that may be inquiring, he would also be happy to make a recommendation on her behalf or talk to any coach who might be interested. He added, "We've played you twice now, and she killed us both times. Jackie hurt us more than any other player in the state." This was from the coach of arguably the most dominant girls team in NJ those two years. I thanked him for his offer but let him know that I wasn't even sure if she wanted to play in college, maybe feeling a lit bit of burnout. He totally understood, saying he had already seen that in a lot of girls.

The highlight tape would get seen by precious few. It wasn't long after her season concluded that Jackie announced that she "just wanted to be a regular student" in her next school, which turned out to be Florida Atlantic University. I was not about to question her decision or try to talk her out of it, but in the back of my mind I thought that maybe she would miss it and change her mind someday. I even sent a copy of the tape to the coach of FAU, who otherwise wouldn't even know that Jackie existed. In the end it didn't matter. Jackie never changed her mind.

I suppose it's easy to think that Jackie was wasting a talent she had, just throwing it all away. But that would be the wrong way to look at it. For any player who ever picks up a basketball, there always has to be a last game...a final game. Maybe it was a little harder for me to accept because Jackie had achieved a high level of success, certainly more individual success than I ever had, and could have continued to excel at the next level. In fact, in the one-point loss to Red Bank Catholic her junior year that ended her season at 26-1, Jackie was the sole person amongst the top 14 players in that game not to go on to play college basketball. Yet the fact that she could have easily played and likely excelled doesn't mean she should have. I would argue that she did it the right way, that she was being true to herself and not just continuing to play just to please other people. She was at peace walking away from the game...there was no reason for me not to be as well. I decided to be happy for what I had witnessed Jackie do on the court in those K-12 years, rather than dwell upon what might have been if she had made a different decision.

Looking back at Jackie's career, it was easy to see both the similarities and the differences between herself and me. We were both important and consistent players on our respective teams, but not the high scorers or eye-catching players by any means, and of course we both played on standout teams that made historic runs for their respective schools. Jackie also had my wiry frame, and while I considered myself a good athlete, Jackie certainly had me beat in that category. I refined my game at Gumbert Park while Jackie refined hers on the AAU circuit. I had to work at it to become a better player. Jackie was a natural if there ever was one.

Speaking of natural, there was one photo that I had trouble getting out of my mind. It was the photo of Jackie scoring the 1,000th point of her career from the foul line. What is so striking about the photo, which was taken by a photographer standing directly behind the baseline and the basket, was how relaxed Jackie looked in her follow through the moment after the ball had left her hand. In fact, it's so striking that anyone looking at the photograph would swear that Jackie had posed for the photo as opposed to being an action photo from a real game. I asked Jackie later why she was smiling in the picture. "Because I knew it was going in," was her reply.

Moments later that game was halted, and Jackie was surrounded by happy teammates who presented her with flowers and balloons for the obligatory photos for the occasion. Even Mom and Dad had to get out of the stands to be part of the picture taking. Jackie seemed a bit embarrassed by all the attention, especially the pictures with her parents, which caused her to shake her head as if this was all very silly.

The money shot taken by Jackie and captured by the baseline photographer

A little over four years after Jackie played her last game I was walking through a mall when I noticed an artist who was displaying several large colorful sketches she had done of famous people using actual photographs as her subject. I was admiring the sketches of the Beatles, Elvis and others when I thought to myself how cool it would be to have one made of Jackie from that baseline photo. A few minutes later I had arranged the deal with the artist and a month later I had the sketch, which was true to the original photograph while also adding a certain mystique at the same time.

There were only two things left to do: put it in a nice frame and add a few words to the picture. Borrowing some words from my earlier poem about my high school team, I labeled the picture "A Player to Remember", and then added more than a few words below the sketch to try to capture the essence of Jackie Reddy, the basketball player. It read:

It is a picture etched in my mind,

that night you calmly stepped up to the line,

with the count at nine hundred and ninety nine...

then, smiling, you casually tickled the twine.

Yes, your 1000th point that night you did score.

You achieved all that and so much more,

all those days and nights on the hardwood floor,

the memories of which I'll always adore.

Like the early days in the CYO,

where you often put on a one girl show,

or Warren Buffet's jet to Amarillo,

or Hampden, Virginia, where the tears would flow.

Your first game at Trenton in the 9th grade...

the countless number of 3-pointers you made...

The weekends away and the price you paid...

the elegant brand of hoops you played.

The incredible run of your junior year...

a team on a mission, a team without peer...

twenty six and 0, so incredibly near...

then a heartbreaking loss, a heartbreaking tear.

A Player to Remember
Jackie Reddy, #15

Notre Dame, 1998-2002

All the wins, records and points you amassed,

now seem like a blur. It went by so fast...

but fittingly, you saved your best for last...

the game of your life would define your past.

Then you walked away, just as you vowed.

The games are now over; gone is the crowd;

quiet are the gyms you once made loud,

but the scoreboard is clear: you did yourself proud!

And through it all you remained the same...

unmoved by stats, indifferent to fame...

but in the end they all knew your name...

because of one thing...you could play the game!

Jackie, thanks for all the great memories...may all your shots in life be swishes...from your biggest fan...love always, Dad

Indeed, I was and still am thankful for all those memories. I presented the framed picture with poem to Jackie on Thanksgiving Day, 2006. She cried.

XIV. A Saturday in March (Mar 16 – Apr 11, 1972)

"We were 24-2 now, with two more days to go.
It didn't matter who we'd play; It was going to be our show."

from *A Team to Remember*, November 18, 2000

I woke up early on Thursday morning. In fact, I woke up several times during the night. Trying to sleep with your ankle elevated is not the most comfortable or natural thing to do. But keeping it elevated was one of the keys to minimizing the swelling and speeding up my recovery…at least that was the common belief at that time. I can still hear D'Andrea's mantra – "Ice and elevate".

Going to school was out of the question this day. There was just a little more than 48 hours until our state finals game, 54 to be exact, and getting my ankle healed in time was my top priority. In my mind I already knew I was going to play, but my body was still indicating otherwise. Sprained ankles can be a bitch, and mine was still hurting pretty badly. Getting out of bed and walking around only made it feel worse. I quickly realized that I had better keep it elevated with the ice bag on it as much as I could throughout the day. Then I would drive over to the gym later in the afternoon so I could at least watch practice and listen in to whatever Horne was planning for our final opponent.

Not only was my injury causing me to miss school and practice as had my earlier thigh bruise sustained right after the Jefferson game, but it also caused me to miss another surprise visit from the media. This time it was a radio station that showed up to do interviews for a pregame show the station was putting together to air before Saturday's game that they would also be broadcasting. The station representatives came around lunch time and interviewed several of our players in the cafeteria. Dave Phillips described to me at practice what I had missed. For some reason the interviewer decided to have a little fun with Goski by tripping him up with a trick question. *"Tim, what year in school are you?"* the radio guy asked, to which Goski replied *"Junior."* The radio guy then asked *"How come?"* Goski hesitated, not being sure how to answer, before replying, "*'Cause I'm not a senior.*" Goski had answered with a bit of a snarly tone that said, "*That was a stupid question.*" According to Moose the question and Tim's response drew laughter from the crowd gathered around him. It also prompted the interviewer to comment that he had never seen Goski lose his cool like that on the court, which of course got more laughs at Tim's expense. Supposedly the station interviewer was going to catch up with me by phone, but I had no idea when that might be.

The other thing that I got caught up on at practice on was the details of the wild game that followed ours the previous night. I hadn't even read about Triton's comeback win by the time I went into practice on Thursday, but by the time I left there I had heard several accounts of the surprising comeback victory by the all-white Triton team over the all-black Trenton team, which was punctuated by the mini riot that followed. It sounded like anyone in the stands had to get out of the way quickly to avoid getting jostled around by the suddenly angry mob of Trenton fans who had just witnessed their team's season getting snuffed out in dramatic fashion.

Meanwhile, Horne was focused on more important things, like how we were going to beat Triton on Saturday. He prepared his practice agenda ahead of time like he always did but had to make a few last-minute adjustments to account for my absence from practice, or at least my ability to participate in drills. Consequently, he nixed the 4 on 4 defensive drill that we often did, as well as a 3 on 2/2 on 1 fast break drill he had planned for the day's session. What was originally slotted as a short practice that would end at 5:15 would now end closer to 5. Still, it had the usual characteristics that most Horne practices bore: a mix of individual and team drills that focused on both fundamentals and game specific situations. Out of bounds plays were part of that. Beating their press was another key part. Last, but not least, was clamping down on their stocky point guard who had plucked victory from the jaws of defeat in their upset win over Trenton the night before.

I had used crutches to get myself from the car to the gym that day, trying to minimize any unnecessary use of my ankle, not to mention trying to justify my absence from school that day. But once I was inside, I ditched

Figure 6

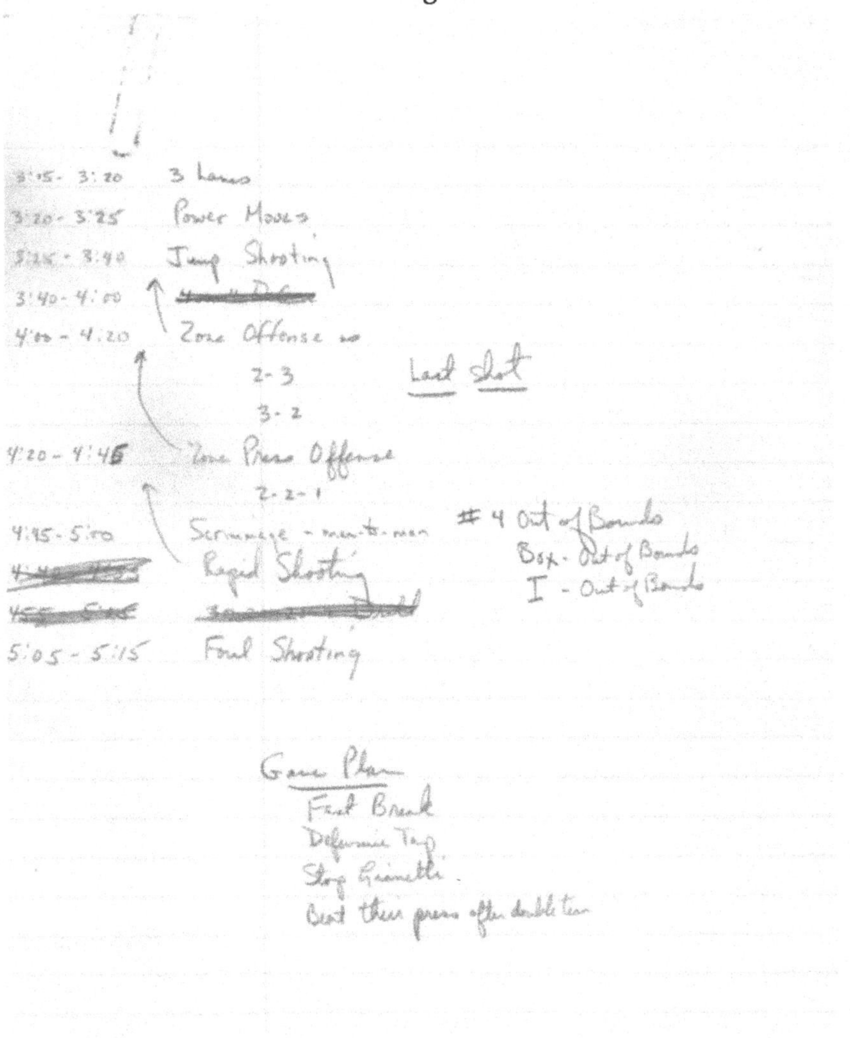

```
3:15 - 3:20    3 Lanes
3:20 - 3:25    Power Moves
3:25 - 3:40    Jump Shooting
3:40 - 4:00    ↑   Defense
4:00 - 4:20    |   Zone Offense
                       2-3            Last Shot
                       3-2
4:20 - 4:45    |   Zone Press Offense
                       2-2-1
4:45 - 5:00    |   Scrimmage - man-to-man    # 4 Out of Bounds
                   Rapid Shooting             Box - Out of Bounds
                                              I - Out of Bounds
5:05 - 5:15    Foul Shooting

               Game Plan
                 Fast Break
                 Defensive Trap
                 Stop Gianelli.
                 Beat their press after double team
```

the crutches to put on the appearance of someone who would be able to play in a couple of days. I shot foul shots for a while, and when I tired of that I just stood by and watched my teammates go at it in a few drills. When you're not an active player you have the luxury of observing some things you might not otherwise catch. I saw a confident team out there, even a bit cocky once again, having finally redeemed ourselves after our two earlier losses. Goski, Novacek and Jester would exchange verbal barbs that were somewhere between trash talking and just plain joking, but they would still be playing hard in between Horne's whistles. Of course, Pfeiffer and Simmons would make sure of that, not to mention Lee, who was now inserted in the starting five and was commanding more respect. As much as I wanted to be out there on the court, it was still pretty cool to watch from the sidelines.

At this point in the season, Horne wasn't going to let us or himself get too worked up in practice. He was more interested in a little fine tuning around the edges, and he certainly didn't want to risk any more injuries. So, a relatively short scrimmage at the end of practice was all we did, allowing us to wrap up right at 5 with some foul shooting. Horne's parting words that day were to go get some rest. It had been a late night the night before with getting back home a little after 11. For me it was more ice and elevation that evening, plus a chance to read about our game and the Triton game I had missed.

The next morning, which happened to be St Patrick's Day, it was back to school time. I'm not even sure if I knew what the rule was, but I wasn't about to take a chance by missing school again and then not being able to play on Saturday. Besides that, I needed to be moving around on the ankle more if I was going to be able to go hard on it a little more than 24 hours later. I tried to disguise my limp as I went from one class to the next that day, and then each class itself provided another 40 minutes of rest and biding time.

Finally, 3:15 rolled around and it was time for our last practice of the year. I didn't dress for it as Horne and I both agreed there was no point. I would more or less repeat my actions of the prior day, shooting free throws on one of the outer baskets and then watching my teammates go through their final drills. The previous day's practice had been, with the exception of the day Horne had thrown us all out early, our shortest practice of the year. On this day he topped that with our shortest one of all. He decided we were ready for our final exam, at least as ready as we were ever going to be. Maybe he believed that some extra rest would do us all a little good. We all knew what was at stake – the school's first Group IV state championship. Before we concluded practice Horne told us that if we just played our game and kept Leonetti in check we should beat this team and we had a chance to be the #1 ranked team in NJ, bringing up a topic that had previously been taboo for players to talk about, at least in practice anyway. I guess it was OK now. We had given our head coach everything he had asked for, and he had given us everything we could have hoped for. Now we had to win just one more game the next day. We walked off our home court for the last time together at around 4:30 pm.

I had heard there was a party of over at Laura Saunder's house that afternoon, maybe something to do with St. Patrick's Day. I wasn't quite sure. Since Laura and Judy Smith were best friends, I decided to venture over there given the little bit of extra free time that Horne had just bestowed upon us. As it turned out, people were leaving just as I was arriving, but Laura invited me in anyways. The next thing I know it's just the three of us sitting on her couch in their family room, talking about the big game the next day. In my mind I am thinking that I may have another shot at this girl, not that I knew how to take it. In any event, it was one of those moments I wished could be frozen in time – a girl I dreamed about was at my side, while the game I had dreamed about for years was one now one day away.

I was home before 6 and got a message from my mom that the radio station had called and wanted me to call them back. It turned out they hadn't forgotten me. I returned the call and answered his questions. The one that I remember in particular was his question, "What was it like to lose after you win so often?" I responded that it was no fun and that the second loss was quite devasting, but that the first loss was more embarrassing than anything and that "I just felt like hiding." When the radio show aired the next day, the narrator aptly followed up my quote with "But nobody has to hide today."

After the interview I headed over to 7-Eleven to grab a couple of papers to see if anything more was being said about our final game. In the *Daily Journal* I was surprised to see an article titled: **"Westfield Gives Lee Job Of Guarding Triton Star."** The article itself stated that Reddy "is not expected to see action." I obviously was planning otherwise. I suppose I was putting a lot of faith in the next tape job I would receive from D'Andrea, because it had only been 48 hours since the injury and I hadn't yet tested it in earnest. I was also putting a lot of faith that icing and elevating was helping the healing process and that 48 hours was in fact enough time for this one to heal just enough.

One step I thought to help my cause was to switch to high top sneakers for the final game, thinking that they might give my ankle a little extra support. I had never worn high tops my entire life, but I made the decision that the next day would be my first day wearing them. The only remaining question was whether I should wear two of them or just one. Maybe I would make a fashion statement in the process? I made arrangements with my dad to go downtown the next morning to pick up a new pair of high-top Converse.

There was nothing else left to do but to kill a little time watching TV in the basement, along with my last dose of ice and elevation. I was oblivious to any St. Patrick's Day celebrations that might have been going on in the outside world. I had only one celebration on my mind…the one I hoped would take place the next day.

March 18, 1972

I was up by 8 on Saturday morning and started walking around to get the blood flowing around my ankle. It always seemed to hurt more once you reverted from a horizontal to a vertical position and the blood rushed to that area and compounded the swelling. But it was pretty much now or never, and I had to start treating the ankle as if it were already healed and ready to go. I was still limping around, but there was no question in my mind that it felt better than 48 hours earlier and that things would be OK once D'Andrea got it all wrapped up.

At 10 my dad and I went down to the Leader, the downtown sporting goods shop, where I sat down to try on a pair of size 11 and a half high tops in the legendary Converse brand. There wasn't much support in these old canvas sneakers, but it's all we had at the time. Adidas and Puma were just hitting the scene around this time and were much more expensive. My father plunked down the $4 for the new pair of Converse and then we headed back home. Once there I took the red and blue shoelaces out of the low top sneakers I had been wearing all season and laced up my new high tops with them. This was no time to interrupt the statement we had been making all season with our colored laces and wrist bands. I did, however, reject the notion of wearing the high top on only the right foot. I was concerned that it just might not feel right when I got out on the court, not to mention that I simply wasn't bold enough to be that different.

At 11 I sat down for my pre-game meal, which was a fried hamburger that was eaten with a fork and a little bit of salt, but without a bun or any ketchup. I had applesauce on the side and of course a tall glass of milk to wash it all down. It was an early lunch but necessitated by our early 2 pm game time. I'm sure it didn't compare favorably to the pre-game steaks that the football team supposedly had on the mornings of their game days. Nor would it measure to today's standards for a smart pre-game meal. It was still red meat, though, and would give me the energy necessary to get me through the afternoon's battle.

I left the house at 11:30 for the high school, where we would board the bus for the ride to Princeton at noon. The bus ride took a little less than an hour, along a route that I was unfamiliar with. Then, without warning, Jadwin Gym appeared right off to our side.

I was still moving a bit gingerly on my ankle as I disembarked the bus. It seemed as if it had stiffened up a bit during our brief bus ride, and Scott Novacek, who was right behind me, took notice. "You're going to play like that?", Scott asked with a bit of his characteristic nervous laughter. I just smiled back at him without answering. From that point on I was determined not to show any limp the rest of the way into the locker room. Trainer D'Andrea would take over from there.

We walked into the cavernous Jadwin Gym for the second time in four days. Based on our still fresh experience of our semifinal game against Hackensack, we wouldn't have to worry about adapting to the Jadwin environment, at least that's how we felt about it. We had played a pretty decent game that night, with a reasonable number of turnovers and decent shooting percentage. We even had one of our best free throw shooting nights of the season, shooting 80% as a team. There was no reason to think we couldn't pick up where we left off the other night.

We proceeded to get dressed with plenty of time to spare, but my tape job required a few extra minutes stretched out on the training table. Some of the guys, particularly Goski and Novacek, were teasing me about getting ready to play after being absent the past couple of days, and that I was about to make a Willis Reed-like appearance when we went out for warmups. Less than two years earlier Reed had famously made a dramatic appearance shortly before the tipoff of Game 7 between the Knicks and the Lakers in the NBA finals. Reed had gotten shot up with cortisone for his injured hamstring and then scored the first two baskets for the Knicks while hobbling around the court. The Knicks then rallied around him to thoroughly outplay the Lakers for their first NBA championship. I didn't particularly care about making a similar entrance with all eyes focused on me; all I wanted was the same outcome that Reed and the Knicks had gotten.

Since we had arrived with plenty of time to spare, Horne let us venture out of the locker room at about 1:25 for a little shoot-around and to get reacquainted with the Jadwin surroundings. As fate would have it, I wasn't quite ready to go at that moment, so the rest of the team headed out there without me. D'Andrea was just finishing up, which meant I still had to put on two pairs of socks, sandwiched around our dark blue knee-high stockings, and then my new Converse high tops. Finally, with everything laced up, I could begin to test the ankle in earnest with all the protection that it was going to get now in place. I needed a few moments to get used to the uncomfortable sensation of the heavy tape wrapped around all sides of my ankle...very rigid and restrictive... but I didn't have much choice. I had just a few short minutes to get used to it.

After a few short jab steps and a little bit of running in place inside the locker room, there was nothing else left to do but to join my teammates out on the court doing my Willis Reed imitation. I wasn't looking for any extra attention, but sure enough, my teammates spotted me as I made my way towards one corner of the court where our team was getting loose just shooting around. When I reached the court Goski tossed me a ball and then others stopped to watch me take a few dribbles and then my first shot from 17 feet off the left elbow. I missed, but at least it got rid of some of the tension and the unwanted attention. Everyone else resumed their own warmups while I continued testing my heavily taped ankle over the next few minutes. Thankfully, it was feeling ok, distinctly better than on Wednesday night, with a manageable level of discomfort. Horne then called us back into the locker room where he reviewed the game plan and everybody's defensive assignments. There was no rah-rah speech to propel us out onto the court.

That wasn't Horne's style and we didn't need that to propel us anyway. Horne was as calm and as matter of fact as ever. I guess you stick with what got you there.

We took the court again just after 1:45 for our normal warmup routine of two layup lines. Eddie Ciemniecki from Linden, one of our conquerors this season, gave us an encouraging "Come on, guys" as we walked right by him on our way from the locker room to the court. He was on our side at least for this day, perhaps hoping to see Union County finish on top in the state tournament, and possibly just out of respect for us having beaten the team that thwarted them five times that season.

The next 10 minutes gave us a chance to burn off a little adrenaline and get comfortable with our surroundings once again. The crowd size, which the papers would put somewhere between 4,300 and 4,500, was pretty decent and certainly more than we were used to playing in front of. In this case, however, the spacious confines of Jadwin Gym made the crowd seem fewer in number than it actually was. The fans were situated mostly on the two sidelines, with the baseline seats relatively empty at each end. Ten

Novacek lays the ball in during warmups

The wait is over...it's time to play one game for all the marbles

minutes later the buzzer sounded and it was time for the coaches' final instructions and the player introductions – at forward, #24 Tom Pfeiffer, at the other forward, #22 Larry Simmons, at center, #23 Scott Novacek, at guard, #11 Tim Goski, and at the other guard, #12 Steve Reddy. Finally, the national anthem was played, followed by our last brief huddle before tipoff. Now there was nothing left to do but play one game for the Group IV State Championship!

We controlled the opening tip and then surveyed Triton's defense. They had dropped right back into a 2-1-2 zone, with their big guy, Richie Radziewicz, roaming the middle of the zone. He was about 6'5" with particularly long arms, which could make penetrating the zone defense even trickier. We were deliberate on our first possession, at least until I put the ball on the floor looking for a seam in the zone. Not a good idea – my path was quickly shut off and then a moment later I was stripped of the ball as I tried to reverse direction just as a double team was arriving. Triton would come back on their first possession and drained an 18-footer from the top of the key. They immediately went into their full court press and forced another turnover when they intercepted Goski's long pass downcourt.

Fortunately, our tentative start on offense would be offset by solid defense and rebounding at the other end of the court. Triton did not score another field goal for about four minutes. Meanwhile, we just tried to get our footing on offense. Pfeiffer missed a jumper from the left side, and then I missed a runner coming across the left side of the lane. Goski finally broke the ice with a made free throw after getting fouled on a fast break. Shortly after that, Simmons added another made free throw after getting fouled hauling in a rebound. On the next possession, Novacek made a nice strip on a driving Leonetti, which ignited a fast break with Pfeiffer coming down the left side, who then spotted Goski flashing across the lane toward the baseline. Pfeiffer hit Goski with a pass, and Tim immediately pivoted and rose up for a short six-footer. The only problem was that Radziewicz was right in his face, so Tim had to launch a high archer to keep it out of Radziewiccz's reach, which he was quite capable of doing. Tim drained the.

Goski takes and makes a difficult baseline jumper over a tall defender

This angle shows the extreme arc Goski used on the shot

tough shot for our first field goal, giving us a 4-2 lead after about two and a
half minutes After a turnover by each team and a missed shot by Triton,
Goski found himself open on the right baseline and walked into a 15-footer
that he swished to give us a 6-2 lead.

Goski rises up for a 15-footer along the right baseline

Triton was fouled on their next possession but missed the free throw. Novacek grabbed the defensive rebound and made the outlet to Goski on the right side. Tim made his way up court on a semi-fast break, cutting back over toward the left side of the court as he crossed the mid court stripe. Meanwhile, Novacek had made a bee line down the middle of the court towards our basket. When Tim reached the top of the key, he spotted Scott in the middle of the lane and slid a pass to him through the defense. Novacek caught it in stride, came to a quick jump stop, and went up for a short banker from the right side of the rim with a defender on his back. Two more points and a foul on the play.

Scott failed to convert the free throw, but we still led 8-2. Triton finally broke their dry spell with a made free throw, followed by a made jump shot on their next possession with 2:40 left in the quarter. On our next possession a missed shot resulted in a jump ball, which Pfeiffer tipped back to me. A Triton defender had lunged for the ball, leaving me an opening to drive

Goski advances the ball with Novacek and Simmons to his left

Goski makes a slick pass to Novacek in the middle of the lane

Novacek converts the basket after receiving Goski's feed

My drive down the lane is challenged in front of the rim

down the lane. I took two dribbles towards the rim and rose up as two defenders converged on me. One may have gotten a piece of the ball, but definitely got a piece of my wrist as well. No call ever came, but Pfeiffer was waiting in the lane to scoop up the loose ball and quickly put it back up and in. 10-5, Westfield.

This angle shows me getting fouled, but no call would be made

We went back and forth with Triton the rest of the first quarter, each team making a couple more field goals. Goski made another short high arching baseline jumper similar to his first one, and Novacek added a free throw. We led 15-11 when the buzzer sounded. That wasn't too bad a start, especially considering the rash of turnovers we committed in the period – eight in all, although a few of them seemed like pretty sketchy calls. Triton had committed a few as well though, and were shooting poorly so far; thus, we managed to come out of the first quarter on top. If we could cut back on the turnovers, our chances looked pretty good.

The early part of the second period would go our way. In the first minute Goski and Novacek each scored field goals, with Goski racking up his eighth and ninth points already. Then Tim hit Pfeiffer on a fast break, and Tom drained a 15-footer from the left baseline. On Triton's next possession, Pfeiffer drew a charge in the lane on a driving Tom Dorsey. Pfeiffer would go to the other end of the court and knock down both foul shots to give us a 23-11 lead. We had now scored 10 straight, including the last basket of the first period. On Triton's next possession they would miss a running shot in the lane, which Goski ripped down off the rim and immediately hooked an outlet pass to Novacek who was heading up the left side of the court. Scott then continued up court with a right-hand dribble. We had a 2 on 1 fast break at this point as I was heading up the right side of the court. Scott, favoring his right hand, decided to cut across the lane, from left to right, as he approached the basket. Then, in one twisting motion, he rose up in the lane and putting a running eight-foot bank shot with his momentum still carrying diagonally across the lane. He nailed it! Novacek had shown uncommon agility for a big guy and made a high degree of difficulty shot given how fast he was moving and the angle he was taking.

Novacek in the unusual position of leading a 2 on 1 break

Scott missed a chance to hit me as he crossed into the lane

Scott rises up over the defender as he moves across the lane

The reverse angle shows Novacek's acrobatic move in the lane

We now led 25-11 and were starting to take control. There were six minutes left in the second period. Things were looking good.

Jester, shortly after entering the game for Simmons, pulled down a defensive rebound, but before he could make the outlet pass a scrappy defender stripped the ball loose to a teammate who gathered it and scored at close range. Jester quickly made up for it on our next possession when he pulled down an offensive rebound after a Novacek miss from close range and put it right back up and in. It was now 27-13 with four and a half minutes remaining. Before Jester's miscue, we had gone three and a half minutes without one. We seemingly couldn't stand prosperity, though, because Jester's turnover seemingly unleashed an avalanche of additional turnovers.

Over those last four plus minutes of the second period we went scoreless and only got off two shots. Instead of taking shots, we committed seven straight turnovers the rest of the period in a bit of a horror show. Pretty much everyone on our squad was getting into the act with an assortment of bad passes, fumbled balls, and bad catches. Naturally, Triton was able to close the gap during this bad stretch, with the scoreboard reading 27-22 as we headed into the locker room at halftime. They had scored nine straight during this stretch, and we were fortunate they hadn't scored any more.

Horne was beside himself at halftime. We had squandered most of the 14-point lead we had built up in the first 10 minutes, thanks mostly to just plain sloppy play. Seventeen turnovers for the first half, and still we had a five-point lead. Our game plan of pushing the ball up court to create transition baskets was largely responsible for the lead we had built up, but a rash of turnovers will kill any team's momentum and ultimately lead to baskets for the other side. The vast majority of our turnovers were self-inflicted and couldn't be attributed to Triton's defensive efforts, although a few certainly were. This was the good news though – if we could just clean up our sloppiness, we should be able to finish the job. Further helping our cause was that Triton was not showing us much offensively. They were content to fire up jump shots from any spot if there appeared to be any opening at all. At the halfway point they were shooting a very low percentage, including Leonetti, who was putting more shots than any Triton player and clearly had the green light to shoot at any time. I was given the assignment of guarding him, and I'm not sure that I was necessarily guarding him well, but many of his shots were taken off the dribble or on the move as he worked to create any type of opening. I had a lot of help defending Leonetti as he beat me a couple of times on drives right into the lane. Fortunately, he had not yet hurt us in any meaningful way.

Horne was reluctant to pull the plug on pushing the ball up the court in the hopes of getting a few easy transition baskets. He was willing to roll the dice that we would somehow cut down on our unforced errors. He didn't want to turn it into a purely half-court game, with us going up against the 2-1-2 zone and them going against our man-to-man defense. Horne may have felt that would somewhat neutralize the offensive weapons that we had, turning it into a more even game, perhaps coming down to which team shot better in the second half. Also, no one was in foul trouble at this point, so Horne saw no reason to change things up at the defensive end. So far, we were winning the game at that end of the court.

The third period was a mixed bag of results. On the negative side, the turnover machine continued to produce at a rate of about one per minute. We racked up seven more during the period, bringing our game total up to 24. As in the first half, most of our turnovers came on bad passes, although a couple came on travelling calls that were again very questionable. The refs seemingly had their own criteria this day when it came to travelling and palming violations. The only saving grace was that these bad calls were going both ways. Triton also appeared to get hosed on two or three very questionable travelling and palming violations, including on a couple of fast break opportunities.

The good news was that we continued to make it difficult for Triton to score. They were getting nothing inside, except for an occasional offensive rebound. Their scoring attempts were all jump shots from a variety of spots on the court. Their offense appeared to be just a free-lance offense with Leonetti controlling the ball the majority of the time. However, their other players were not hesitant to shoot at all whenever they saw an opening.

The third quarter was a slog, with baskets coming slowly each way. Our five-point lead was maintained throughout the period, give or take a bucket. Each team made four field goals along the way. Of course, we didn't do ourselves any favor, though, by going 0-for-4 from the foul line during that stretch. The period ended with the scoreboard reading 35-30, Westfield.

We now had eight minutes left in our season and the state championship hung in the balance. Our lead seemed and felt tenuous at best. We had been unable to rebuild the big lead we had early in the second period, and now it felt more like we were just trying to hold onto the slim lead we still had.

During the break Horne decided he had seen enough, and he made a calculated decision that we should slow the game down and be more deliberate on offense. Hopefully this would lead to less bad passes and more good, open shots. While attacking a zone defense wasn't necessarily our strength, Horne felt it was a risk worth taking given the five point lead we had at the time. He was also counting on our defense to make it tough for them to score at the other end.

Novacek won the fourth-quarter tap, his third won tap of the day, and we immediately showed more patience on the first possession. After 14 passes, I took and made a 16-footer from the right wing on a feed from Goski.

I knock down a jumper early in the fourth quarter

We stopped them on their next possession, after which I got fouled on a steal attempt and made the one free throw, giving us a 38-30 lead. After stopping Triton once more, we again were patient on offense until the ball reached me on the left baseline, about 16 feet out. I saw one of Triton's big guys come at me, and then a slight opening along the baseline. I took two dribbles to my left trying to slide past the defender along the baseline. When I made my move, the defender stuck his right foot out further to his right, widening his stance, and put his chest up into my shoulder as I tried to slide by him. I had gotten a half step around him when the whistle blew for an offensive foul! A terrible call that game films would later validate as just that - terrible.

A dubious offensive call prevented us from grabbing a 10-point lead.

As if that wasn't unfortunate enough, the bad luck seemingly followed us down to the other end of the court on Triton's next possession. Radziewicz tried a hook shot from the middle of the lane. The ball hit the back of the rim and came off to the left side of the lane, where Pfeiffer, Novacek, and Simmons all went up and appeared to get a hand on the ball simultaneously some six feet from the rim. The next thing we see is the ball heading back towards the rim, and then right through it. No Triton player had even left their feet to go after the rebound. It was impossible to tell from

Novacek, Simmons and Pfeiffer all go up for the rebound

Everyone watches the batted ball go through the hoop

game film who had tipped the ball in because it appeared that all three had gotten a hand on it, although Simmons would later claim responsibility for the unfortunate batted ball. Regardless of whose hand it came off of, Triton got credit for the basket. Now it was a 38-32 game. That was a four-point swing that kept us from regaining a commanding 10-point margin.

Novacek and I failed to connect on a pass inside the lane the next time down court. Triton made us pay at the other end with an offensive rebound and put back to make it 38-34. Horne then called a timeout to regroup with 4:42 left on the clock. The timeout backfired when I forced a pass up the left sideline when Triton went back into their full court press. The ball got deflected and recovered by Triton near midcourt. Then, as if to bail me out, Pfeiffer intercepted a pass to the wing on the very next possession and headed down court for what appeared to be an easy layup. Tom slowed up just a hair to time his steps as he approached the basket, and that fraction of a second allowed the pursuing Triton player to get close enough of Tom to break up the layup attempt – barely. Pfeiffer got two free throws instead but missed both to keep the score steady at 38-34.

Triton now had a second chance to narrow the gap to two points, but Leonetti was also unable to convert a one and one after getting fouled by Novacek near midcourt. Four minutes now remained. For the first four minutes of the final period, we had been very patient on offense as Horne had instructed, but the next time down court I threw patience out the window when I received the ball on the left wing about 27 feet out. Seeing the defender too far off me, I took a dribble towards the basket. Then another. Finally, the defender started toward me, and I took a third dribble down the left side of the lane to get around him. Now, with my momentum taking me towards the rim, I was committed to getting there somehow and took one more dribble. One of their bigger defenders, who was stationed near the low block and watching out for the pass to Simmons along the left baseline, now turned to help stop my drive, but I jumped to my right to avoid him while putting up a running hook shot off the board from just inside the lane. Fortunately, I was able to draw a foul on the low post defender who bumped me in mid-air with his right side – two free throws were coming my way. Meanwhile, Horne was none too pleased with my drive to the basket. Four dribbles directly into the teeth of the zone defense was not exactly his idea of how to attack the zone or how to be patient. I turned toward the bench with my arms outstretched asking "What?" I got his answer instantly. Perhaps I could have redeemed myself in that moment by making the free throws, but instead I missed both. We had now missed four straight free throws and were 1-for-7 in the second half, not helping our cause one bit.

I dribble into Triton's zone, trying to exploit a slight opening

We stopped Triton on its next possession, but then I gave it right back after I was double teamed on the right wing, and another one of their long arms got into a passing lane...my fourth turnover of the period and fifth of the game. They were now off on a fast break headed the other way. The ball quickly got into Leonetti's hands who fed it to one of the big guys racing down the right side of the court. The Triton player caught it in stride, took one dribble, and rose up for the driving layup attempt. But the whistle had already blown! No basket – travelling! Their coach must have

I get an earful from Horne who didn't like my foray into the lane

been livid because this was a terrible call, as game film later confirmed. Thus, the see-saw battle continued, with even the bad calls appearing to more or less even out as the game went on. The score remained 38-34 in our favor, with 3:05 remaining on the clock.

Then came a play that I still can't explain to this day. After a few short passes against Triton's zone, Goski hit me in the left corner. I then proceeded to exit the corner with the dribble back in Tim's direction near the top of the key. But having gotten past the corner defender fairly easily, I now saw a lot of real estate between me and the basket, so I made a left hand turn in that direction. Then, contrary to everything that Horne had been harping on and had just called me out on, I put my head down on a mission to get to the basket again, essentially doubling down on dumb. Using eight dribbles in total I had weaved my way through the entire left side of their zone. I had arrived at my destination with a jump stop, but unfortunately with nowhere to go.

I saw an opening in the defense and cut in that direction

As the defense converged, I got low with the dribble

I've gone as far as I can go, but now what?

I was directly underneath the basket but *behind* the backboard, barely inbounds, and surrounded by four defenders. There was virtually no way to get the ball to a teammate, assuming I could even find one in the now crowded lane area. I was looking only up towards the rim. I had no choice at this point but to get the ball up for a shot attempt. I pump faked once, then sprung up and out from behind the backboard and gave the ball a good hard flick with the wrist in the hopes of getting it up on the glass somewhere above the rim. I think Triton's defenders were leery of committing a foul in that sequence, so they just kept their arms up around me to limit my operating room. I was able to keep the ball clear of the rim on its way up to the top of the backboard. It finally kissed the very top of the backboard surface above the right side of the rim before beginning its descent. Then, as if the basketball gods were looking down and said: "You deserve this one," the ball caromed straight down and through the rim without touching it.

I get off a prayer of a shot while jumping back into the court

The ball hits high on the board... then my prayer was answered

I let loose with an Ali-like right cross to express my approval of the made shot. Meanwhile, Horne had to be beside himself even as the ball went through the hoop. Fortunately, played continued, so I was spared the obligation of looking over towards the bench in Horne's direction. Better still, our lead had just increased to 40-34 with 2:47 showing on the clock. Those two points had to ease his anxiety just a bit.

Leonetti, to his credit, was like a bull who kept charging. I played soft defense on the next possession as he came at me, not moving my feet enough as he got by me to my right. Having been beaten with his dribble, I swiped from behind but missed, and he took one more dribble and then put up a 10-foot runner from the middle of the lane. It was long, but he drew the foul from Simmons who had stepped up into his path. After missing his first four free throws earlier, Leonetti drained these two. 40-36.

On our next possession Horne's desire for patience on offense prevailed as we managed to make 16 passes without even coming close to taking a shot or making a turnover. Horne then signaled for a timeout and with 1:53 left and we headed for the sideline. Horne again stressed patience and to be ready for more defensive pressure from Triton as the clock ran down.

We set up a sideline out of bounds play to resume the action. Ten more passes ensued, mostly around the perimeter of the defense. Their defense was forced to spread out more in pursuit of the ball. Then Goski became guilty of the same thing I succumbed to – seeing an opening and going for it. From just above the foul line he took two dribbles into the lane, relatively unobstructed. But then he met the Triton interior wall about eight feet in front of the rim. At this point, Goski had already committed to attacking the basket as opposed to pulling up for a short jumper. So, he jumped off one foot and then brought the ball over to his left side with both hands, shielding the ball from the defenders, before trying an underhanded scoop shot from the left side of the rim with defenders still pinned on his back side. It was an athletic move by a talented offensive player, and while the ball appeared destined to go in, it did not. Instead, it rolled off the front iron into Triton hands with 1:18 now showing on the clock.

...and deftly keeps the ball away from the defender

Goski's athletic move is countered by great defense in the paint

Leonetti was now immediately coming back the other way in attack mode. He drove the ball into the lane area and then shoveled it over to an open Cliff Crews along the left baseline. Crews went up the for the 15-footer and drained it. Our lead had just been cut in half at 40-38, our smallest lead since early in the game!

Triton was in their full court press after every score. Pfeiffer received the inbound pass and easily beat the defender up the right sideline and was fouled in the process with just over a minute remaining, earning him a one and one at the line. Tom missed again. Pfeiffer had been our second-best free thrower all season, but after making his first two today, he now had missed four straight, making us 1-for-8 in the second half.

Simmons came up huge on the ensuing rebound, getting his hands on the loose ball in the lane and forcing a jump ball. Larry then followed it up by winning the tap straight back to Pfeiffer, allowing us to retain possession while clinging to our two point lead. The reprieve proved to be short lived, however, when Pfeiffer called for a very questionable palming violation as the Triton defense was coming further out to pressure us. Game film would later confirm another terrible call had been made. Unfortunately, it was our turn to bear the brunt.

Now here came Leonetti back the other way once again. While never flashy, he was adept at working his way into the lane with his dribble in either direction. Once again, I got beat to my right as Leonetti maneuvered his way down the left side of the lane before putting up another floater. He missed, but Radziewicz had inside position and was fouled by Pfeiffer while attempting a quick put back on the short rebound. At this stage, Triton was more or less matching our futility from the foul line and was only 6-for-19 for the game. They missed again! The rebound went out of bounds off both Simmons and Novacek who each had inside position yet somehow had the ball escape their fingertips. Another chance for Triton. Triton ran a play designed for Leonetti, who inbounded the ball but then used a baseline screen to get open and receive a return pass. I was able to stay close to him this time as he spun and in one motion put up a forced jumper from the left baseline. Leonetti's shot resulted in air ball that landed safely in Simmons hands!

We quickly advanced the ball to half court when Horne called another timeout with 28 seconds remaining. All we had to do was play a little keep away and maybe make a foul shot to put the game away. Horne set up the sideline out of bounds play with Goski breaking into the backcourt where he received the inbound pass from Pfeiffer. I had moved over to the opposite sideline as a relief valve in case we needed another option to inbound the ball. Goski started advancing the ball but had a couple of guys running at him, so he lobbed it over to me near the right sideline and the midcourt stripe. I was wide open when I caught the ball but then saw Dorsey and another guy quickly coming towards me as I advanced it into the front court. I reversed my dribble and briefly turned my back as I did so. It was only a split second, but in that split-second Dorsey managed to cleanly poke the ball free. I immediately went into a dead sprint back

I'm in good shape here, but the defense is starting to come at me

Dorsey picks my pocket clean when I fail to protect my dribble

I'm right on Dorsey's side, planning on blocking any shot attempt

...but he shielded the ball with his body as I tried in vain to reach it

towards Triton's basket while Dorsey recovered the ball near half court and without breaking stride also began racing towards the basket. We were essentially side by side the whole way, but with me gaining ground ever so slightly. I thought I had gained enough ground where I could swat his ball away as he went in for a layup attempt. I was wrong. On the dead run with me draped all over him, the shorter Dorsey somehow got off a lefty layup attempt that eluded my fully extended right arm, with the ball then hitting the top left corner of the box on the backboard and then went straight through the hoop! On top of that, the whistle blew – I had fouled Dorsey and given him the "and one" opportunity for a three point play and a chance to take the lead!

Their fans went nuts. Their players were ecstatic. Meanwhile I felt a wall of gloom suddenly overwhelm me as our relatively secure lead that we had held virtually the entire game had just been snatched away in seconds. I had been extremely careless in protecting the ball in our front court as the double team approached me, and then I compounded my error by committing the cardinal sin of fouling Dorsey, giving Triton a golden

Triton has reason to celebrate…they were now 18 seconds from victory

opportunity to take the lead with just 18 seconds on the clock. I helplessly looked over to the bench for something, maybe some kind of consolation or encouragement. I think we all did. I could only hope and pray that Dorsey would miss the "and one" free throw.

For the second time in three minutes, my prayers were answered! Dorsey missed and Simmons hauled in the rebound, prompting Horne to call our last timeout. I used most of the timeout trying to recompose myself and block out of my mind what had just happened. Despite my blunder, we were still in the driver's seat with a chance to win the game in the remaining seconds.

Triton again reverted to full court pressure coming out of the timeout to make our task more difficult with the clock winding down. The inbound pass went to Novacek, who eventually got it back to me after avoiding all the pressure around him. I was still a nervous mess at this point and treading very cautiously up the court, simultaneously looking to get rid of it as soon as I could find an open target. Pfeiffer became that guy, up in the forecourt near the sideline. Tom caught the ball with about six seconds left, and he made his way toward the foul line area. He eluded one defender before pulling up just inside the lane for a 14-footer with about three seconds left, over the outstretched arm of Radziewicz. The ball was a bit short, just grazing the front iron, but a hand deflected the ball down to the left side of the rim, where it landed in the hands of Goski who had snuck into the lane while Pfeiffer was getting off his shot. Tim quickly put up the little three-foot chippie bank shot, rushing it a bit to the beat the clock. He missed it! The buzzer sounded. We were going to overtime!

We had had so many opportunities to win the game in regulation, but we hadn't capitalized on them, so now all we could do was walk back to the bench and regroup. It's one of the toughest things to do in sports – to overcome a blown opportunity to secure a victory, and then just moments later you have to resume playing with the score effectively zero-zero. You simply can't dwell on what just happened; instead, you have to focus on what's about to happen. I was still unnerved about the colossal blunder I had committed just moments earlier, but at least thankful that we had our chance to overcome it. Horne knew best of all not to look back. Composure was one of his big strengths and he wasn't about to lose it now. His demeanor and calm tone helped us all refocus on the task at hand.

Triton won the jump ball to start the overtime session, although Leonetti appeared to get away with a backcourt violation after retrieving the tipped ball. A few seconds later Dorsey missed a 17-footer. I got the long rebound and then we displayed the kind of patience that Horne had been preaching. The only problem was that while we were being deliberate, we also weren't doing much to attack the zone and create a good shot. Yes, we had guys rotating through the middle of the zone near the foul line, but we weren't always looking to make that pass, content with keeping the ball on the perimeter. Finally, after 15 passes in the forecourt, I received the ball while open on the right wing and let it fly from about 15 feet. I had knocked down my two other jump shots in the game from almost the exact same spot, but the third was not a charm. The score remained 40-40 with 2:04 remaining.

Triton, in contrast to us, didn't take much time to get their next shot off. Cliff Crews came driving across the foul line and, seeing an opening, headed down the right side of the lane with Pfeiffer right alongside of him. As Crews went up for the running hook, Tom went right up with him and made a perfect block with his left hand, but then the ball came straight down into his lap as his momentum carried him out of bounds just to the right of the lane. Triton set up an out-of-bounds play with the ball being inbounded from the baseline. They had four players lined up just below the foul line with our defenders between them and the basket. They made a simple screen and cut between the two guys in the middle of the four-person line. Simmons got picked off for a split second, allowing his guy to slip down the right side of the lane where he received the inbound pass and then went up for the quick layup. Larry got there a fraction too late to defend the shot, but miraculously the ball rolled around and out of the rim. Like Goski's last-second shot to end regulation, this one had also been rushed just enough to cause the error.

Simmons then gobbled up the defensive rebound and we were headed the other way with 1:45 remaining. Goski walked the ball up slowly and

Novacek rises up and hits a 15 foot baseline shot to give us the lead

then hit me on the right wing about 20 feet out. Novacek ventured out from the lane area along the baseline some 15 feet out. The defense didn't come out on Scott right away, so I got him the ball. Scott turned to face the basket and rose up without hesitation for an open baseline jumper. He swished the 15-footer. We were finally back in the lead with 1:31 left!

Triton wasted no time trying to retie the game, and within about 15 seconds got off a 17-foot jump shot from the right side of the key. Novacek was there again to haul in the defensive rebound, his 18th rebound of the game, and quickly got the outlet pass to me on the left wing. I immediately launched a pass up the left side to a streaking Pfeiffer who had released as soon as he saw Novacek secure the ball. Tom now had a clear path to the basket, with only one defender with a chance to cut him off. Simmons was streaking down the right side giving us a 2 on 1 fast break advantage. Tom did what he should have, which was force the defender to block his path to the basket, in which case he could dump the ball off to an open Simmons for the easy basket. But the defender never did block his path, so Tom continued his assault on the basket hoping to lay it in unobstructed.

Pfeiffer heads down the left side a 2 on 1 fast break...

Only a smack across the temple prevented a sure basket by Pfeiffer

He got ever so close. The defender arrived just soon enough to disrupt Tom's layup attempt with a forearm across Tom's right temple. It was an all-out effort by the defender to disrupt the play, but the ref was in perfect position and couldn't possibly miss this one. Once again, the layup attempt narrowly missed, but Tom still had two foul shots coming his way with 1:10

left in overtime. Tom missed the first free throw. We would find out later that Al Pfeiffer had moved himself to the upper portion of Jadwin and had taken to watch the late game action through his binoculars. Maybe the tension was getting to him, or he was afraid of what he might see…or might yell. He peered through the binoculars again and saw Tom miss the second. We were now 1-for-10 from the line in the second half, but we still led by 42-40.

Leonetti brought his troops back the other way, with another chance to tie the game again, and he wasn't about to get gun shy either, bad shooting game or not. He obviously had a lot a confidence that was not going to be shaken in a single game. Perhaps he was a little Goski-like in that regard. I was able to stay in front of him on this possession, so he gave it up to a teammate and headed down the lane and camped out on the low block. A few seconds later, he flashed out and got the ball back some 12 feet out. I was still right on him, but he spun back to the baseline and drove along the baseline toward the basket, only to find Simmons in his path. Leonetti put up a runner as he approached the lane, but Larry held his ground and drew the charging call he was hoping for. It also happened to be foul #5 for Leonetti – he was done for the day!

We clung to a two-point lead with 45 seconds to go, similar to where we stood at the end of regulation. We now had to inbound the ball near the corner where the sideline and baseline converge. Pfeiffer was able to get it into Goski in the corner as the rest of us started to clear out. Tim had only Dorsey to contend with at this point, essentially the one-on-one full court drill that we had done almost every day all season. Tim put the ball on the floor to start heading out of the corner and up the court. But the basketball gods had other plans.

On Tim's second dribble, the ball uncharacteristically clipped the outside of his left foot and then took a 45 degree bounce away from across the baseline and out of bounds! I had played hundreds of hours with Tim and had never seen him do that. Nor did I ever see it after that day either. Like many other games, basketball is also a game of inches. In this case, it was a fraction of an inch. It was our 31st turnover of the game.

Goski's dribble clips his left foot and goes out of bounds

As fate would have it, Triton would capitalize on the miscue. The inbounds play yielded an open 15-foot jumper from the left wing that was off the mark and which Novacek hauled in for his 19th rebound. But in his haste to get the ball to Goski, he threw a bounce pass across the lower portion of the lane that an alert defender anticipated and snatched. But the Triton player also rushed a quick shot underneath which came off the rim. However, a crashing Radziewicz timed the rebound perfectly and a put in a little two-foot bank shot all in one motion!

We advanced the ball into the front court and Horne and signaled for our last timeout. The scoreboard now read 42 all, with 25 seconds left. We simply couldn't shake the tenacious Triton squad that was acting like a dog that wouldn't let go of its favorite bone. We now faced an eerily similar situation that we had at the end of regulation. We had the ball with the score tied but were going to have to earn one more basket to claim victory.

The plan this time was to try to get the ball to Goski with a few seconds left and a chance to attack the basket and create his own shot. We came out of the huddle with more purpose. We had regained our footing and were no longer shell shocked by Triton's late charge that had sent the game into overtime. We could win it right here with a few seconds of good execution.

After the timeout, Pfeiffer inbounded the ball to Goski in the backcourt. We then proceeded to run the clock down with a series of short quick passes ... Goski to Pfeiffer ... Pfeiffer to Novacek ... back to Pfeiffer ... Pfeiffer to Reddy ... Reddy to Goski.

Goski prepares to make a move with 6 seconds left and a tie score

Goski caught the ball with his back to the basket about 20 feet out on the right side. Six seconds left. Tim looked over his right shoulder as if he might drive in the direction of the foul lane. Dorsey was up on him very tight. Instead, Goski drop stepped with his left foot while beginning his dribble to Dorsey's left. Tim got a half step on Dorsey as he took his second dribble towards the baseline before pulling up for a 12-foot jumper ... but the whistle had already blown. Goski's half step advantage had caused Dorsey to reach in as he took his second dribble closer to the basket. Dorsey fell to the ground on the play hoping to draw a charge, but the ref clearly got this one right as he signaled the reach-in foul.

Dorsey reaches in as Goski begins to drive past him

Tim was going to the line to shoot a one and one with four seconds left. He was confident. He told Scott not to worry…that it was over. He had been our best foul shooter for the season at 78 percent. He was just 1-for-2 in this game, but that didn't matter though; he was ready for this moment. He was going to close the game out right here. Novacek, Simmons and Pfeiffer took their spots on the foul lane, while I moved back just beyond half court to be ready to defend. With four seconds left, Triton still had time to advance the ball and get a shot off.

Tim's shot looked good but caught the back portion of the rim and careened high towards the left side of the lane. A sea of hands went up for the ball, but only two got their hands on it. Fortunately, they both belonged to Novacek. What happened next was so remarkable that anyone would need to watch a replay several times to fully appreciate it. But we didn't

Novacek uses both arms to secure the rebound after Goski's miss

Novacek's rebound from the reverse angle

have replay back then. The closest thing we had was black and white film, but even that wouldn't show up on any news broadcast, let alone ESPN, which hadn't been conceived yet. No, for decades the play would only be truly seen by a small handful of people. Even those who were there that day could not possibly fully see or appreciate what happened in the two seconds after Goski's shot drew iron.

Novacek's rebound was remarkable enough in that the ball somehow found its way into Scott's hands over the outstretched hands of the taller Radzewicz, who also had longer arms and inside position on Scott. By the time Scott's feet touched the ground, he was surrounded by Triton's three tallest players like a tripod. But the ball never came down. It stayed seven feet above the floor, surrounded by a sea of arms and sandwiched between his own two hands. He was simultaneously securing the ball while immediately beginning his elevation back up off the floor, despite all the traffic.

Almost every single player you see in that situation would bring the ball down two or three feet to gather themselves before they go up again,

Novacek holds on tight with both hands while keeping the ball up

Novacek goes right back up with it before the defense can stop him

especially in heavy traffic. Every player needs some amount of room for their arms to move in an upward motion to propel their whole body upwards. Every player but Scott, that is. He had been doing it all year – going up with two hands, grabbing it with two hands, and then going right back up. But never had he had to do it with practically an entire defense sandwiched around him.

Scott managed to get a good 12 inches or so off the ground, despite the quick takeoff from a constrained space. The ball went up a similar distance with his arms still in the same half bent position they had been in since he got his two hands on it. Then he released the ball just a fraction before Radzewicz could get his outstretched arm in the ball's path.

Before you knew it, the ball had left Nova's hands in a bit of a low line drive towards the backboard. But it was a perfect line drive, off the board and through the hoop without touching the rim! It all happened so fast, so there had to be at least one second left, if not two as the ball went through the hoop. We immediately started retreating back up court, but Triton was slow to signal for a timeout, appearing to be a little shell shocked at the

Novacek gets the last shot off in heavy traffic

Novacek was the first to celebrate his big basket, and deservedly so

remarkable put-back. By the time they did, it was too late. The buzzer sounded … it was over!!

In the immediate aftermath, Novacek raised both arms triumphantly as he ran back towards half court. Once the buzzer sounded, Goski raised his as well, but out of exasperation with himself for missing the foul shot. Meanwhile, I did a couple of pogo stick jumps in the backcourt before rushing in with both arms raised to meet Goski and Simmons at the half court circle. The crowd was starting to pour onto the court, but before they could reach us the three of us converged at half court. I was celebrating the moment, but Tim's head was in a different place. He just crouched and then sat down at center court almost as if to self-protest his own failure at the end of the game, all while fans were now rushing all around him. Larry, meanwhile, just stood hands on hips, seemingly joining Goski in an anti-celebration posture. His body language suggested that we had no business celebrating after playing such a sloppy game. My mind would have been saying the same thing, but I let the euphoria of the moment trump all the other emotions inside me.

As the buzzer sounds, Goski raises his arms for a different reason

The anti-celebration celebration

Heads are bowed on both sides; ours would be easier to raise again

Goski always got on himself for poor play…this day was no different

It's a moment of a lifetime…and emotions are running the gamut

The crowd flooded the court in a manner that became a familiar sight in college basketball arenas in the decades that would follow. It wasn't such a common sight back in 1972, but we were fortunate to be part of one when it's your own fans pouring onto the court. Triton had to endure the flip side of that scene, where they have to exit the court while trying their best to stay out of the way and ignore the onrushing fans of the team that just beat you. The scene very much exemplified the thrill of victory and the agony of defeat.

Once the spontaneous on court celebration had run its course, we gravitated toward the locker room, but not before soaking up every pat on the back from friends and familiar faces all around us. Novacek was on the receiving end of the majority of those congratulations, and rightfully so. Westfield's Mr. Big was literally standing head and shoulders above the crowd in that very moment. Perhaps quite fittingly, the final scoreboard still read 42-42 when we left the court that day.

Make way for the hero...Mr. Big is coming through

Pfeiffer is congratulated by JV Coach Ed Tirone as players exit the court

March 18, 1972…the day the score was tied

Back in the locker room emotions almost instantly became more subdued. Despite the heroics of Novacek, several of us were having trouble shaking the mistakes each of us had made and almost cost us the game. Tim was still kicking himself for the missed foul shot after Horne's final play had set him up to win it. I was still reeling from my colossal mistake at the end of regulation, while Tom was kicking himself for the six straight foul shots missed in the second half. Even Larry was mad at himself for less egregious errors made during the game.

Then, two things happened to help change our collective mood. Horne gathered us quickly to give us a final message for the day, a much needed one at that. His message was: "Guys, we didn't play our best today, but we still did enough to win. There's a team in the other locker that feels a lot worse than we do right now. So, let's focus on everything we achieved this season rather than today's game." We all agreed. How can you possibly be down when you just won the state championship?

Horne left our presence at that point to talk to reporters, either off to one end of the locker room or just outside it. His departure coincided with the almost magical appearance of a bottle of champagne from the depths of someone's gym bag. Rumor had it that it emerged from Goski's bag, but we didn't care what the source was and there certainly wasn't any time to conduct an audit. Everyone's mood was suddenly lifted. Several hands were trying to get on it, first to help open it, and then to taste a bit of the bubbly. It wasn't like we had 10 of these bottles to waste and spray around. We had to make the most of the one bottle we had … and boy did we ever!!

I think Larry got the first shot at getting the bottle opened, although there were several hands in there trying to give him help. At some point, Nova gained control of the bottle and finished the job. Tim was right there to taste the first rush of champagne rising from the now overflowing bottle. Other heads quickly converged on the bottle as we formed a huddle of another kind. Only some of us got a taste of it while the rest of us had to settle for being part of the spectacle. Tim eventually grabbed it back … after all, it was *supposedly his* bottle. Then Rat got a clean gulp or two in before

A bottle of champagne suddenly appears in the locker room...

...and it takes a lot of teamwork to get it open...

...when all else fails, you can always turn to Mr. Big

Reverse assist – from Novacek to Goski!

One last huddle...

Pfeiffer and I look on, oblivious to Dorsey's offer of congratulations

In the end, Rat was not to be denied.

A serious mismatch: D'Andrea's one hand versus Novacek's two

BJ and Rat are all smiles as Nova continues to assert himself

D'Andrea couldn't help but smile when he finally secured the bottle

yielding the bottle to Scott. Trainer D'Andrea then arrived on the scene and tried to break up the fun, but Nova was too quick for him. He grabbed the bottle with both hands and spun away from D'Andrea, then raised the bottle with his back to D'Andrea. Scott got his money's worth before finally yielding the bottle back to our trainer!

After our own special celebration had played out, we turned our attention to the legion of reporters and photographers who had suddenly gained access to our locker room, not an everyday occurrence for a high school basketball game! We did our part and dutifully answered the reporters' questions and of course had a few pictures taken for their newspaper articles that would come out over the next couple of days. I wasn't particularly enthused about having to talk about this game given how sloppy it was and how I had almost blown it at the end, but at least it gave me a chance to give Novacek credit for bailing me out with his late game heroics. Of course, they also asked me about my ankle, which held up fine and did not adversely affect my play at all. No, I couldn't blame all the turnovers on that.

We happily pose for the newspapers' cameras

I wouldn't even realize what the game stats were for another couple of days. While the papers would report that we committed 34 turnovers on this day, our team statisticians only recorded 32, a figure that would later be corroborated by the game film. Our sloppy play extended to almost all the starters, with Pfeiffer being charged with eight turnovers, Goski seven, and myself with six, with all but one of mine occurring in the fourth quarter, including the most critical one of all. In our defense, at least four or five of those calls were phantom turnovers according to game film. Regardless, it was an astounding total for a winning team, perhaps setting some kind of dubious record. We also finished shooting a horrific 6-for-18 from the free throw line, including 1-for-11 in the second half...definitely not a winning formula!

So how did we ultimately win the game? For starters, we had an incredible 54-31 rebounding advantage. Triton somehow also exceeded our futility at the foul line by shooting a woeful 6-for-21. But perhaps even more telling was Triton's 18 for 64 from the field, which is just over 28%. Their star Bruce Leonetti only scored 10 points himself on 4-of-16 shooting. Our defense almost certainly contributed to Triton's poor shooting as they got off hardly any shots inside the paint, and many of their longer shots were either rushed or contested. They say that defense wins championships. Ours certainly did help us win on this day – barely.

The box score looked like this:

Triton Regional

	FG-FGA	FT-FTA	Reb	PF	Pts
Leonetti	4-16	2-6	3	5	10
Dorsey	2-8	0-2	2	5	4
Radziewicz	3-7	3-9	14	0	9
Crews	6-19	1-2	4	2	13
Prudence	2-8	0-1	7	2	4
Tannuck	1-5	0-1	1	0	2
Thorn	0-1	0-1	0	0	0
Totals	**18-64**	**6-21**	**31**	**14**	**42**

Westfield

	FG-FGA	FT-FTA	Reb	PF	Pts
Goski	5-11	1-2	4	3	11
Pfeiffer	3-6	2-8	5	2	8
Jester	1-1	0-0	9	1	2
Novacek	7-18	1-3	20	4	15
Lee	0-0	0-0	0	0	0
Reddy	3-7	1-3	3	3	7
Simmons	0-4	1-2	13	4	1
Totals	**19-47**	**6-18**	**54**	**17**	**44**

Goski and Novacek went back out on the court and took down one of the nets which Scott then wore around his neck when he reentered the locker room. Pfeiffer and I were a bit more subdued as were still shaking our heads at how we had failed to win the way we should have. He was more miffed at his own missed foul shots while I was dwelling on my fourth-quarter turnovers that almost did us in.

Athletic director John Lay entertains questions from sports writers

Novacek and Goski are also in demand with reporters

There was another thing that was bothering Tom and me – namely, that we had probably just blown our chance to end up with the No. 1 overall state ranking from the *Star-Ledger*. There were other highly ranked teams competing for titles in the other Groups - in particular, Roselle and East Orange. While Group IV schools generally would have an edge given that they play more games against bigger schools, that was now highly in doubt given the way we had limped across the finish line. I mentioned it to Horne in the locker room and he agreed that we had probably blown that opportunity.

Nova looks quite content with the day's outcome...I look much less so

The bus ride home was an easy one. Regardless of our play that day, there would be a lot of happy people back home, and the Goski household was hosting a party for everyone associated with the team. Novacek continued

Next stop: home of the 1971-72 Group IV state champs

to assert himself and claim hero's status when he somehow got the coaches to let his girlfriend, Ellen Cooney (Mike's older sister), come on the bus for the ride home. Scott and Ellen spent much of the ride home hiding under Scott's jacket, trying to avoid the catcalls from the rest of the team. Meanwhile, Pfeiffer and I rode in the back of the bus where he told me something that I needed to hear: "Years from now, people won't care how we won, just that we won." It made sense…I believed him. He put my mind at ease. It was another way of saying what Horne had said back in the locker room. Yes, we had played a terrible game, but we still had a tremendous season and we got the "W" that we set out for today. So what if it wasn't perfect? We were still bringing home the bacon. We were still going to get off that bus as state champs, something Tom and I had dreamed about since the fifth grade. I was thankful for that. I was thankful for everything the season had given me.

The rest of the day is a little bit of a blur to me. I remember cruising around town, looking for a party to unwind at. I was still a bit overwhelmed with ambivalence, a bit embarrassed at our sloppy performance and my careless play at the end, but also buoyed by the fact that we still got the outcome that mattered in the end. At one point I crossed paths with grammar school friend Kevin Harrington, who congratulated me and then asked the question: "Steve, why did you foul that guy?" in a tone that also said, "What were you thinking?" I sheepishly responded with the truth: "I thought I could block the shot."

I did spend some time at Tim Goski's house that evening, where there was a houseful of parents, coaches, cheerleaders and players there, not to mention a countless number of Goski children. The cheerleaders had prepared a three-foot-high cake for the occasion, but I suspect that many parents were more interested in drinks to calm down their nerves after what we had just put them through. Our play had sent Al Pfeiffer to the rafters and Sig Goski, according to Tim, had needed a valium during the game and was accommodated by one of the other parents who came well prepared for a nail biter.

I would find out at a later date that my fellow starters had spent a portion of the evening at a celebratory dinner at the Sleepy Hollow Inn, all accompanied by girlfriends. While I never asked, I surmised that was the reason I wasn't included...I was missing the requisite girlfriend. I understood. Life is not perfect. We had won the big game, but I didn't get the girl in the end. Our season didn't have the perfect fairy tale ending...but it was pretty darn close.

When I got home that night the realization that the season was now over started to set in. No more games, no more practices. All good things must come to an end. But one thing wasn't ending – in fact, it had just begun: the right to call ourselves STATE CHAMPS!

The next morning was bittersweet reading about the game because it only served to remind us how horrific the turnovers and foul shooting had been. Of course, it wasn't all bad. We crushed them on the boards, and we didn't collapse after blowing our big lead late in the game. Furthermore, we had beaten a team that was 25-1 going in and had won 24 in a row, not too shabby. Of course, there was also Nova's heroics that deserved real praise and was the difference in the end.

That afternoon Pfeiffer and I went over to Overlook Hospital in Summit to visit my father's good friend Lank Siebert, who had been hospitalized for gall bladder surgery a few days earlier and was still recuperating. For better or worse, being the true sports fan that he was, Lank had listened to our championship game on the radio. Lank was one of those guys who would tell it like it was, just like Tom's dad or Howard Cosell. His first comment was about all the turnovers. Then it was the foul shooting. Tom and I took it in stride, though, as we were there to wish him a quick recovery, not to defend our prior day's performance. Besides, how could we defend it?

Monday in school principal Al Bobal officially congratulated the team over the school intercom. Later that week, the Star-Ledger confirmed that we had blown the No. 1 state ranking. Horne's source there said we had the inside track going into the final game, but our finale was eclipsed by the Mike Dabney-led East Orange team that won the Group III title handily in their final game. The final Star Ledger Top Twenty had East Orange on top at 24-2, Westfield second at 25-2, Jefferson third at 23-2, and Group I champ Roselle fourth at 26-2. A true banner year for Union County teams, which finished 2nd, 3rd, and 4th, along with Linden finishing 8th at 16-8 and Cranford 16th at 16-6.

Meanwhile, a few of my teammates were already on to their spring sports. BJ and Chip Danker were already out on the baseball field, while Lee was hitting the links. Like Steve, I also had a good chance of being amongst the top golfers on the golf team, but I just wasn't ready to think about anything else. I chose to take a pass and "just be a regular student".

The next time that I touched a basketball was the following Monday, nine days after we won the states. My ankle finally felt good enough to play on it without any tape, so there we were - Goski, Novacek, Cooney and myself - down at the Westfield Y playing in pickup games. I remember sitting along the wall waiting our turn to play. Were the other players thinking about us any differently? Like "those guys over there are the state champs".

That Thursday we got word that the Holy Trinity gym was going to be open that night for pickup games. A few local guys and Gumbert regulars were expected. We hoped to get all five of our starters down there for a little encore performance just 12 days after winning it all. Pfeiffer ended up having a conflict, so he never made it that night. The reality of our team status was starting to set in. The starting five of Pfeiffer, Simmons, Novacek, Reddy and Goski had had their run. That team was done and part of history now.

An official stamp was put on that a few weeks later at the winter sports banquet when our whole team was there to collect our state championship trophies. As mere teenagers who hadn't even finished high school yet, it was impossible for us to fully appreciate the trophies we were handed that night or what we had accomplished during that championship season. Those things were going to take more time. There was one more thing we had no way of knowing on that April night. It would be the last time that all 12 players and Coach Horne were in the same room together.

XV. All You Can Be

Tim Goski's varsity career at Westfield High got off to a very inauspicious debut. It began with Tim scoring a single point while fouling out of his very first game. A week later he sat the final six minutes of a tight game against rival Scotch Plains, and then got benched at the start of our 5th game a few days later. These were not the kind of results Goski had in mind when he transferred from crosstown rival Holy Trinity just one year earlier. He would later confide in me that he had gone home and cried after that Scotch Plains game, a game I had celebrated because we had finally beaten a team that consistently had our number.

Therein lies one of the more intriguing aspects of basketball – that it is simultaneously both a team sport and one where individual performances are both scrutinized and celebrated. For a team to realize its potential, it requires an almost perfect blend of individual contributions and critical interactions with teammates. Good chemistry is often attributed to those teams that excel in the latter department, where those teammates appear to be on same page, as if they were part of one body and one mind. Our 1971-72 team had good chemistry. More famously, the 1969-70 New York Knicks showed the basketball world what good chemistry looked like when they stormed their way to their first NBA championship.

Still, any team needs enough talent for good chemistry to be able to make a difference and allow a team to be able to compete for league titles. Not every team can have a Michael Jordan or a Lebron or a Kobe, but even those guys have shown that it's often how their talents blends with those of their teammates that dictates how well their team fares in the end.

While it's a beautiful thing to watch a championship team playing at an optimal level and making the game look easy, there can be no denying that it's the standout players the fans often come to see, because they, well, *stand out*. Almost every team has a "star" player, one who is deemed their top dog, the one to look out for and to defend against. It's true at almost any level – in CYO, high school, college, the pros…and even on the playground.

The final team stats for our 1971-72 season might suggest we had no stars on our team that year. It all comes down to how you define "star player." Tim Goski's season scoring average of 15.1 might have been a bit deceiving. It was lower than the average score of most star high school players, but it was clear to all of us that Tim was in fact a rising star, on his way up in the basketball world. After all, he was only 16 when we won the state championship in March 1972, and had been playing basketball in earnest for just two or three years. Anyone paying attention could see that he was working his butt off and improving at a rapid pace. Goski was able to quickly overcome his rocky start and increase his individual output while also playing within the team construct required by his head coach. Perhaps our championship season disguised his progress a bit because the team's success will almost always overshadow the individual success of its players, and that was certainly the case for our team. But once it was over, he was back to the playground to continue his upward trajectory.

It wasn't just full-court pick-up games that Tim would seek out. There was a lot of one-on-one as well. I remember several of those sessions - sometimes it was just the two us, other times we were joined by Mike Cooney or Jimmy Masters. Goski's offensive moves were so proficient that you had to play tremendous defense just to stay with him and contest his shots, hopefully forcing a couple of misses along the way. Of course, the best defense against Goski was good offense, because we'd always be playing winner's out which meant your own made shot got you the ball back. The best way to keep the ball out of Tim's hands was to score on every one of your possessions, which itself requires maximum effort and almost flawless play. I was often able to beat Tim the first game on any given day, but I would burn energy at a rate that I couldn't sustain, becoming exhausted in only two or three games.

Thanksgiving break in 1973 was a good example of this. Goski and I crashed Horne's practice one morning to find a basket where we could play some one-on-one. We found one in the wrestling gym where I proceeded to beat Tim in the first game 11-0, which a pissed-off Tim punctuated by kicking the ball straight up to the ceiling, just narrowly missing one of the hanging lamps. As usual, though, my advantage was short-lived. As soon as I missed a couple of shots, Goski got rolling and I quickly got exhausted. He ran the table on me for the reminder of that morning.

During my freshman year at Bucknell, I would only get to see Westfield and Goski play one time, which was during Christmas break. My brother Mark, who hadn't seen any of our games the previous year, was also in town and decided to catch this game, largely based on my encouragement and after talking up Goski and Novacek. The game was essentially a rematch of the buzzer-beating game we played against Roselle Catholic the prior year, only this one would take place in Westfield's gym. We attended the game separately and did not sit together, but I did see Mark out in the foyer at halftime after a woeful first half by Westfield in which they trailed 43-28. Mark shook his head and said they look awful, further commenting that Westfield was playing without any energy and that Goski was too nonchalant. Rick Gomez, a junior standout for Roselle Catholic and regular fixture at Gumbert during the summer, had indeed looked like the better player in the first half. Whatever their issues were, Horne snapped them out of it at halftime as WHS looked like a different team the second half. They chipped away at the lead until the very last minute when Goski finally tied the game at 64 with 16 seconds left. Then after a missed free throw, Westfield regained possession and with the clock running down, Goski was able to power the ball to right side of the key and drill a low arcing 18-footer off the glass for the game winner as the place went nuts! I remember seeing my brother again in the foyer in the immediate aftermath. He shook his head again, this time with a big smile on his face. "Unbelievable!" was the first thing he said, having just witnessed a remarkable comeback win powered by Goski's game-high 20 points.

Tim's continued improvement that season earned him first team all-state honors from the *Star-Ledger* and many college scholarship offers. Goski selected the University of Georgia and quickly made his mark there by starting and making the All-SEC Freshman first team. He would later tell me about playing against the North Carolina State team that featured the great David Thompson and the little water bug Monte Towe. Tim said Towe tried to steal the ball from him and Tim just spun around him leaving him grasping at air!

The summer of 1974 was another active one at Gumbert, but something happened before Goski returned to Georgia for his sophomore year. I will never do justice to exactly what happened those next few months, but it went something like this. Tim had an older brother and sister that were living in a commune up in Connecticut led by a "Brother Julius." Tim had gone to visit them that summer and at some point after the season was underway, he decided to bail on Georgia and all his basketball commitments and join his two siblings in the commune. Some five months later Tim's dad and other family members went up there and effectively kidnapped him out of the place under the false guise of his mother being very ill. Tim's dad had then arranged for him to go through a form of deprogramming with the renowned Ted Patrick to clear Tim's head of whatever had compelled him to seemingly throw away the opportunities that basketball had given him. Once cured, Tim then spent the next three months or so travelling with Patrick and helping him help others in similar situations, as there were apparently many such cults around the country that had become the new homes of many disillusioned youth.

By the fall of 1975, Goski had almost come full circle and returned to Georgia, scholarship still intact, although he wasn't immediately eligible for NCAA play. He would leave Georgia a second time, this time for good, by the end of the year, but that didn't mean Tim's basketball career was over. Over the next two and a half years, Tim would attend local Union County College, while working part time for the trucking business run by his older brother Joe, and the local CYO. During this period he continued to tear up the local basketball courts whether it be Gumbert, the Westfield Y, UCC pickup games, rec league games, or the highly regarded Jersey Shore Basketball League (JSBL). Tim's basketball prowess and local reputation continued to flourish in these settings, as he was simply a playground player at his core. To fully appreciate how good he became, you had to witness it yourself and be at one of those playgrounds or gyms where those skills and accompanying trash talking would be on full display.

One good example was when a college friend of mine named Jeff Rhoads came to live in Westfield for a brief period, sharing a house with Alan Deombeleg, and ventured down to the Westfield Y one Saturday afternoon. Alan would later recount Jeff describing Tim Goski playing at the Y that day and how he would come down and start firing up jumpers from barely over half court and was hitting shots from all over the court and that he was "freakin' unconscious." It wasn't clear if Jeff was more disbelieving in the shots that Goski had been *taking* or the ones he'd been *making*. Well, Alan just laughed and told Jeff that Goski was like that all the time...he had seen it too often to be surprised at what Jeff was describing. Jeff was incredulous that what he saw might be the norm for Goski, but Alan knew better.

Goski would impress many others during this time in his early twenties. Tim described the exposure he got at the JSBL, "Lots of people would come and players - some Knicks and Sixers would play but mostly NJ guys and lots of legends. John Somogyi played there. Eddie Mast (Knicks) was on my team. I busted Elnardo Webster's ass (St Peter's) for 26 one night and got an offer to play in Israel right after the game. GREAT place to play." Goski turned down the offer as he already had an invitation to try out with the Detroit Pistons that summer of 1978. He also had a Plan B which was a scholarship offer he had received from East Texas State.

Tim later recounted the story of attending the Pistons' 1978 rookie camp where high draft picks John Long, Terry Tyler, and Andre McCarter would also be vying for a spot on the team. Tim said he busted his butt through the two days of triple sessions, sometimes having to leave the court to go puke in the bathroom, only to return and kick some more ass on the court. While he didn't have the same physical gifts these other guys had, Goski was still supremely confident and believed he could play with all those guys. Pistons assistant coach Richie Adubato agreed and told Tim he "could play in this league", but was not able to offer Tim a spot on the team at that time. As it turned out, Long and Tyler filled the two available spots that year and went on to have long and productive NBA careers.

So Goski went with his Plan B and headed down to Texas in the fall of 1978 with a full scholarship in hand to play NAIA ball down at East Texas State. Tim was having a great first year there until he broke his foot, but he played through it with the help of some injections so he could be part of the Lone Star Conference Tournament and NAIA Tournament. He was honored with a selection to the first team for the Lone Star Conference. The next season he continued to excel until it all came crashing down when he blew out his knee. Injuries and Father Time are the two things that are most likely to end a basketball career, and in Tim's case it was injury. It seemed like a cruel irony. One day you are the toast of the town and capable of doing things on a court that no one else is capable of. The next day it may be physically impossible for you. But that's life, I suppose. Things are given, and things are taken away.

Tim's basketball achievements were formally recognized in 2000 when he was inducted into the Westfield Athletic Hall of Fame (WAHOF). Over the years many of the WAHOF inductees were multisport athletes and made their impact in a broader fashion. Others like Tim earned their way solely based on their achievements in a single sport. Tim was the first athlete to get inducted into the WAHOF for basketball alone, and to this day remains one of only five athletes to do so, with the others being Boo Bowers, Bob King, Bob Felter and Spud Monroe. Any comparison of those players, or any other players for that matter, is hard to make without caveats, but I did get to see a lot of Felter, and a little bit of King in game films, and Bowers and Monroe in a couple of Horne's practices. I am undoubtedly a bit biased, but there is no doubt in my mind that Goski was the most talented to ever play at WHS. Those other inductees all scored more points than Tim, but Tim's 67-8 won-lost record during his three years at WHS speaks volumes. Furthermore, Tim didn't have the physical tools the others had to work with. This was a 6-foot-1 guy, not particularly strong or quick, who earned everything he achieved on the court through hard work. That much I witnessed firsthand. When you consider Tim's subsequent achievements at Georgia and East Texas State, his almost legendary reputation at Gumbert, the Westfield Y, and various rec leagues, the Jersey Shore League and his NBA tryouts to boot, it's hard to imagine another player who deserves top billing in the annals of Westfield hoops. Tim even earned the respect of prison inmates one day at Sing Sing when they dubbed the long-haired Goski "White Jesus" after he put up some 60 points against them one Saturday afternoon.

I remember being at the WAHOF ceremony when Tim was inducted and seeing one of Tim's twin boys. The younger Goski was about 18 at the time, longish hair, and certainly didn't give me the impression that he had followed in his father's basketball footsteps. I'm not even sure if the twins had played any basketball at all. I wondered that night if they had any idea of what their dad had been able to do on the basketball court. Was there any way they could ever really appreciate it?

While Tim's calling in life, or at least the early portion of it, may have been to be the best basketball player he could be, the twins had a different calling. Less than a year after the WAHOF ceremony, 9/11 happened. The following day Christopher Goski enlisted in the Marines. His brother Michael was not far behind, graduating from Army boot camp in June 2003. Between Iraq and Afghanistan, both would serve several tours of duty over the next decade and experience the harsh realities of war. Along the way, Chris would graduate to the Marines Corp Special Operations Forces and Michael would join the Green Berets. They had both become very good at what they did.

But their story would have a tragic ending. Once back home, after a decade of serving their country, each would succumb to the deleterious long-term effects that war can bring upon a person. Christopher, who was battling depression, took his own life in 2012. Four years later, Michael, who struggled after losing his brother and best friend, lost his own battle with substance abuse. It is a heartbreaking story that was chronicled in a feature article in the *Wall Street Journal* entitled *"BROTHERS IN ARMS: THE TRAGEDY IN SMALL-TOWN AMERICA,"* as well as a 17-minute video that told of their story and included interviews with Tim and his wife Kathy. At the end of the video Tim says that yes, he was proud of them and that maybe they did what they were meant to do on this earth. How could you not be proud of your children who spend more than 10 years fighting for their country?

The video also includes a portion of the eulogy that Michael Goski delivered at his brother's funeral in 2012. I was particularly struck by the following words he said on that day: "Chris was not a victim. He was a warrior...he willingly stepped forward in defense of his country. He did so to the best of his ability, firm in his beliefs, and in the knowledge that he went in defense of his family and his home." Just like Pat Tillman had done at the height of his pro football career, the Goski twins had stepped up and were more than willing to take one for the team. Their team was a much more important one than you will find written on any basketball jersey. Theirs was Team America.

The Army's recruiting slogan for more than two decades leading into 9/11 had been, "Be All You Can Be." It seemed particularly fitting in the case of the Goski twins. In fact, the more I thought about it, the more it seemed appropriate advice for anyone. Life's too short to take it on in a half-assed manner. Go all in, or don't go in at all. That slogan reminded me of another saying that my junior high coaches had posted on our locker room wall. It read: "Today I Gave Everything I Had to Give. Whatever I Saved, I Lost Forever." I think it's fair to say that Tim and his twin boys had heeded the advice contained in those slogans, and each one, in their own way, gave everything they had to give.

XVI. The Test of Time (Apr 12, 1972 – Present)

Our high school graduation was just around the corner for the four seniors on our team, which meant in just a few short weeks we would all go our separate ways to begin the next phase of our lives. Our championship team was about to be further dismantled by time's relentless march. However, before those significant milestones were etched in stone, our starting five did manage to have one final curtain call on a June evening down at Gumbert when we took the court together for the last time. Fittingly, we ran the table that evening and defended our home court. That doesn't mean we played like the same team though. Goski was now back in his element - the playground - and we didn't have Horne on the sidelines to ensure disciplined play. It didn't matter, though; we were king of the hill for one more night.

Just two months later, our seniors were off to college: Pfeiffer to Bridgeport, Simmons to Seton Hall, Lee to William and Mary, and me to Bucknell. Now our team was not only disbanded, but physically separated which further reinforced the notion that we were part of the past now...our team could no longer be referred to in the present tense.

For the next four years while I attended Bucknell, which was a three-hour drive from Westfield, I experienced the same separation from Westfield that my brother Mark had experience the prior four years. Mark had not seen a single game of our championship season during his senior year at Bucknell, and once I got there as a freshman, it became clear to me why. You quickly establish a new life on a college campus, and between academic life, new friends, fraternity life and sports, you hardly have time to think about high school anymore, let alone driving several hours to go see one of their games.

While I was at Bucknell playing freshman hoops, amongst other things, I would remain somewhat oblivious to what was happening back in Westfield during the early months of 1973. As it turned out, the second act of Goski and Novacek, along with their supporting cast, was an impressive one, no matter how you slice it. Their team won their first 21 games, which when combined with the final six games from the prior season, set a school record with 27 straight victories. That winning streak began after our meltdown loss to Linden my senior year and ended with another loss to Linden the following year, both losses occurring during the Union County Tournament. Westfield still had an excellent chance in the state tournament, but was upended by Weequahic when Novacek and Masters both played in a weakened state after battling the flu. Their final record stood at 24-2, one victory shy of the prior year's team. Goski, Novacek, Jester, Cooney and Phillips all finished their two varsity years with a remarkable record of 49-4.

The class of '73 would soon graduate, another summer would pass, and then all of my former teammates were also gone from WHS. My ex-teammates and I made a respectable showing at the next level. Goski had a full ride to University of Georgia where he was making his mark starting as a freshman. Scott Novacek passed up a full ride at Rutgers and joined me at Bucknell and became a part time starter as a freshman (he would later regret his decision to forgo Rutgers where he could have been part of an elite NCAA Final Four team). Meanwhile, Tom Pfeiffer had a full scholarship to play football at Bridgeport University and was excelling there as a defensive back. Larry Simmons also returned to the football field at Seton Hall, grabbing 8 interceptions on their club team that only lost one game and would become an NCAA team the following year. Steve Lee would make his mark on the golf team at William and Mary over his four years. Bob Jester went to NC State and later Trenton State, where he would play baseball after getting drafted by the San Francisco Giants and almost joining their farm team as a pitcher.

Six months after graduating from Bucknell, I got a big assist from Novacek who was in the middle of his senior year there. During his January break, we ventured down to a club in the Bridgewater area on a Saturday night and picked up a couple of sisters. He got the better looking one of course, but a week later he was back at Bucknell. Three weeks after that, I went out on a first date with the sister Scott left behind. 11 months later, Susan Koterba and I got engaged.

A few years later in 1982 we heard from John Belis, the sportswriter at the Courier-News, who was planning a feature article for the 10th anniversary of our championship. This prompted the first reunion of any kind, but it only involved half the team plus our head coach (See Epilogue). Still, it provided a brief forum for the handful of us to do a little reminiscing.

We would get another brief reprieve from the demands of daily life 18 years later when our team was formally recognized with its induction into the Westfield Athletic Hall of Fame in November of 2000. Ten middle aged men and their head coach reconvened for the occasion to celebrate once more what we had achieved together as young boys. While life continued to march forward, our basketball triumph continued to stand still in our collective memory banks.

While nostalgia tugged at our hearts for a few brief hours, life had more important demands on all of us. The daily grind of long commutes and the long hours required to earn a decent living would have been challenging enough, but life, like basketball, comes with curve balls that we are often unprepared for. Stressful events like divorce or the loss of a parent or sibling would start to become more commonplace amongst members of our team. Layoffs from longtime employers were also experienced. Then on top of all that 9/11 comes along to make basketball seem like a luxury that none of us can justify spending any time either playing or watching.

The years that followed would continue to keep us all preoccupied with our jobs and family obligations. At age 49 I took a job up in Springfield, MA., and would spend the next 13 years going back and forth between there and our home in Bucks County, PA. I had barely any contact with my former teammates during this entire period, with the exception of Tom Pfeiffer, which unfortunately was not under the best of circumstances.

When Tom attended Horne Man's retirement dinner in June 2003, he was a perfectly healthy 49-year-old. Within a few months Tom was diagnosed with throat cancer. Tom had never smoked. The cancer got to an advanced stage pretty quickly and Tom had to undergo both chemo and radiation. It seems like he has been fighting off a series of complications ever since. At some point it had spread to one of his lungs and after various consultations he made the difficult decision to have that lung removed. He had several infections that landed him back in the hospital for a week or two at a time. The radiation treatment also wreaked long term havoc on his teeth, which is a long-term risk and common side effect. Amidst all of this, while the cancer was being held at bay, Tom's throat was never fully back to normal, which made eating a difficult and laborious task. To offset this, Tom had to go on mostly liquid diets or use a feeding tube for at least part of his eating and nutrition. Not surprisingly, Tom's weight dropped a lot, from 180 to 155ish. This happened twice – first after the initial bout with cancer and all the necessary treatment, but he eventually got stronger and gained most of it back. Then he went through another cycle with all the eating difficulties, but again he has fought his way back up.

Are you getting the impression that Tom is a fighter?

Tom had to make another very difficult choice several years ago. There was a way to fix the throat restriction and swallowing discomfort, not to mention the constant battle to keep his strength and weight up, but it meant taking out his larynx and replacing that with an artificial voice box. After careful deliberation, Tom made that tough choice, and now he can only speak in an artificial voice that is difficult to understand. Not only does it take effort for him to talk, but it can also be very difficult for the listener to understand him and frustrating for Tom that he often can't connect.

But he's still fighting through it all. A few years ago, Larry Simmons, Coach Horne, Bruce Cant and I attended Tom's daughter's wedding and saw him walk her down the aisle. He was a real trooper that night - you could see that all the festivities wore him down a bit, and having only one lung also means that he can get out of breath very easily. But he was all in for his daughter's big day.

It's been hard to see Tom battle through one obstacle after another. Cancer is the kind of thing you wouldn't wish on your worst enemy. But Tom, being the trooper that he is, continues to fight through it every day. You'll never hear him complain about the hand he was dealt. Once you know Tom's story, it's hard to feel sorry for yourself about anything that might be bothering you. It's like the old commercial used to say…when you have your health, you have just about everything.

It was late summer of 2017 when Neil Horne III emailed me about some other unsettling news - the tragic deaths of Tim Goski's twin boys. He shared the featured article, and I watched the 17-minute video, which was heartbreaking. I hadn't seen or talked to Tim since the WAHOF reunion 17 years earlier, which I immediately started feeling guilty about. Despite the tragic circumstances, it was still good to see Tim's face and hear his voice once again after all those years.

I couldn't imagine what Tim and Kathy must be going through. I knew I had to call Tim, but I just wasn't sure how or when to do it. One thing that might make the call a little easier was that these tragic deaths had not just occurred – they were now more than one and five years old at this point, so maybe Tim and Kathy had a chance to heal a little bit with some passage of time. Then again, how much can one heal after losing two of your own children like that?

A few weeks later I had dinner with Scott Novacek after attending a wedding in Florida, which served to reinforce my need to reach out to Tim. A few evenings later I made that long overdue call. The phone rang and then I heard Tim's voice:

"Tim?", I asked.

"Yes", he replied.

"It's Steve Reddy."

"Redeye! How are you, man?", he immediately blurted out.

It was good to hear those words and that reaction. I immediately got to the main reason for my call, that I had recently heard the tragic news and that I wanted him to know how sorry I was. Tim was at ease discussing the loss of Michael and Christopher. It appeared to be a form of therapy for him, but he also said that you never get over it. It's a blessing that he comes from a large family that inherently forms a strong support system. I happened to marry into a large Polish family myself, so I had seen first-hand how those large families can help cushion the blow in times of grieving. After a while I mentioned that I had just seen Scott and that we had broached the idea of another reunion. Tim again said he would be up for it, especially since he still had several family members living in the Jersey area and regularly went back there to visit. That was all I needed to hear. Without Tim, it wouldn't have been the same. Of course, I could have said the same thing about Pfeiffer, but I was confident that Tom would be there when the time came. With Tim on board, it was now just a matter of tracking down the other guys.

Four months later, eleven players and a head coach reconvened in Westfield for a whirlwind 24-hour reunion. The bonds that were formed among us 46 years earlier were on full display and seemingly stronger than ever. Previously dormant memories rose to the surface. For 24 hours, we *were* in high school once again. In the aftermath of that reunion, those bonds and memories ultimately convinced me to write this book.

About a year and a half later my wife and I were at the local tavern in our hometown of Washington Crossing, PA, when Bill Napier, WHS class of '71, surprised me as he walked in with his wife and sat down next to us. Bill and I had gone to Wilson School together and played stickball back in our grammar school days. At WHS a few years later he starred on both the football team, where he set school records as a wide receiver, and the baseball team as a catcher.

During our conversation that night we talked about Westfield's winning ways and how the '72 hoops team was able to more or less match the football team's exploits during the great 48-game unbeaten streak that Napier's teams had just started a couple of years earlier. At one point he asked me how we were able to do that, or more to the point, why were we the only Westfield hoops team to be able to win the state championship? It was a question I had wondered about many times to myself, and thought I knew the answer, but I wasn't willing to share it that night: "You're going to have to read the book to find out, I joked." My book marketing campaign had just unofficially begun.

So how did it happen? Why have we remained the only team to do it? I came up with several reasons that were contributing factors, but whenever I tried to rank them in importance, I was unable to do so. They all seem to be somewhat equally important contributing factors as far as I can tell. Here they are:

1. A Dream - I was inspired by my older brothers who played for their respective high school teams. I dreamed of following in their footsteps. Tom Pfeiffer and I shared the dream that was born in those Friday night games we attended while in grammar school.

2. Good infrastructure - Westfield had good facilities that included Saturday morning basketball clinics at Washington School and Gumbert Park pickup games during the summer months. They also

had knowledgeable boosters and parents who organized and ran those youth clinics and then watched the Gumbert action regularly on summer evenings.

3. Great coaching in Junior High – I/we learned so many important fundamental skills from our junior high coaches, Gralewski and Leonzi, especially on the defensive end, and that continued in 10th grade under Ed Tirone. They also taught us discipline and conditioning. I had no idea what being in shape meant until Gralewski introduced me to suicides...lots of them.

4. A winning culture, led by Gary Kehler - You couldn't help but be inspired by the winning ways of the football team under coach Kehler. "That guy must really know what he is doing," I used to think to myself. It made you believe that if you did things the right way, you would win.

5. Enough talent/depth – We had a deep pool of good athletes and good basketball players between the classes of '72 and '73, each of which had strong JV teams in 1970 and 1971, respectively. This provided us with a strong bench that saved us in many cases.

6. Defense and Rebounding – We excelled in defense thanks to team defensive concepts that were drilled into us at the junior high level and reinforced in high school. We outrebounded our opponents in 23 of 27 game despite lacking height. Some of this could be attributed to boxing out more effectively than our opponents and some of it from guys who just went after the ball. A team almost always has a chance if they can outplay their opponents in these two categories.

7. Junior horsepower – Tim Goski and Scott Novacek provided us with the firepower to go up against and neutralize other teams' big guns, like Leo Nolan, Norm Hobbie, and Bruce Watson. They were

consistent as well, with one of them being the high scorer in all but five of our games.

8. Great balance & chemistry – Counterbalancing the firepower of the juniors was the steady but perhaps less noticeable strength of the seniors. While Goski and Novacek distinguished themselves individually, they were both still a little bit green as juniors and still improving and learning to play the right way. The seniors helped ensure that because collectively we could play defense, rebound, handle the ball, and score when necessary. This carried through to the bench as well and was evident in practice every day. The result was great chemistry and a very balanced team with no particular weaknesses that other teams might exploit.

9. Unselfishness – Perhaps a cousin of good balance and good chemistry, we never showed any signs of selfish play or concerns about personal stats. Scoring and shot attempts were usually spread around more than most teams. No one tried to do too much on their own or play hero ball.

10. The Horne factor – Coach Horne was masterful in managing the players he had to work with. Goski was a burgeoning star, but Horne wisely benched him a couple of times early in the season to get him to play the right way. Novacek was a bit unorthodox, but Horne made him less so. Horne's meticulous preparation and practices, with emphasis on both team and individual fundamentals and skills, got us as prepared as we could be for specific opponents and game situations. His cool at the end of close games no doubt rubbed off on us and helped us come through in most of those close ones.

11. Belief - We believed we could beat anyone. This was perhaps more important than anything but may have simply been the manifestation of all the other previous factors listed above. Some of it came from success on the football field and the town's culture of

winning. Some of it came from recent success of our JV teams. Some of it came from all the experience gained from tough competition on the courts at Gumbert. Some of it came from seeing Simmons and Novacek being able to dominate the boards against bigger opponents. Finally, being able to knock off our prior years' nemesis (Scotch Plains) and then pull out other close games made us realize that sky was the limit.

12. Luck – Every successful season has some amount of good luck associated with it. We were virtually injury free all season, and who knows what would have happened if I hadn't made the last second shot early in the season, or if Jefferson's Watson hadn't dunked the ball on that breakaway, or if Tom Dorsey hadn't missed his foul shot with 18 seconds left in the state final? On the other hand, I prefer to believe more in what we were taught, that you make your own luck and that "the harder I work, the luckier I get." I like to think that we created a lot of our own luck that season.

There you have it. My dozen reasons we were able to do what we did, and perhaps why no one else has. An almost perfect storm. I suppose that many teams have several of these going for them in any given year, but how many can get them all? All twelve? Or even close to twelve? I think we've seen the answer. One. There are too many headwinds today. Kehler is gone. The real Gumbert is gone. Too many kids are learning from parental coaches rather than coaches who are all in and know the game. Families are smaller these days with fewer older brothers to inspire their younger siblings. There are more distractions these days, and too much wanting of instant gratification such that the price of greatness has become further out of the reach of the typical kid.

Perhaps John Lay, our athletic director at the time we won our championship and former head coach of some of WHS's great teams from the late '50s and early '60s, knew something that the rest of us didn't quite realize at the time when he said: "This team had something special, an ingredient you may only find once in a lifetime."

We had the track record to support Lay's statement - Watchung Conference champs. State champs. 25-2 record. Best record in school history. Won seven games by two points or less. Won five games overcoming fourth-quarter deficits of six or more points. Won our final four games by a total of 11 points. Our last three opponents had a combined record of 72-4 not counting games against us, 72-8 after playing us. Won two games in overtime. Won one game by one at the buzzer. Unbeaten at home. Beat every team that we played. Beat the No. 1-ranked team in the state in their gym. Became the No. 1-ranked team in the state.

We met and stood up to pretty much every challenge we faced that year. Now, half a century later, we've withstood the test of time as well. Lay coached three teams that came very close during his tenure, each losing only three games, with one of those being a state final game. Of course, the '72-'73 team may have had the best chance to equal or top our team. Horne felt that the '73 team may have had a slight edge based on pure basketball talent, with the addition of Jimmy Masters and Buddy Robinson, but maybe didn't have quite the balance or chemistry or confidence that our team had. Goski echoed this, feeling that everyone knew their roles and played them well, and that unselfish play was the key in '72. Still, the '73 team came very close with a 24-2 record, narrowly losing in the states with both Novacek and Masters hampered by the flu. It still fell three victories short of a second state title, showing again how elusive the big prize can be. There's been a real drought ever since and no one else has made a serious run at it. In retrospect, Lay's statement seems somewhat prophetic. He said it only 10 years after losing by three points in his state final, but now it has been a lifetime … in fact, it's been a hundred years, and we're still the one, still the only …

That season was truly everything I could have hoped for, and more broadly, basketball has paid me countless dividends. I've made most of my good, long-time friends through hoops. I learned about teamwork, about discipline, about what it takes to be successful at something. I learned about the power of believing in yourself and what you can achieve when you do. I learned what a skill is. I'm probably the only person in the world who thinks their eighth grade typing class made them a better basketball player, but I believe that. Basketball gave me confidence. It also taught me how to lose - I'll never forget John Thompson explaining how his Georgetown players were able to clap for the victorious Villanova Wildcats after their devasting 1984 NCAA finals defeat: "We know how to win, and we know how to lose." It taught me how to get up after losing and what you can learn from losing. It taught me about conditioning and what it means to be in shape. It helped me to get in shape and stay in reasonable shape as the years went by. It also taught me about diversity and how people from different backgrounds can come together in pursuit of a common goal. I saw that in Westfield, at Bucknell, at the playground, at the Y and even in prison. Basketball even found me a wife (thanks, Scott), which led to a beautiful family. Finally, basketball has provided me an endless collection of memories that will stay with me until the day I die.

While many of those memories are oriented around winning and losing, I've come to appreciate that it's not just the end result that matters, but everything that happens along the way. Like the old saying goes, it's not whether you win or lose but how you play the game. But how you play the game depends on all the practice and preparation you put in ahead of time, both individually and as a team. In the end all you can do is try to be the best player or best team you can be and hope it's good enough. I've always been a bit haunted by the razor thin margin by which we prevailed in 1972. We were 18 seconds and one made foul shot away from being on the losing end of the championship game. What if that moment or any other play hadn't gone our way? All the great memories might have been overshadowed by one nightmarish finish. Our reunions likely never would have happened. There would be no poem or no song (see appendices), and maybe it would have been Tom Dorsey writing this book.

But only one scenario plays out in the end, and we were good enough in that scenario. While the highlight of my basketball career may have occurred at age 17, I believe my real achievement was that I gave it my best shot, likely realized most of my potential, and, like my daughter, learned how to play the game pretty darn well. As for winning and losing, you take your victories however and whenever you can get them, and then move onto the next challenge that comes along, whether it be on the hardwood floor or somewhere else. Lord knows that life has no shortage of challenges as you move through it. The ones on the athletic field are the most fun to take on, but there's also no avoiding the others that take place in a classroom, at a job site, in a hospital, on a battlefield, or even at home. People lose jobs. People get divorced. People get sick. They get old. They get cancer. Loved ones die. People die. Losing a game, by comparison, is nothing.

A bit ironically, as I'm in the middle of writing this book, Bruce Johnson, a WHS alumnus and long-time sportswriter for the Westfield Leader, let me know that Westfield is having a good season, one of its best in years. On the Monday of President's Weekend, I decide to take in a game while I could. I met Larry Simmons, Coach Horne, and Neil III for lunch in town and then Larry and I headed over to the high school to catch the second half of the game there. They looked good, with decent size, too. One kid stood out. I would find out later his name was Griffin Rooney. Larry and I had the same reaction. He reminded us of Tim Goski. He was about the same height, was solidly built, and appeared to play with a bit of a chip on his shoulder like Tim used to. He also played very well that day, including draining some threes against the other team's zone. Larry and I agreed we should take in another game, hopefully in the upcoming Union County Tournament.

I never did make a UCT game, where WHS would lose a tough one to highly regarded Linden for the second time this season, this time by four points. The loss put their record at 17-6. I did, however, later see my alma mater win a tough second-round state tournament game against Newark East Side, the defending Group IV champions, overcoming an eight point second half deficit. It was an exciting win that culminated with a good portion of the crowd spilling onto the court at the final buzzer, joining with the players as they celebrated their win.

For their next round game three nights later, Bruce Johnson, Larry and I were in the seats to watch Westfield battle highly rated Watchung Hills. Westfield would hang tough for three quarters, trailing by 43-32, before the floodgates opened and Watchung Hills pulled away with a 30-point win at 77-47.

Westfield had fought valiantly and showed nice flashes but didn't quite have the goods that night. Westfield finished their season at 21-7, their best record in more than four decades.

The following Tuesday Simmons and I returned to watch Watchung Hills lose a nail biter to an equally tough Elizabeth team, losing on a game winning jump shot with 2 seconds left. The game had been everything Larry and I had hoped to see – extremely hard fought, well played, and evenly matched. It reminded us of our battles with Jefferson our senior year. I felt bad for Watchung Hills, which was vying for its first sectional title…yet another reminder of how hard it was to win the whole thing.

Watchung Hills' season ended abruptly that night. The next night the NBA suspended its season just as abruptly due to the Covid-19 pandemic. Two days later the NJ state tournament was halted for the same reason. I felt bad for all the kids. It's tough enough when one team loses a close one in a championship game, but when everyone's season ends abruptly for other reasons, that is truly sad. This was the kind of thing that only happened in wartime. But I suppose we were at war … this time with a virus. How lucky was my generation that we never had to deal with any of these wartime scenarios? Every year, every season, games that were scheduled got played. That was taken for granted. Now, it seems, nothing can be taken for granted anymore.

But whoever said life was fair? Whoever said that you only got good bounces in the game of life? No one needs to tell me the answer. I've seen my lifelong friend Tom Pfeiffer have to battle cancer and all its side effects for 17 years now. I've seen my backcourt mate Tim Goski have to suffer the loss of two of his three sons. I've seen my teammate Scott Novacek have to endure a tough divorce and the loss of both parents and a brother all within a few short years. I've seen my good friend Larry Simmons try his best to raise a son as a single parent and struggle to keep him on the right path. No, I have no illusions as to the challenges that life may bring, or whether there are any guarantees, other than death and taxes, of course.

Fortunately, you can still find a safe haven out there if you look for it in the right place. I found mine on the hardwood floor, between the lines … in a place where you make your own luck, where the harder you work, the luckier you get … where there are no bad bounces, where the balls have no points ….

Of course, even the safe havens might throw you a curve ball once in a while and test you when you least expect it. That happened to me in

January of 2021. I was checking in on Tom Pfeiffer via text as I had been doing at somewhat regular intervals the past few years. At this particular time I was going through the process of dotting "i"s and crossing "t"s for this book, so I decided to tap into Tom's memory to corroborate one specific point. I asked Tom about the night we voted for captains. "I was just trying to confirm that it was 4 rounds of voting, not 3," I texted. "I DON'T want to know who switched their vote - I never asked anyone about that". Tom's reply came back quickly: "I remember you and Larry being tied after two rounds and the third round between you and Larry was going to be the last one…So it went four total rounds." That was the confirmation I was looking for. Then came these additional words that stunned me. I read the words a second time and then a third: "I am sorry to tell you but it was me. I understand if you cannot forgive me. You remember our junior year we had tri-captains and honor was diluted. I was selfish and you deserved my support. I've been carrying that around for 49 years and telling you does not help, but you deserve the truth after all you have done for me."

After all I had done for him? This was the guy I'd been friends with since the first grade, who had never turned his back on me when I was both a physical and social weakling, and who would one day be part of my wedding party. But Tom had caught me completely off guard. I had been playing bridge with my wife and a couple of friends at the time and now my mind was racing, trying to process the incoming missile that just struck. It didn't take long – just a matter of seconds. Tom's admission and explanation, while a complete surprise, made perfect sense. If Tom had felt a need to distance himself from the mediocrity of our junior year via this action, who was I to second guess that? Besides, he *had* supported me by voting for me in each of the two prior votes. Then there was the undeniable fact that I had put Tom in that difficult position, between a rock and a hard place, with only a few moments to make a decision.

For 49 years Tom had been carrying around the guilt associated with his decision in that brief moment, but for 49 years he had been unaware that I had voted for Larry each time. Now the shoe was on the other foot. Now it was my turn to come clean about having put Tom in that awkward position and thus being the one responsible for him having to carry that guilt for so long. I had to try to put Tom's mind at ease because of the actions

I took that same day such a long time ago. As soon as I did, Tom was naturally a bit miffed at me – first, for creating that burden he had been bearing for so long, and second, for putting him in a position where felt he needed to risk our friendship by coming clean. I truly felt bad at that moment, because my naivety as a teenager had unwittingly created a real long-term burden for Tom to bear. I quickly apologized for my earlier stupidity and for causing the whole situation and reassured him that his admission didn't change a thing.

Tom may have thought our friendship was being put to the test, but there was no way I was going to let this come between us. Tom and I had shared a dream together...then we chased it together...ultimately, we realized it together. When you are honest with yourself, it's easier to see the truth everywhere else. Tom had not slighted me that Monday after practice just four days before our first game. That much was very clear to me. We all did that day what we thought was the right thing to do. In fact, it was unanimous – the three of us had all voted for Larry. Perhaps it was all just part of God's plan.

In July 2021 the three of us reconvened at Tom's home in Milford, CT where we lamented the hardships of getting and being old before shifting our focus to the more pleasant memories of events and days we had experienced together such a long time ago. This day was just another of the constant reminders that we aren't spring chickens anymore, so it seems we find ourselves spending more time recalling the days when we were. Maybe that just occurs naturally. Physical limitations or ailments may restrict us to simpler lifestyles than those that we enjoyed in our younger days, but thankfully friendships never go out of style and they never get old. Nor do the memories of those precious days we all spent together.

When I look back at the last 50 years, I count my lucky stars for the good life I've enjoyed...make that the good *basketball* life I've enjoyed. Indeed, basketball has been inextricably woven into my being, it's part of who I am, part of my DNA. As for 1972, I can't help but be reminded of the final scene in *Field of Dreams* when Ray Kinsella asks: "Is there a heaven?". "Oh yeah," the answer comes back. "It's the place dreams come true." Maybe heaven came to Westfield in the winter of 1972. Maybe that *was* heaven.

These days I have a choice at the end of each day. I can turn on the TV and watch the news and hear about this conflict or that, where opinions differ wildly and where happy stories seem to be nowhere in sight. Or I can watch a game that will be over in an hour or two and have an objective

The captains and me in July 2021

outcome. And if that doesn't do it for me, I might just close my eyes and allow myself to drift off to a simpler time with the music of Don McClean playing in my ears, with my own lyrics playing in my mind ...

> *Now it's been almost fifty years*
> *Since we filled those gyms and heard those cheers.*
> *I can still hear them now.*
> *Our gym housed a boyhood dream*
> *Where good players blossomed as a team.*
> *We dared to win, and Horne Man showed us how.*
> *Yes, something drove us deep inside*
> *In a football school full of pride.*

We put all we had into it,
With a will that said: "Let's do it!"
Yes, we did that year what precious few
Ever dreamed we'd ever do
And became the best the town ever knew…
State Champs of '72.

So bye-bye good Ol' Westfield High.
That championship season was our all-time high
When we learned the meaning of never-say-die,
And together we all touched the sky.

EPILOGUE

Each passing year after high school brought with it the further separation of our championship team. While Tim Goski's travels took him a number of places, Tom Pfeiffer stayed in Connecticut after graduating from Bridgeport, Larry Simmons went back to school at Greenville Tech in South Carolina, and Scott Novacek moved to San Francisco to pursue opportunities in the shipping industry. Others like Mike Cooney, Steve Lee, Bob Jester and Dave Phillips also ended up outside New Jersey's borders right after college. Pretty soon we got to the point where our championship season already seemed like a distant memory.

Ten years later, six players and coach pose in Westfield's gym along with their championship trophy. From left: Bob Jester, Tom Pfeiffer, Steve Reddy, Mike Cooney, Larry Simmons, Neil Horne, Tim Goski

In March 1982, six of us (Goski, Pfeiffer, Simmons, Jester, Cooney and myself), along with Coach Horne, reunited in Westfield's gym on a Friday afternoon where John Belis and the Courier-News took pictures and interviewed us about our banner year. A few days later, on March 9, 1982, the Courier-News published Belis's article that was titled: **"Devil of a Team"**, with the subtitle **"Westfield players still bound together by state basketball title they won 10 years ago"**.

Belis did an excellent job summarizing our memorable season: "Ten years ago this winter, a handful of unheralded basketball players from Westfield came out of nowhere to win the Group 4 state tournament. It was one of the most remarkable Cinderella stories ever written." But the article didn't just document what happened that season, it contained comments from seven players who now had the benefit of 10 years hindsight and reflection. That commentary, which was artfully immersed into Belis's article, put into words for the first time what our championship season had meant to the players who made it happen:

"We complimented each other in a very unique way.... When we were playing as a team, nobody could beat us." – MIKE COONEY

"If we'd played Jefferson 10 times we'd have won 9 or 10 of those games. All of them would have been close and Horne would've made the difference every time." – BOB JESTER

"Until that season, I was a pretty wild person basketball-wise, I was totally into run -and-gun. I had to learn to play under control. Our offense was structured but there was still room for individual play, too. " – TIM GOSKI

"Man for man, we weren't really a super team. We just ran a few offenses really well and we were very well drilled. We'd wear out a lot of those teams and then we'd come up with those last-second shots to win." – SCOTT NOVACEK

"We were really disappointed we didn't play better in the state finals.... I was still a little down the next day but Pfeiffer told me that years from now nobody would remember how we played, just that we won." – STEVE REDDY

"Defense was always the most exciting part of the game to me. I liked trying to shut out a player or shut him down.... I didn't even take shooting practice seriously because I figured the team could win without my scoring." – LARRY SIMMONS

"We played together, there was no selfishness. It was a real team effort.... That's why there will always be a bond among us.... It's great to go back to the gym and see that state banner hanging on the wall. When they ask me for my ticket at

the door, I just point up to the banner and say, 'See that? That's my ticket.'" –
TOM PFEIFFER.

It truly was a banner year, both figuratively and literally. The banner
Tom was referring to was very real. WHS had hung a nice, full-sized banner
right up near the scoreboard. The blue banner with white lettering and Blue
Devil insignia spelled out our NJISAA Group IV State Championship and
25-2 Won/Loss record.

A portion of our banner can be seen in this 1984 photo

Before you knew it, we would be separated by hundreds of miles, with
our lives marching on in different directions, making high school a distant
memory once again.

Students aren't the only ones who move on after high school. Coaches do too. Neil Horne Jr. would coach at WHS for seven years before he would move on. He enjoyed more coaching success at Somerville High, and then at Union Catholic. It was there that Coach Horne proved he wasn't a one trick pony, by orchestrating what was likely the biggest upset in the history of NJ state championship basketball. Horne devised a unique game plan for his unranked Union Catholic squad, which then went out and played a near perfect game to upset heavily favored CBA, a nationally ranked team that had been ranked #1 in NJ by the Star Ledger the entire season. CBA had the best player in the state that year, McDonald's All-American point guard John Crotty, along with 6'8 forward Marc Dowdell, an eventual starter for Villanova, and two other players who enjoyed D-1 hoops success. Not only was coach Horne able to produce the brilliant state final game that had eluded us, but he got to do while coaching his son Neil III as one of his starting guards. Coach Horne was rewarded for his sustained coaching success with his induction into the NJ Scholastic Coaches Association Hall of Fame in 1995 and, more recently, into Union Catholic's Hall of Fame.

Shortly after our 10-year reunion in 1982, my wife and I moved out of New Jersey but never ventured too far away from the Garden State. Our first stop was Audubon, PA, near Valley Forge, which was followed by Bucks County, PA eight years later, and we've been there ever since.

I was doing long train commutes every day to New York City those first several years after moving to Bucks County and would still get back to Westfield somewhat regularly to visit my parents who still had their house on Kimball Avenue. In 1995, my 81-year-old father got diagnosed with pancreatic cancer after literally going almost four decades without a sick day. It took the first few months of that year for doctors to diagnose my father's illness, and then the next three months his decline accelerated. In late July Coach Horne heard of my dad's condition and called me up. A few days later he came over to my dad's house and the three of us reminisced a bit while watching the state final game film again. I probably hadn't seen the game film in more than two decades, but it was the perfect time to watch it again given my dad's condition. I think that night was the last time I saw my father smile. He passed away three weeks later.

It was the summer of 2000 when I got a call from Bruce Johnson, acting in a capacity that I wasn't familiar with – that of Trustee of the Westfield Athletic Hall of Fame ("WAHOF"). I didn't even know there was such a thing. Bruce delivered the news that our hoops team would be going into the Hall of Fame that November. I would later learn that there were inductions every other year starting in 1994, with most of the inductees being individual athletes, along with one team each of those years. Ours would be only the fourth team in any sport to get inducted. That was pretty cool.

Soon after we were planning our first real reunion around the November 20 Hall of Fame date. The ceremony was on a Monday night, and 10 of our 12 players, along with Coach Horne and his wife Rose, reunited for dinner at the Jolly Trolley in downtown Westfield two nights earlier. It was great to see everyone, middle aged though we were. More than 28 years had now passed since our championship run, so we were ripe for a night of reminiscing. I decided to write a poem for the occasion, one that tried to retell our story. I had done something similar for a fraternity reunion about 10 years earlier that had been a big hit, so I figured something like that was worthy of this occasion. At the end of dinner, I read the poem, which I had entitled "A Team to Remember", to my unsuspecting teammates. They ate it up, in part because it included lots of details about certain events that had good memories associated with them.

The next morning, we attempted to turn back the clock in a different way – a bunch of us got back out on the court together at Maxim Junior High in Plainfield where Mark Jackson was the principal. There we were again … Goski, Novacek, Simmons, Cooney, Jester, Jackson, Lee and me, along with Richard Goski and a friend who crashed the party…out on the court again for our last hurrah. It wasn't very pretty like the good old days, but you could still see evidence of our signature traits. Cooney still had the sweet jumper, Tim still had the shot fakes and hesitation moves that would get you leaning off balance, Larry could still get up to snatch a ball out of the air, Nova could still use his broad shoulders and short bank shots to dominate inside, and Jackson still set a pick that felt like a brick wall.

There was one other thing that had caught our attention in the weeks leading up to the ceremony: our championship banner no longer hung from the gym wall. This was disconcerting, at least to me, to the point where I needed to find out why. That banner had a special meaning to me, and I often thought of Pfeiffer's quote in Belis's feature article when he referred to that banner as being his permanent ticket into the gym.

Going back to school isn't so bad when it's for this reason

I inquired with Ed Tranchina, the current WHS athletic director and another Trustee of the WAHOF, that Monday afternoon. I remember walking in unannounced, introducing myself, and asking about the whereabouts of the banner. His response was something to the effect that the banner had been taken down to be cleaned at some point, but I don't think he offered any explanation as to why it had not gone back up immediately afterwards. While Ed may have said that he would look into it, I didn't leave there very confident that our banner would re-appear on the gym wall any time soon. Regardless, that was going to have to be a battle for another day. This was no time to dwell on a negative. That night we were going into the Hall of Fame!

The event was held at The Westwood, a banquet hall in neighboring Garwood, and was very well attended. Nine of our twelve team members, along with Coach Horne, were present 28 years after our season, missing only Pfeiffer, Chip Danker and Greg Allen. We had a good showing of parents as well, with the Novaceks and Jesters present along with Tim's mom and my mom. Not only was our team being honored this night, but so was Tim Goski who was individually being inducted for his achievements on the basketball court.

Fittingly, Coach Horne graciously accepted the WAHOF plaque on behalf of our team and heaped praise on the players that he coached that season, but the reality is that he deserved it every bit as much as we did. Many in the banquet room had witnessed our season 28 years earlier, with a string of down-to-the-wire games that overwhelmingly went our way. Everyone who had witnessed it knew it wouldn't have been possible without Horne at the helm. Horne concluded his remarks by reading the last quarter of my poem to the audience, which ended with:

So Bye-Bye Miss American Pie.
That championship season was our all-time high.
But these old boys aren't ready to die.
No, this team will never die.
'Cause good teams come and good teams go,
But there never ever was as great a show,
As the one we put on back in '72
When Horne and his boys made the dream come true.

But time marches on. Before you knew it we were all saying our goodbyes, heading back to hotels and airports, and then to our daily routines. It was back to the salt mines again.

I had been unemployed for a few months when Neil Horne III called me in the spring of 2003 to ask me if I would speak at his dad's retirement dinner later that year. Neil III had asked a few former players to speak that night, to rekindle some of his best coaching memories. The occasion

From left: M Cooney, B Jester, D Phillips, S Novacek, S Reddy, L Simmons, N Horne, S Lee, M Jackson, T Goski

A night to remember for Coach Horne and Tim Goski

afforded us another opportunity for a mini reunion of sorts. Just three short years after our WAHOF reunion, seven of us – Bob Jester, Mark Jackson,Greg Allen, Scott Novacek, Larry Simmons, Tom Pfeiffer, and I reunited for the occasion.

When it was my turn to speak, I recalled several specific instances that the typical Westfield fan would not have been aware of. Like how Horne finally realized that Goski was going to take the first shot every game, so he decided it was better to design a play for him to at least get a better shot. Or how he put Goski in the back of the one-three-one zone defense, telling him at the time it was because Tim was quicker than anyone and that spot required more running, when in reality it was because Horne didn't want Tim to cheat on defense and take off early to the other end (which we only found out years later). Then there was the priceless look on Horne's face when Novacek presented a small baggy full of hair clippings in the locker room right before the second Cranford game. Topping all those was the time when Horne masterfully put the hammer down and threw us all out of practice when we needed a wake-up call more than we needed the practice.

We presented Horne with a gift that night – a framed picture of a professionally printed version of my earlier poem *A Team to Remember,* along with a prominent footnote below it stating:

"Dedicated to our coach Neil Horne, who in 1971-72 led us to a 25-2 season and the Group IV NJSIAA State Championship, still the best record and only Group IV Title in Westfield High School's history as of this date, June 27, 2003. Thank you, Coach, for one special year together and a lifetime of great memories."

I went a step further though. I decided the occasion deserved a song as well. So, I wrote lyrics to the tune of Don McClean's hit song *American Pie,* purchased an instrumental version of the song, hired one of my son's friends to sing the lead vocals, and then went to a small local recording studio three days before the dinner to record *Ol' Westfield High.* The song, like the poem, told the story of our season. It was played toward the end of my talk, but in retrospect was probably overkill and a bit too long for the occasion. To this day the song has only been heard by a handful of people beyond those in attendance that night. But who knows? Maybe that will change someday.

Coach Horne accepts his gift at his retirement dinner in 2003

While Tom Pfeiffer would face a series of health issues in the ensuing years, I continued to be blessed with good health, save a bum hip that I had replaced at age 53 and a couple of meniscus tears in my right knee that finally put me on the sidelines for good at age 57. The only real bump in the road I faced was getting laid off from a well-paying job and then ultimately taking another position more than 200 miles away. Moving can be a bitch, especially when your kids get into their junior high and high school years. But so can long-distance commuting or trying to maintain two homes that far apart. I chose the latter over moving and did the long commute for 13 years. It certainly wasn't easy, but hey – sometimes life can be hard, and I wasn't about to complain. I still had my good health which meant I had just about everything.

I was relieved of that somewhat demanding lifestyle in an instant when I got another unexpected pink slip at age 62. After months of never quite finding the right next job, I began to think that it just might never come. Yet I was OK with that, having saved enough over the years to be able to retire by that point. Besides, I was in good health and now I would have extra time to do some things that I might never have considered prior to that. There are certainly worse things in life that not having to get up every morning and then commuting long distances to and from work.

In early November 2017 my wife Susan and I were attending a wedding in the Florida Keys, and I was able to connect with Scott Novacek, another teammate that I had not seen or talked to for about 10 years. After college Scott had spent about two decades living on the West Coast, where he got his MBA and started a successful international container business. He ultimately sold that and moved to South Florida to be closer to his aging parents while beginning a new career in residential real estate, one that keeps him busy to this day. More recently, Scott did have the misfortune of losing both his parents and his younger brother Todd, all within a few short years. He then went through a divorce. Despite those recent hardships, Scott was upbeat and looked great for 63, still sporting those broad shoulders and strong forearms. He looked like he could still get out there and play. In fact, he said he still does get out for a little bit of outdoor pickup games.

Scott said he had seen Tim within the past year and that, at least by outward appearance, he was doing OK. I decided right there that I would call him as soon as I got home. We also talked about the idea of another reunion. After all, it had now been 17 years since we last gathered at the WAHOF reunion. We were all middle aged back then, but now we were close to retirement age and most of our kids were grown up. I agreed to contact a few of the guys to gauge interest.

After connecting with Tim, I got a hold of Mike Cooney, who needed no convincing at all. In fact, Mike informed me he had attended Michael Goski's funeral in Texas and was able to spend some time with Tim and his family, a commendable act indeed. That only reinforced the bond that existed between us and that this reunion needed to happen. Mike helped track down several of the guys and plan the details. We eventually settled on Saturday, March 10, 2018 for the event. While this would be our fourth reunion since high school, it would be the first one not prompted by any other event.

About a month before the reunion, I made a visit to Westfield to check out Ferraro's Restaurant, which we were targeting for our reunion dinner. I only knew it as a pizza place when I was in high school, but it has come a long way since those early days and was now one of the nicest restaurants

On the streets of Fort Lauderdale with Westfield's Mr. Big

in Westfield. While there, Neil Horne III introduced me to Chuck Murray, the guy who ran the place and who would presumably set us up for our reunion dinner. Not only was Ferraro's touted as a great restaurant, but Chuck was rumored to be a big basketball fan and had a kid somewhere in the WHS basketball program. This guy was super busy but also a bundle of energy as he showed us around to a few private or semi-private rooms we might want to reserve. Even though I hadn't been inside Ferraro's for decades, something about him seemed familiar. Then it hit me! Chuck was the cocky little guard I had run into down at the Westfield Y when I was 35 and just starting a new job in Manhattan. The quickness and energy that had gotten my attention on the basketball court some 28 years earlier I was now observing as he made his way about his current court. "I remember you", I said, smiling, "from down at the Y!" "Yeah, that was probably me", he would reply. That pretty much sealed the deal for me – the place was perfect for our reunion a month later. We took the Wine Room.

There was a chance that we would have all 12 players together for the first time in 46 years. Greg Allen was the biggest question mark as we hadn't gotten any responses from him. Ironically, he was also the only one who still lived in Westfield, so there was still a chance.

Finally, the weekend of March 10 arrived. Scott flew into Newark and drove down to my house the evening before. The next morning, I told Susan as we were leaving that for the next 24 hours Scott and I were 17 years old and back in high school – that's what it felt like. We grabbed a DVD player, three game DVDs, and the basketball that my daughter Jackie had marked up and made the 65-minute drive to Westfield. Before lunch we drove by the houses we had grown up in, or at least the spots where they used to be.

We then headed over to Charlie Brown's on North Avenue where eight of us met for lunch. From there it was on to the high school where we had reserved the large cafeteria and would hang out and watch videos of our old games. We were up to 10 players at this point, missing only BJ and Greg Allen. A few others joined our little party, including Coach Horne and Neil III, Bruce Johnson, Bobby Davis (who was from the Class of '74), and a handful of parents and kids from the current varsity and JV teams. We watched the video of the first Scotch Plains and Jefferson games and last, but not least, the state final game against Triton. Many notable plays were given replays, and while there was no audio for these games, we supplied plenty of our own commentary. It had been 23 years since I had seen the finals game back when my father had died, and for most of the team it may have been twice as long. Coach Horne's dad had somehow taken several extra minutes of footage of the state final that I didn't know even existed. It was priceless. It even had some reverse angle footage, including Nova's game-winning rebound and shot, and the immediate aftermath of the game both on the court and back in the locker room. This extra footage was finally seeing the light of days after all those years!

On the way to Ferraro's for dinner, a short walk from the Westfield Inn, Mark Jackson and Larry Simmons pulled up alongside in Mark's car and had some good news – they had found Greg Allen! And he would be joining us soon for dinner! We had just gotten one step closer…we now just needed BJ to show up at Ferraro's to give us our baker's dozen of 12 players plus one coach in one room for the first time in 46 years!

Hanging out in the bar area of Westfield's nicest restaurant with former teammates all around me, having a beer and shooting the breeze prior to dinner was priceless. Spud Monroe, another WHS standout from the Class of '77, and Bruce Johnson were at one end of the bar talking with Goski and Simmons, no doubt recalling certain moments from the good old days. The rest of us huddled nearby and got caught up while waiting to be called into the Wine Room. Meanwhile, I was holding in one hand a small duffle bag with a special basketball inside it. A few days earlier my daughter Jackie had put her artistic talents to work and marked up the ball to commemorate our special season, but we still needed to decide what to do with the ball. My initial thought was to donate it to WHS thinking they would want to display it in one of their trophy cases. Another possibility was to give it to Ferraro's to further remember our celebratory night there. A few of us kicked around the options, but when it came time to move into the Wine Room, I still wasn't sure what I would do with or say about the ball.

It was a bit after 7 pm when we were ushered into the Wine Room. Greg Allen had indeed arrived, which was a beautiful thing to behold, but there was still no BJ at the scene and our calls to him were going unanswered. Jester had forewarned me two days earlier that a work obligation would prevent him from making the afternoon film session but said that he would be there for the dinner. There was nothing else we could at that point…it was game time. We settled into our room, with 11 players, Coach Horne and his wife Rose, and Neil III. Bruce Johnson had been invited to join us for the team dinner, but he ultimately chose not to attend

that portion. I never asked him why, but I suspected he may have felt out of place and declined out of respect for the team. Bobby Davis, on the other hand, did not feel so inhibited and summarily took a seat at one end of the table, directly opposite Pfeiffer and me at the other end.

I decided the time was right to address some team issues while we waited for our food and drinks to arrive. I got everyone's attention and then turned to face Tim. "Tim", I began, "on behalf of the team, I want to say that we are all happy that you are here, we are sorry for your loss, we thank Michael and Christopher for their service, and may their souls rest in peace." "Here. Here.", someone else chimed in, and we all raised our glasses in a salute to Tim's fallen sons. Tim clearly appreciated the gesture.

I then turned my attention to the next topic that needed addressing – that of our team ball and what to do with it. I reached down into the bag by my foot and pulled out the special ball. "A week ago, this ball was just another ball at a Dick's Sporting Goods. Now it's been transformed into something more meaningful. But we still need to figure out where it should go from here." I then began mentioning our options and discarding them one by one, before proclaiming: "Fuck it." Turning to Pfeiffer, I then said "You deserve this. You should have it." Tom's face lit up as I handed him the ball. Unfortunately, Tom couldn't express himself vocally but his facial reaction said it all. He then requested, via text, that we all sign the ball. I had been planning on that anyway, so I pulled the black Sharpie out of my bag and made the first signature before passing the ball to my right. In retrospect, it was obvious right away that this was the right choice, that the only fitting home for that ball was Tom Pfeiffer's home. Fortunately, Mark Jackson didn't have any such misconceptions about the available options and he helped me see the clear right choice a few minutes before dinner.

With the two elephants in the room out of the way, I couldn't resist sharing my Joe Weider/Bob Martin story as most of them were totally unaware of it. That meant recounting the multiple "What are you doing here, Reddy?" incidents, and my dad telling me "You'll never get your money back" when it came to spending the $100 on Joe Weider's weight training program. I had brought with me a few of the bonus pamphlets the program came with, that I had preserved in mint condition over the years, perhaps unconsciously saving them for this night, and passed them around the table. These included invaluable "how to" pamphlets such as *"How to Overcome Shyness, Bashfulness, and an Inferiority Complex"* and *"Sex Education for the Body Builder"* pamphlets that perhaps I should have paid more attention to when I first got them! I ended my little speech by telling my teammates that if I saw Martin now, I'd probably say "Yeah, Martin, I am here to read about myself, and what are you gonna do about it?", which I punctuated by standing up and doing my most intimidating muscle flex with both arms in front of me. There, I had finally answered Bob Martin's question from 46 years earlier…I would be intimidated by him no more! But just then Bobby Davis interrupted the laughter with an insightful question: "But would you thank him?" to which I replied with barely a pause: "Probably." It wasn't lost on me at all that Bob Martin had inspired, or perhaps *scared* me into being a better athlete.

The rest of the evening was magical. Along with great food and drink, and recalling those most memorable moments from our season, it included

Standing from left: N Horne Jr, M Cooney, S Lee, S Reddy, T Goski, C Danker,
G Allen. Seated from left: D Phillips, T Pfeiffer, L Simmons, S Novacek, M Jackson

a call with our JV coach Ed Tirone, a surprise visit from Richie Scialabba, and the first nearly complete team photos in 46 years. Several of us capped off the evening by huddling in Mike Cooney's room to milk the reunion for all it was worth. The following morning eight of us reconvened one more time at the Westfield Diner before it was time to finally go our separate ways. The 24 hours were finally up...we weren't in high school anymore.

The next couple of days there were a lot of thank yous and pictures exchanged. The reunion certainly lived up to everyone's hopes. I think we left there with the realization that our team had withstood the test of time. We now had a better appreciation for what had happened nearly half a century earlier, and for the friendships that were still intact all these years later.

That Sunday evening, after being home for just a few hours, I sat down to memorialize our successful weekend with one last email to my teammates, which I labeled *A Night to Remember*. Toward the end of the email, I hinted that the only thing left to do was write the book, and not to doubt that it might still happen.

I frankly didn't think a book was in the cards at that moment, as I had thought about it several times over the past few years and always came to the same conclusion – it would be a lot of work and ultimately not enough readers who would care. I probably waited too long if I was ever going to write one. But my thinking was starting to shift on this. When I had mentioned the possibility of a book to Bruce Johnson, he responded with "you may need to write the book to prove that it happened", which I took as a subtle reference to the banner being gone, taking with it the fading memories of what we had achieved decades earlier. That resonated with me. With the memory of our special season suddenly jogged, I would now start to think of this again with a fresh perspective.

From left: S Reddy, T Pfeiffer, M Jackson, M Cooney, L Simmons, B Jester

A few months later a few of us had a little reunion encore with a small gathering at Tom Pfeiffer's home in Connecticut. Among other things it provided the opportunity for Bob Jester to reconnect with Tom for the first time since Tom's battle with cancer began shortly after Horne's retirement in 2003. Consequently, there are now 13 signatures on the ball that sits on Tom's mantel.

2018 morphed into 2019, and that winter I found myself in Westfield's gym after Bruce Johnson had alerted me to the very competitive current hoops team, Westfield's best in many years. I got to witness Westfield pull out a fourth quarter comeback against Newark East Side, the 2019 Group IV champion, in a second round state tournament game. While I was there that evening, I took a couple of pictures of the one basketball banner that is still

With Tim Goski in Scotch Plains in September 2019

hanging. I could certainly take solace in that our year 72 shows up three times, along with the 65 and 68 from my older brothers' teams. I sent them both the picture and we were all a bit surprised to learn that my brother Tom's '65 team was still the last WHS team to win the Union County tournament 55 years earlier! It was also neat to see that all three Reddy brothers had made their mark on WHS hoops history.

Every number tells a story…

Before I left that evening, I took one more picture out in the foyer where a recently redesigned trophy case lined the entrance into the gym. Unfortunately, the team trophy that had been awarded 48 years earlier for the Group IV state championship had somehow been lost or discarded at some point over the years, another victim of passing time, lack of space, and fading memories. But in its place now sits a new trophy, a round one that I suspect will be around for a while. Who knows? Maybe the number of people who are familiar with the story behind that special ball will increase over time rather than pass away along with the people who made it happen. As with many things, only time will tell.

The trophy case outside Westfield's gym now includes this ball

The 50th anniversary of that championship season is quickly approaching, and there will be another reunion to celebrate the brief time we all spent together decades ago. Sadly, our teammate and brother Greg Allen won't physically be there, having passed away in August of 2020. But he will be there in spirit, because he'll always be part of our team and it's the team we'll be celebrating. Individually we may have been good, some of us perhaps even very good, but what we achieved as a team trumped everything we accomplished as individuals. If ever there was an example of the whole being greater than the sum of its parts, our team was it. In the years ahead all of Greg's teammates and our head coach will pass away one by one, but I am confident that the memory of our team will survive us all, validating that we were...no, that we *are still*, in fact, a team to remember.

In Memoriam

Gregory Owen Allen

(May 7, 1955 – August 25, 2020)

A year ago, Greg Allen, our teammate, passed away. He was the first of the team to do so. Our heart-felt condolences go out to his mother and family.

Greg was a two-sport athlete. A stalwart defensive end for two state championship WHS football teams and an integral member of the 71-72 state championship basketball team, about which this book is written. As teammates, across multiple years and sports, we were all intimately involved with each other's lives - in class, on the field and in the community. We all came to know Greg, principally, as a fine person. His easy, welcoming manner enabled him to connect with people from all walks of high school life. He was also an excellent student, his academic accomplishments rivaling his athletic ones.

Our last connection with Greg was at our all-team reunion in March 2018. Laughs and memories were shared, and the evening ended with the strength of our collective bond reaffirmed. Now, well into our 60's, we could all look around the table and acknowledge that the most lasting legacy of our championship season was the relationships we have all maintained. Empty though his seat at the table of future reunions will be, Greg's presence and spirit will remain with us always.

Appendix I

Schedule & Results
for
The 1971-72 WHS Varsity Boys Basketball Team

25 Wins, 2 Losses

Date	H/A	Winning Team	Score	Losing Team	Score		Game
12/10/71	A	Westfield	46	Gov Livingston	29		Reg
12/14/71	H	Westfield	73	So. Plainfield	50		Reg
12/17/71	H	Westfield	66	Scotch Plains	62		Reg
12/21/71	H	Westfield	73	Dayton Reg	43		Reg
12/23/71	A	Westfield	75	Union	59		Reg
12/28/71	A	Westfield	69	Roselle Catholic	68		Reg
1/4/72	A	Westfield	59	Johnson Reg	44		Reg
1/6/72	H	Westfield	80	Hillside	56		Reg
1/8/72	A	Westfield	64	Colonia	56	OT	Reg
1/11/72	A	Westfield	48	T. Jefferson	47		Reg
1/14/72	H	Westfield	67	Cranford	27		Reg
1/18/72	A	Westfield	69	Scotch Plains	46		Reg
1/21/72	H	Westfield	83	Rahway	53		Reg
1/28/72	H	Westfield	74	Johnson Reg	56		Reg
2/2/72	A	Westfield	98	Rahway	59		Reg
2/4/72	A	Cranford	82	Westfield	78		Reg
2/8/72	H	Westfield	71	Gov Livingston	54		Reg
2/11/72	H	Westfield	58	Linden	56		Reg
2/16/72	A	Westfield	81	Kenilworth	48		UCT
2/19/72	A	Westfield	65	Hillside	56		UCT
2/23/72	A	Linden	54	Westfield	51		UCT
2/26/72	A	Westfield	75	Hillside	58		Reg
3/1/72	A	Westfield	88	Parsippany Hills	43		Grp-IV
3/7/72	A	Westfield	61	Cranford	59		Grp-IV
3/11/72	A	Westfield	52	T. Jefferson	50		Grp-IV
3/15/72	A	Westfield	56	Hackensack	51		Grp-IV
3/18/82	A	Westfield	44	Triton Reg	42	OT	Grp-IV

Season Statistics
for
The 1971-72 WHS Varsity Boys Basketball Team

Season Totals

	GP	FGM	FGA	FG%	FTM	FTA	FT%	PTS	O-REB	D-REB	T-REB	ASST	T/O	AS/TO	STLS	BLKS
T Goski	27	168	359	46.8%	71	91	78.0%	407	43	47	90	125	123	1.02	78	5
S Novacek	26	167	356	46.9%	37	72	51.4%	371	150	129	279	19	66	0.29	39	39
T Pfeiffer	27	125	266	47.0%	68	89	76.4%	318	88	85	173	59	61	0.97	76	16
S Reddy	26	90	177	50.8%	57	90	63.3%	237	14	41	55	93	69	1.35	50	4
L Simmons	27	79	190	41.6%	37	68	54.4%	195	142	163	305	44	75	0.59	51	24
B Jester	26	34	69	49.3%	31	58	53.4%	99	33	59	92	8	25	0.32	9	5
M Cooney	21	29	67	43.3%	9	11	81.8%	67	8	16	24	14	28	0.50	10	1
S Lee	16	16	37	43.2%	15	29	51.7%	47	11	3	14	8	19	0.42	6	1
M Jackson	15	10	28	35.7%	13	16	81.3%	33	15	10	25	8	11	0.73	5	3
D Phillips	16	13	33	39.4%	0	4	0.0%	26	10	14	24	1	7	0.14	1	0
G Allen	14	5	20	25.0%	2	7	28.6%	12	4	7	11	3	11	0.27	3	0
C Danker	13	3	6	50.0%	6	11	54.5%	12	2	5	7	2	6	0.33	4	0
WHS		739	1608	46.0%	346	546	63.4%	1824	520	579	1099	384	501	0.77	332	98
Opponents		541	1414	38.3%	321	519	61.8%	1403	282	440	722	229	632	0.36	207	56

Per Game Averages

	GP	FGM	FGA	FG%	FTM	FTA	FT%	PTS	O-REB	D-REB	T-REB	ASST	T/O	AS/TO	STLS	BLKS
T Goski	27	6.2	13.3	46.8%	2.6	3.4	78.0%	15.1	1.6	1.7	3.3	4.6	4.6	1.02	2.9	0.2
S Novacek	26	6.4	13.7	46.9%	1.4	2.8	51.4%	14.3	5.8	5.0	10.7	0.7	2.5	0.29	1.5	1.5
T Pfeiffer	27	4.6	9.9	47.0%	2.5	3.3	76.4%	11.8	3.3	3.1	6.4	2.2	2.3	0.97	2.8	0.6
S Reddy	26	3.5	6.8	50.8%	2.2	3.5	63.3%	9.1	0.5	1.6	2.1	3.6	2.7	1.35	1.9	0.2
L Simmons	27	2.9	7.0	41.6%	1.4	2.5	54.4%	7.2	5.3	6.0	11.3	1.6	2.8	0.59	1.9	0.9
B Jester	26	1.3	2.7	49.3%	1.2	2.2	53.4%	3.8	1.3	2.3	3.5	0.3	1.0	0.32	0.3	0.2
M Cooney	21	1.4	3.2	43.3%	0.4	0.5	81.8%	3.2	0.4	0.8	1.1	0.7	1.3	0.50	0.5	0.0
S Lee	16	1.0	2.3	43.2%	0.9	1.8	51.7%	2.9	0.7	0.2	0.9	0.5	1.2	0.42	0.4	0.1
M Jackson	15	0.7	1.9	35.7%	0.9	1.1	81.3%	2.2	1.0	0.7	1.7	0.5	0.7	0.73	0.3	0.2
D Phillips	16	0.8	2.1	39.4%	0.0	0.3	0.0%	1.6	0.6	0.9	1.5	0.1	0.4	0.14	0.1	0.0
G Allen	14	0.4	1.4	25.0%	0.1	0.5	28.6%	0.9	0.3	0.5	0.8	0.2	0.8	0.27	0.2	0.0
C Danker	13	0.2	0.5	50.0%	0.5	0.8	54.5%	0.9	0.2	0.4	0.5	0.2	0.5	0.33	0.3	0.0
WHS		27.4	59.6	46.0%	12.8	20.2	63.4%	67.6	19.3	21.4	40.7	14.2	18.6	0.77	12.3	3.6
Opponents		20.0	52.4	38.3%	11.9	19.2	61.8%	52.0	10.4	16.3	26.7	8.5	23.4	0.36	7.7	2.1

Appendix II

<u>A Team to Remember</u>

November 18, 2000

Way back almost thirty years ago,
Back when Gary Kehler ran the town's best show,
A new Westfield legend was about to be born,
And it all started with a man named Horne.

It was June '71 when he came to town
And made his presence felt at Gumbert playground
Where his boys-to-be refined their skills
And gave the locals their share of cheap thrills.

Night in and night out at Gumbert Park,
They'd knock heads with their rivals till well after dark,
Then cruise the town trying to stay cool,
In the nearest municipal swimming pool.

September soon came with Maggie May
And gridiron glory every Saturday;
Undefeated again in '71,
Extending onward their incredible run.

Horne's boys, meanwhile, awaited their turn,
As their simmering passion started to burn.
They decided: 'Enough of this football crap,
It's time to put Westfield hoops on the map!'

So in preseason, the players got tough,
The defense was physical and the fouls were rough.
When our football teammates joined the fray,
No one could wait for opening day.

The rumors were flying, the hoopsters were good,
How high they would soar was not yet understood.
Horne remained focused on opening night,
When he unleashed the fury on Berkeley Heights.

A week later Scotch Plains came to town,
But Miller and Ray Ray left with a frown.
The cagers had passed their first real test,
But still had not yet shown their best.

While Nova and Larry flexed their basketball muscle,
Red-eye and Piker relied on sheer hustle.
But Tim-eye was often in a world of his own,
And more often than not, he was in the zone.

There was BJ and Cooney and the Rat factor too,
Moose and Allen, Jax and Chiperoo.
With the Horne man commanding his basketball troops,
The team brought the fans a new brand of hoops.

The wins piled up, but not with scare,
With buzzer-beaters and overtimes the standard fare.
Then came Jeff in Elizabethtown,
But like all the others, the Jeffs would go down.

Now we were something, turning heads left and right,
Next on our hit list, Cranford – Friday night.
So Cranford brung it on, the Maz and Hobbie show,
But we wiped 'em out by 40 and our legend did grow.

Each and every victory was more and more fun,
Would we ever lose a game, were we number one?
Our cockiness was oozing, it showed on all our faces;
So when practice got shoddy, Horne put us in our places.

'Go home, get out of here, you guys stink today.'
While our rematch with Cranford was only three days away.
I guess it was an omen, a sign for the worst;
Cranford got revenge and our bubble finally burst.

Losing was a downer, the antithesis of fun;
Horne treated us to suicides and full court one-on-one.
Curse words were a flyin', with 'bastards' everywhere.
The big men served their notice: 'Don't bring that bleep in here.'

But winning was our forte, it's what we had to do,
To make it all worth it, to make the dream come true.
So we got back on track, back to 19-1;
Winning was the remedy. Winning was our fun.

We wanted that county tournament, where Jefferson would loom.
But Eddie and Freddie had other ideas, and Linden was our doom.
It wasn't supposed to happen, we came apart at the seams,
A painful unraveling of our basketball dreams.

But Horne man would have none of it, there were still games to play,
And what happened next, my friends, is why we're here today.
We tore apart that Hillside team and claimed the conference crown,
Then we whipped Parsippany and mowed their giants down.

Now Cranford stood between us and our final destiny.
We played loose, won by a deuce, and the games were down to three.
Now Jefferson was waiting, it was our day of reckoning:
The loser would go home for good, the winner would be king.

The place was jammed with thousands, in every corner people stood.
But it was déjà vu all over again; we sent 'em home for good.
And while the juniors were our big guns, or so the story goes,
We were saved by Piker's defense, and Larry's clutch free throws.

We had done what disbelievers said we couldn't do.
Yet we still had some work left; we had to win our final two.
Hackensack was next, but we would cut them down to size;
Goski would work his magic before their very eyes.

When Red-eye turned his ankle, Horne put Rat in there.
Soon Hackensack was off their track; that Rat was everywhere.
We won that game by five, but it was never really in doubt.
We liked to entertain the fans, we liked to hear them shout.

We were 24-2 now, with two more days to go.
It didn't matter who we'd play, it was going to be our show.
So Red-eye made his entrance like a limping Willis Reed;
Then we turned to face our foe: Triton of Runnemede.

We cruised for a while, and built a double-digit lead,
But we let it get away and at halftime Horne was teed.
The second half was ugly as we played in disarray;
And as fate would have it, it came down to one play.

Timmi stood at the line, poised to bring us glory,
But Nova grabbed his wayward shot; the rest is history.
The celebration started, the crowd went insane.
Back in the locker room, it was raining cold champagne.

We were mad at how we'd played that day; we barely got it done.
We hardly looked like a team that could be called number one.
But Piker reassured me, as we rode into the sun:
'Years from now, they won't care how, only that we won.'

Tom's been proven right, of course; we've made the Hall of Fame.
We did the thing we had to do, we won our final game.
Yes, we were very fortunate; we got to live our dream.
It was a Cinderella season; it was an extra special team.

So bye-bye Miss American Pie.
That championship season was our all-time high,
But these old boys aren't ready to die.
No, this team will never die.

'Cause good teams come and good teams go,
But there never ever was as great a show
As the one we put on back in '72,
When Horne and his boys made the dream come true.

Appendix III

<u>Ol' Westfield High</u>

June, 2003
(sung to the tune of "American Pie")

<u>Intro</u>
Long, long time ago,
I can still remember how those close games used to make 'em smile.
And we knew when we took the court,
That we'd do justice to our sport,
And we would make 'em happy for a while.
But February made us quiver,
With every tirade Horne delivered,
Another disciplined practice,
No rankings would distract us,
Then all the efforts that we'd applied,
Paid off with Nova's deuce inside,
And we became champs the whole state-wide,
The day the score was tied.
So…

<u>Chorus</u>
Bye-bye good Ol' Westfield High
That championship season was our all-time high
When we learned the meaning of never-say-die,
And together we all touched the sky; together we all touched the sky.

Verse 1

It was June of '71 when Horne came to town,
and made his presence felt at the local playground,
where his boys-to-be refined their skills,
Night in and night out at Gumbert Park,
we'd knock heads with our rivals till well after dark,
and gave the locals their share of cheap thrills.
September soon came with Maggie May,
and gridiron glory every Saturday;
undefeated in '71,
extending their incredible run.
Horne's boys, meanwhile, awaited their turn,
their simmering passion starting to burn,
Oh, how I to this day yearn
To play those games once more.
And we were singin' …

Chorus

Verse 2

The rumors were flying, the cagers were good,
how high they would soar was not yet understood.
Not even Horne knew what the season would bring.
While Nova and Larry flexed their inside muscle,
Redeye and Piker relied on sheer hustle,
And you could count on Timmi doin' his own thing.
There was BJ and Cooney and the Rat factor too,
Moose and Allen, Jax and Chipperoo.
With the Horne man commanding his troops,
He brought the fans a new brand of hoops.
He unleashed the fury on Berkeley Heights,
The wins started piling up left and right,
Now we were the ticket on Friday night,
The hottest show in town.
And we were singin' …

Chorus

Verse 3

When Cranford came to town with their high scoring show,
We wiped 'em out by 40 and our legend did grow.
Basketball should always be that fun.
Our cockiness was oozing; we wore it on our faces;
but when practice got ragged, Horne put us in our places.
Unimpressed that we were now ranked number one.
'Go home. Get out. You didn't come to play',
And our rematch with Cranford was just 3 days away.
I guess it was a sign for the worst;
Cranford beat us and our bubble finally burst.
After 15 and 0, losin' wasn't any fun;
Horne treated us to suicides and one-on-one.
But when we lost to Linden we were surely done,
Or so it seemed that day.
And we were singin' …

Chorus

Verse 4

Yes, there were still games left to play,
And Horne Man said what he had to say.
We all knew what we had to do then.
So we crushed Hillside and Parsipanny,
Then we nipped Cranford as if destiny
Demanded our rematch with Jefferson.
So in every corner the people stood,
And watched as we sent them home for good.
We had made it to that state final game;
It would put us in the Hall of Fame.
We played bad that day and barely got it done.
But Pfeif reassured me as we rode into the sun,
'Years from now, all they'll know is that we won
the game we had to win.
And we were singin' …

Chorus

Verse 5

Now it's been more than thirty years
Since we filled those gyms and heard those cheers.
I can still hear them now.
Our gym housed a boyhood dream
Where good players blossomed as a team.
We dared to win, and Horne Man showed us how.
Yes, something drove us deep inside
In a football school full of pride.
We put all we had into it,
With a will that said: "Let's do it."
Yes, we did that year what precious few
Ever dreamed we'd ever do
And became the best the town ever knew...
State Champs of '72.
So...

Chorus

Acknowledgments

There are many people to thank for help making this book possible in its final form. First and foremost, I have to thank Bruce Johnson for being a sounding board and providing encouragement in the early stages, indeed when the book was just being planned. Bruce has always been that bridge between the WHS that I experienced and the one that exists today. His feedback on the early drafts were invaluable in convincing me that I was on the right track and that my efforts would be worth it in the end. Bruce and I probably met for lunch a half dozen times during the two years this book was in the works, even though unbeknownst to me Bruce was receiving treatment for a rare form of cancer that was threatening his kidneys. I will be forever grateful for his support and various contributions during this whole process.

Bill Kane, who also played for Coach Horne a few years after I did, not to mention having written a couple of books himself, also provided very helpful feedback throughout. This was particularly true right after the first draft, where he helped me sort out the good from the bad. He was always a great resource whenever I needed advice or faced a key decision on some aspect of the book. Thank you, Bill.

Neil Angis, one of my son's business partners and a former English major at Bucknell with a lot of writing experience, also provided a valuable chapter by chapter critique which ultimately led to some restructuring of the latter portions of the book. Scott Berenson, the spouse of one of my daughter's good friends, also provided a detailed review from the perspective of a reader who, like Neil, knew nothing about Westfield or its history in the athletic department. Neil and Scott both helped me at least try to answer the question as to what the reader unaffiliated with Westfield might care about. Thank you, Neil and Scott.

My son David and eldest daughter Lauren both played key editing roles along the way as well. David correctly highlighted many overused words and phrases that needed and ultimately got a thorough review and makeover. He also appeared to have an eagle eye for any statement that wasn't adding some value and therefore should be trashed. He also wasn't holding back on any critiques – "Come on – where's the good writing?"

being an example of one. I probably acted on 80+% of the various suggestions he made throughout. Lauren, an avid reader, provided an equally critical review. Since I had decided to forego the use of a traditional book editor, Lauren effectively became my Editor in Chief with a detailed critique that included highlighting unnecessary content and poorly or overly worded sentences and paragraphs and suggesting better ways of saying certain things. She was persistent at pointing out things I really didn't want to hear, but which she felt were necessary to make a better book and reading experience. Ultimately, I agreed with and acted upon 80+% of her recommendations as well. Thank you, David and Lauren.

Thank you to my daughter Jacqueline for her help with the design and creation of the book's front and back covers. While I thought I already had a good book cover, she was able to come up an exceptional one, one that subtly illustrates the underlying conflict of a basketball triumph in a football town, and which rivals any cover you might see from a major publisher. Like her skills on a basketball court, her artistic skills also come naturally, as evidenced by her artwork on the championship ball that now sits in Westfield High's trophy case. Thank you, Jackie.

Several people agreed to provide reviews of the nearly final version of the book before its release, for which I am very grateful. These include Jay Jorgenson, Dave Miller, Bruce Moran, Glen Kehler, Jim Baglin, John Belis and Jack Steimel. Dave Miller also provided countless helpful suggestions regarding specific passages in the book to help it read better in addition to his broader review of the book as a whole.

One chapter in particular ("Paradise and a Parking Lot") required interviewing several former players who used to frequent the courts at Gumbert Park around the same time I did. Their recollections were also invaluable in helping to make that chapter possible and bringing Gumbert back to life. Many thanks to John Somogyi, Jack Steimel, Jim Baglin, Richie Sciallaba, Leo Nolan, Steve Solop, Jim Kelly, Jay Boyle, Tom Flaherty, Norm Hobbie, Mike Allocco, Tim Kish, Mike Cooney, Bob Jester and Tim Goski for all their recollections of the evenings spent in that parking lot a half century ago!

Of course, much of the book writing would have been much more difficult, if not impossible, had it not been for Coach Horne's various contributions. These included i) his incredibly detailed practice notes and team statistics that he somehow managed to preserve in nearly mint condition through all these decades, ii) a more complete and better organized scrapbook than I had, iii) game films of three key games and a radio broadcast of a fourth, and iv) additional game and locker room footage for the state final game that his father had taken. Thank you, Coach, for all of those priceless contributions to this project.

Thanks must also go to Westfield High School for graciously permitting the use of various photos, including the official team photo, still shots extracted from game films, photos of football action, yearbook photos, and photos taken for the school newspaper. The Westfield Leader, the Courier-News, and the Daily Journal were also additional valuable sources of game details and action photos. Thank you to Bucknell University for permitting the use of official team photos of their 1974-75 varsity basketball team.

Thank you to all my teammates for being supportive and encouraging of this effort all along the way, and of course for those 125 days we spent together! I hope I have done our team and all of you justice.

I feel like I should also give further kudos to Rudyard Kipling, whose timeless advice was still guiding me as I wrote this book:

"If you can trust yourself when all men doubt you,
But make allowance for their doubting too;"

Finally, and most importantly, the biggest thank you of all goes to my wife Susan. Her patience and understanding of basketball in my life goes beyond words. Throughout the years she's endured all my league playing, coaching, watching, and now writing this book. This book required a team effort and simply would not have been possible if she wasn't part of the home team. Thank you, Susan!

About the Author

Stephen Reddy, a 1972 graduate of Westfield High School in Westfield, NJ, went on to earn a Bachelor of Arts degree from Bucknell University in 1976, majoring in Mathematics. He then enjoyed a long career as an actuary, after becoming a Fellow in the Society of Actuaries (FSA) in 1983. *A ball with no points* is Stephen's first book. He and his wife Susan are semi-retired and live in Bucks County, PA. They have four children, all living in New York City.

Made in USA - North Chelmsford, MA
1287992_9780578948188